**THE ARCHITECT'S GUIDE TO
EFFECTIVE SELF-PRESENTATION
IN THE MARKETPLACE**

ANDREAS LUESCHER

First published 2014
by Routledge
2 Park Square, Milton Park, Abingdon, Oxon OX14 4RN

and by Routledge
711 Third Avenue, New York, NY 10017

Routledge is an imprint of the Taylor & Francis Group, an informa business

© 2014 Andreas Luescher

The right of Andreas Luescher to be identified as author of this work has been asserted by him in accordance with sections 77 and 78 of the Copyright, Designs and Patents Act 1988.

All rights reserved. No part of this book may be reprinted or reproduced or utilised in any form or by any electronic, mechanical, or other means, now known or hereafter invented, including photocopying and recording, or in any information storage or retrieval system, without permission in writing from the publishers.

Trademark notice: Product or corporate names may be trademarks or registered trademarks, and are used only for identification and explanation without intent to infringe.

The publisher makes no representation, express or implied, with regard to the accuracy of the information contained in this book and cannot accept any legal responsibility or liability for any errors or omissions that may be made.

British Library Cataloguing in Publication Data
A catalogue record for this book is available from the British Library

Library of Congress Cataloging in Publication Data
Luescher, Andreas.
The architect's guide to effective self-presentation / Andreas Luescher.
pages cm
Includes index.
1. Architects--Vocational guidance. 2. Architecture--Vocational guidance. I. Title.
NA1995.L79 2013
720.23--dc23
2012050223

ISBN: 978-0-415-78344-6 (hbk)
ISBN: 978-0-415-78345-3 (pbk)

Typeset in Avenir
Designed by Oliver Hutton
Printed and Bound in Great Britain by Ashford Colour Press Ltd, Gosport, Hampshire

THE ARCHITECT'S GUIDE TO EFFECTIVE SELF-PRESENTATION IN THE MARKETPLACE

ANDREAS LUESCHER

Routledge
Taylor & Francis Group
LONDON AND NEW YORK

CONTENTS

Acknowledgements	vi
Contributors	vi
Introduction	viii
Chapter One: Planning an Effective Self-Presentation Campaign	1
Design Helps Us Fashion a Narrative	3
Story Helps Us Build a Theme	3
Symphony Helps Us to See Relationships	4
Empathy Helps Us to Be Human	4
Play Helps Us to Exhibit Improvisation	5
Meaning Helps You Go Beyond	5
Case Studies:	
1 Unorthodox Methods propeller Z	6
2 Mapping a Self-Presentation Strategy Alex Hogrefe	10
3 Presenting, Presencing Nick Axel	16
4 Promotion Proportions Brandon Clifford	24
5 Harnessing the Power of Invention Alexis Pegram-Piper	28
Chapter Two: Creating a Career Plan	35
Planning a Career Means Knowing Yourself and Being Understood	34
Launch Your Career	35
Career Planning: The DIY (Do It Yourself) Way	35
Creating a Competency Profile: Your Tools for Positioning	39
Developing Your Personality Profile	41
Case Studies:	
1 In Defense of Happy Accidents Eric Cesal	42
2 The Medium is the Message Peter Murray	50
3 Self Presentation: Things I Have Learnt, Things I Am Learning and Some Things I May Never Get Vanessa Norwood	54
4 Multiple Paths: Curatorial Fellow, Communicator, Co-Founder and Editor of *CLOG* Julia Van den Hout	60
Chapter Three: The ABCs of CV Résumé	65
Different Résumé Formats	66
Your CV is Your First Impression	67
Standard CV Etiquette: The Ground Rules According to a Career Professional	68
Not Too Much and Not Too Little	68

Targeting Your CV	69
Six Key Characteristics of an Effective CV/Résumé	69
Your Letter of Recommendation	71
Finding a Job Through Your Network	72
How to Build a Network	72
Initial Interactions with Prospective Employers	73
What You Should Do After the Interview	74
Preparing for a Negative Post-Interview Outcome	75

Case Studies:

1 Non-Résumé Jordan J. Lloyd	76
2 Interpretation of a Résumé Bill Mackey	84
3 A Résumé Transformed from Book to Web Lillie Liu	92

Chapter Four: Mapping a Marketing Strategy — 101

Self-Marketing Means Commitment to Your Craft	102
The Keys to Branding: Self-Actualization, Effective Development, and Recognizability	102
Branding: A How and What to Do	103
Relationships, Relationships, Relationships	104
How Social Media Can Help Your Cause … and How It Can Hurt	105
Two Additional Tools for Successful Self-Marketing Campaigns: The Press Kit and the Elevator Speech	106

Case Studies:

1 A Strategic Case Study: A Virtual Brand Amy J. Slattery	108
2 How to Create Identity for a New Architect's Office Henk Döll	116
3 *Opúsculos*: Talking about Architecture André Tavares	122
4 Contre le Marketing (I'm Not) Pascal Monniez	124

Chapter Five: Maintaining an Edge — 127

Don't Stand Still … Be Active	128
Staying Focused Even Through a Recession	129
Never Confuse Means with Ends	129
Always Have "Young" Ideas	129
Maintain Self-Discipline	129

Case Studies:

1 Film is More: Architecture + Storytelling + Film Adam Goss	134
2 The Architect Who Blogs: Notes from On the Road James Benedict Brown	138

Index — 144

ACKNOWLEDGEMENTS

This book is a collaborative effort, and would not have been possible without the shared experiences and wealth of knowledge from the contributors. I am inspired by their work and honored by their diligent participation.

I also would like to recognize those who went out of their way to help me during my research and investigation, particularly Architects ACXT from Madrid, Zehra Abidi from London, Andrew Caruso from Gensler, Washington D.C., Maud Cassaignau from the Monash University in Melbourne, Australia, James Doerfler from California Polytechnic State University at San Luis Obispo, Halldor Gislason from Oslo National Academy of the Arts, Norway, Edgar Gonzalez, Editor in Chief of edgargonzalez.com, Catherine Killen from the University of Virginia, Aram Mooradian from AA London, and Christian Unverzagt from the University of Michigan.

I also owe thanks to the whole Routledge team, particularly Francesca Ford, Commissioning Editor, Jo Endell-Cooper, Deputy Production Editorial Manager, Francesca Galbo, Marketing Assistant, and Laura Williamson, Senior Editorial Assistant, for their steady support and shepherding the project to come to fruition as well as Sarah Fish for an excellent job of copy editing. Finally, I want to thank my daughter Annabelle Luescher for her understanding and immense patience during my occasional absent-mindedness as a parent.

CONTRIBUTORS

Nick Axel engages with the discipline of architecture through a variety of mediums and platforms for expression. He works to reveal latent opportunities for spatial praxis at the limits of agency in the contemporary city. Nick is currently keeping himself occupied in Madrid, Spain. He maintains a highly active online presence at the following location: http://www.nickaxel.net.

James Benedict Brown is a lecturer in Architecture at Norwich University of the Arts in Norwich, England. He tweets @jbenedictbrown and blogs at http://www.combinearchitecture.com. He tries very hard to make sure you can't find any drunken photographs of him on Facebook.

Eric Cesal is a wandering misadventurer who dabbles in architecture, construction and writing. He believes that design, when done well, is fundamentally an act of kindness, that construction is an act of will and writing is a self-indulgence. He is the author of exactly one book: *Down Detour Road: An Architect in Search of Practice*. He currently lives and works in Port Au Prince alongside a kick-ass team of humanitarian architects, and supported by a family of assorted chickens and a half-German, half-Haitian dog named Chans. http://www.ericjcesal.com/about.html

Brandon Clifford received his Master of Architecture from Princeton University in 2011. From 2006–2009 he worked as project manager at Office dA in both Boston and New York where his contributions varied in scale and program – silverware, installations, restaurants, a professional soccer stadium, and numerous urban planning studies. Brandon also served as editor of *Pidgin* magazine from 2009–2011, was the 2011–12 LeFevre Emerging Practitioner Fellow at The Ohio State University Knowlton School of Architecture, and the founder of The Malleablist Movement in architecture. In 2008 Brandon founded Matter Design with Wes McGee as a way of rarefying the overlaps between their respective backgrounds. http://www.matterdesignstudio.com/about/brandon-clifford/

Henk Döll graduated in 1984 at the Faculty of Architecture at Delft University of Technology. As a result of winning and realizing the Kruisplein housing competition in Rotterdam (1980–1985), he was already working during his studies as an independent architect, together with Francine Houben and Roelf Steenhuis. This cooperative firm was transformed in 1983 into Mecanoo Architects, in which he was partner for over twenty years. In 2003 Henk Döll made a new step forward by founding the Döll Group / Döll Architects in Rotterdam. The increasing amount of work in Germany resulted in 2006 in a partnership in Hamburg: Coido architects (Cordsen Ipach + Döll GmbH). Since 2010 Döll has a joint venture with Joint Business Center of International Design Union in Shenzhen. http://www.dollab.nl

Adam Goss, along with partner Red Mike, founded Spirit of Space in Chicago in 2006. He was educated as an architect at the University of Wisconsin-Milwaukee. During a semester of architectural study in Milan, Italy, the passion for understanding the relationship between film and architecture blossomed. Shortly after befriending Red Mike in Italy, the two saw the power of using film to communicate the value of design. With a keen interest in business operations, Adam has taken on the managerial aspects of the firm. In 2008, he became part of the adjunct faculty at the School of the Art Institute in Chicago and began teaching a film and architecture course.

Alex Hogrefe is currently working in Boston M.A. for Paul Lukez Architecture although he has lived most of his life near corn fields in Northwest Ohio. In 2009 while a student at Miami University, Ohio working towards a Master in Architecture he created a website as a means to communicate to his instructors the progress he was making on his thesis work.

CONTRIBUTORS

However, the site since then quickly turned into a place to upload all of his thoughts, work, and experiments, whether it had to do with the thesis or not. http://www.alexhogrefe.com/

Lillie Liu received her Bachelor of Architecture from Carnegie Mellon University (2002) and Master of Architecture and Urbanism from the Architectural Association, Design Research Lab (2007). The work featured in this book was part of a collaboration with AADRL teammates Oznur Erboga, Theodora Ntatsopoulou, and Victor Orive. Lillie is currently a Senior Designer at Zaha Hadid Architects, where she has worked since 2007. She has also taught in the AA Shanghai Visiting School.

Jordan J. Lloyd is currently a PhD researcher at the University of Sheffield School of Architecture, interested in redefining everyday living, from changing the way we live and interact with the world to the future of the economy. His Ph.D. research, Adaptive Design Capacity, is focused on developing a Strategic-Design based methodology rooted in a comprehensive understanding of behavioural and complexity sciences, before applying them to complex entities such as cities. http://jordanjlloyd.me/

Bill Mackey received degrees from the University of Illinois (BS Architectural Studies 1991) and the University of Arizona (B.Arch and M.Arch 1994) with a primary focus on the social construction of space. His work explores human connections to built environments and bridges the theory and practice of social sciences, planning, architecture, and art. As an artist, architect, and educator he freely bounces back and forth between the fields of architecture, art, and the academy. His engagement simultaneously includes public, academic, and professional fields. In 1995, he created Worker, Inc., a company that specializes in promoting change in the built environment. http://www.workerincorporated.com/index.html

Pascal Monniez is founding partner in the Brussels-based M architecture. Catherine Maraite (since 2005) and Natalie Hess (since 2009) are part of the collaborative structure. This association allows them, in addition to the conduct of personal projects, to also work as a team and participate in competitions and response to calls for design concepts. http://www.m-architecture.eu/

Peter Murray is the founder and Chairman of Wordsearch Communications, the leading international consultancy specializing in architecture and real estate. Peter trained as an architect at Bristol University and the Architectural Association and has worked as technical editor of *Architectural Design* (AD), editor of *Building Design* and editor of *RIBA Journal*. In 1983 he founded *Blueprint* magazine with the aim of communicating architecture to a wider audience. Peter also founded the London Festival of Architecture in 2004 and the New London Architecture Centre in 2005.

Vanessa Norwood is Head of Exhibitions at the Architectural Association, one of the world's leading centers for architectural culture and learning. Vanessa has curated and organized a range of renowned exhibitions that celebrate architecture in a wider context. She recently curated "Switzerland: Designed for Life" at the AA Foundation. She previously worked for Wordsearch, Lifschutz Davidson and de Rijke Marsh Morgan.

Alexis Pegram-Piper is a teaching assistant and PhD candidate at the University of Wisconsin-Milwaukee specializing in the field of Rhetoric and Composition. She is currently working on her dissertation in Michigan. Her research interests include Native American rhetorical traditions, conceptions of temporality, and Rhetorical Invention.

Amy J. Slattery is a Senior Architect / Project Manager at Burns & McDonnell and a 2011 recipient of the AIA Young Architects Award. In recent years, Amy served as a Project Architect for the Kauffman Center for the Performing Arts in Kansas City, Missouri as design coordinator with project designer, Moshe Safdie & Associates and as Lead Project Architect of the new state-of-the-art WIN-GEM building for the School of Engineering at UCLA, a collaborative project with Los Angeles architecture firm Moore Ruble Yudell. Amy has been a guest lecturer in professional practice at Yale School of Architecture, the University of Kansas School of Architecture and several other regional universities.

André Tavares, editor at Dafne Editora is a small architectural publisher that was started in 2003 with the purpose of publishing *Sebentas de História da Arquitectura Moderna*, a series of 23 titles on the history of modern architecture, from Jan Van Eyck to Claude Nicolas-Ledoux, all books authored by Domingos Tavares, professor at the Porto School of Architecture and Dafne founder. http://www.dafne.com.pt/

Philipp Tschofen is an Austrian architect and founding partner of propeller Z (1994). Propeller Z also consists of Turkish-born Korkut Akkalay and Austrian architects Kabru and Carmen Wiederin. The collective trained in schools around the world, including Japan and the USA; describing their studio as a "platform for space, content, material, form and program research in all fields". Propeller Z is constantly evolving. http://www.propellerz.at

Julia Van den Hout was born in Amsterdam, the Netherlands, and moved to Chicago in 2000. She holds a BA in Art History and Urban Design and Architecture from NYU, and has led the communications department at Steven Holl Architects since 2008. She is co-founder and editor of the architecture publication *CLOG*. http://www.clog-online.com/

INTRODUCTION

The subject of the book is increasingly universal: presenting oneself in the globalized marketplace. In an age of unprecedented and previously unimagined access to the personal information and virtual identities of others, careful and strategic self-presentation in the global market is a critical skill that is essential for professional success. Although most of the case studies contained in *The Architect's Guide to Effective Self-Presentation in the Marketplace* are examples from the architectural field, the information and advice offered throughout the book is interdisciplinary. With relevant contributions and examples from some of the most exciting professionals working in design today, this book will guide you through the process of developing, organizing, strategizing, and promoting career profiles in written and visual form.

Myself and many of the contributors begin with the premise that effective self-presentation starts with self-actualization – or with the important capacity to know yourself and your own potential. Twenty-five hundred years ago Socrates left us with this great tenet of Western philosophy and thought: "know thyself". This ancient Greek maxim that was inscribed in the forecourt at the Temple of Apollo at Delphi continues to serve us well today. Self-actualization, understanding your own potential, or simply knowing yourself is the first step in building a successful self-marketing campaign and personal brand – which will be discussed throughout this book.

As you read, it will help you to think about your specific, personal interests. According to Holland Codes, who have developed a unique method for categorizing interests, there are six primary types of interests: Realistic, Investigative, Artistic, Social, Enterprising, and Conventional. Readers will come to understand themselves as motivated by one of these interests. This understanding can then be used to present yourself in written, visual or verbal form.

Readers will also learn about presentation in the virtual world and the evolving digital mediums for showcasing their self-presentation (social media, video, etc.). In addition, you will read about the timely and important topic of transforming a presentation from a hard copy to an online demonstration of your skills and experience, or to an interactive web-page.

A recommendation that runs the course of this book is: embrace the unexpected. The different case studies encourage us to embrace the constant challenges presented by blended design. Various contributors urge newcomers to the field to incorporate architecture into broader spheres and professional specialties. A couple of other take-aways that you will find threaded throughout *The Architect's Guide to Effective Self-Presentation in the Marketplace* are as follows:

- Be social and step outside the comfort of your studio or classroom.
- Don't limit yourself by conventional, contemporary parameters, standards, or media.
- Practice design informed by your personal core values.
- Practice design informed by self-actualization, altruism, and equity.
- Always maintain your professional persona and integrity – the digital self never sleeps.
- As a 21st century professional, you must navigate shifting digital networks, mediums, and technologies.
- Maintain your commitment to accessibility throughout your self-presentation campaign.

The first chapter, "Planning An Effective Self-Presentation Campaign", discusses the six theoretical fundamentals of creating a successful self-presentation, which are as follows: 1) design helps us fashion a narrative, 2) story helps us build a theme, 3) symphony helps us to see relationships, 4) empathy helps us to be human, 5) play helps us to exhibit improvisations, and 6) meaning helps you go beyond. This chapter offers you a theoretical underpinning while also providing you with a general purpose for your self-presentation campaign.

The second chapter, "Creating a Career Plan", is a survey of the different ways that a professional career can develop. Although it's very clearly not intended to be a career guide, this chapter provides practical, pertinent information about the thoughts and circumstances that bring individuals from one point to another throughout their professional lives. By offering their own personal experiences written in an interesting and highly accessible tone, the contributors in this chapter convey the significance and complexity of professional careers. You will also take heart in this chapter's message that unexpected detours and course changes can lead to productive, successful, and fulfilling vocations.

The third chapter, "The ABCs of CVs Résumé", discusses the diverse spectrum of styles and techniques currently being used by architecture and design students and young professionals to create their original curricula vitae and résumés. In addition, this chapter gives a brief history of the résumé/CV as a method of introductory self-promotion while also explaining conventional U.S. and European formats and terminology.

The fourth chapter, "Mapping a Marketing Strategy", will explain the range of communication and marketing strategies available to you as you get ready to present yourself in a globalized marketplace. This chapter will also discuss different approaches you can use to stand out and get noticed in the marketplace. Some of the strategies detailed include: self-initiated events and exhibitions, developing your own blog or website, cultivating contacts, exchanging links, submitting work to media outlets, and many more.

The fifth chapter, "Maintaining an Edge" presents specific ideas and techniques to use as you invent your own personal brand and promote that brand in the global marketplace. This final chapter also describes the sense of self-awareness that plays such a critical role in successful self-presentation.

All in all, The *Architect's Guide to Effective Self-Presentation in the Marketplace* is intended to arm you with the practical information you need as you prepare to enter the exciting and competitive fray that is the global professional market. But perhaps even more importantly, this book's utmost purpose is to incite your passion, creativity, and innovation.

PLANNING AN EFFECTIVE SELF-PRESENTATION CAMPAIGN

YOUR ABILITY TO EFFECTIVELY PRESENT YOURSELF, your work, experience, and ideas in the marketplace will prove essential to your future success and self-satisfaction in the architectural field. The first step in attaining this objective is planning a successful self-presentation campaign. An effective self-presentation campaign must continuously navigate the crossroads of culture, ingenuity, economics, and technology. As you prepare to enter the workforce, the field you will be playing on is a multimedia mixture of images, sounds, texts, and symbols. Complicating this interconnected amalgamation further is the fact that the social component inherent in many current technologies often blurs the boundaries between personal and professional selves. Traditional ways of design thinking frequently fall short in today's creative marketplace. This reality often requires professionals to rethink many culturally embedded problem-solving strategies.

In his book *A Whole New Mind: Moving from the Information Age to the Conceptual Age*, Daniel H. Pink contends that the global cultural shifts that will take place in the forthcoming "Conceptual Age" are so profound that they warrant comparisons to past periods of monumental change, including the Renaissance and the Industrial Revolution. Pink (2005) writes, "Today, the defining skills of the previous era – the 'left brain' capabilities that powered the Information Age – are necessary but no longer sufficient. And the capabilities we once disdained or thought frivolous – the 'right-brain' qualities of inventiveness, empathy, joyfulness, and meaning – increasingly will determine who flourishes and who flounders" (p. 3). So as our globalized culture, social structures, and economies become increasingly more dominated by the right hemispheres of our brains, according to Pink, the six essential skills necessary for successfully navigating modern markets in this imminent era are: 1) design, 2) story, 3) symphony, 4) empathy, 5) play, and 6) meaning. Pink (2005) maintains that these six essential aptitudes "are fundamentally human abilities that everyone can master" (p. 11); which is a good thing because he also contends that learning these six essential aptitudes is what our professional success and personal satisfaction will depend upon.

If we apply Pink's six qualities to the constantly evolving, nonlinear route of effective self-presentation campaigns, they translate into a continuously innovative, thoughtful, and dynamic promotion of oneself in the global marketplace. By performing a more in-depth analysis of the six skills (Figure 1) outlined by Pink and by applying them to our own careers and professional fields, we will be better able to thrive and excel in the rapidly changing marketplace he describes.

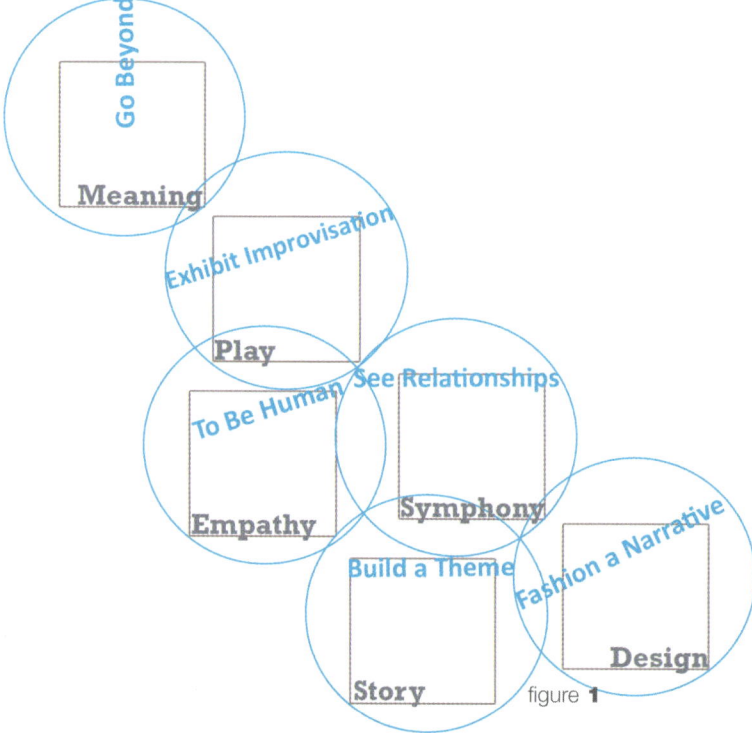

figure **1**

PLANNING AN EFFECTIVE SELF-PRESENTATION CAMPAIGN

☐ DESIGN HELPS US FASHION A NARRATIVE

As an agent of change, design is based on creativity, critical thinking and collaboration. Good designers foster sensitivity to and inclusion of a rich diversity of ideas, beliefs, and values. An exceptional design is not only functional; it is also beautiful, imaginative, and emotionally impactful while simultaneously engaging multiple senses. The act of design can heighten multi-cultural awareness. As designers we should be adept at: freely exploring ideas and envisioning ourselves as multidisciplinary thinkers and designers; expressing ideas clearly in a variety of media and circumstances; attracting and ultimately affecting diverse audiences; and exploring various cultural, professional, and personal contexts as they relate to society.

Design is a beginning, a means – not an ultimate end. In other words, it shouldn't be an afterthought. If you decide to create a PowerPoint component for your presentation, the design of the slides (or any visual aid) begins in the preparation or planning stage, before you have even turned on your computer. It's during the preparation stage that you should take a deep breath, slow down, and quiet your mind so that you may consider your thesis, objectives, messages, and your audience. Only then should you begin to sketch out ideas – on paper or just in your head – that you can turn into tangible realities later. All too often too much emphasis on design for PowerPoint presentations ends up being interpreted by your audience as a collection of recycled bullets, corporate templates, clip art, and seemingly random charts and graphs that are frequently too detailed or cluttered to make effective on-screen visuals and too vague to stand alone as effective self-presentation. Instead, think of design as your chance to fashion your own narrative that your audience can interpret, relate to, remember, and take with them.

☐ STORY HELPS US BUILD A THEME

As human beings, we possess an innate affinity for the craft, act, and experience of story. We are all born storytellers – and storylisteners. Story is not only about storytelling; it's also about listening to stories and becoming part of the narrative. Experiencing being, culture, and self-actualization through story engages our highest facilities of imagination and union with others. Story connects and compels us throughout our lives.

From Aesop, to the Grimm brothers, to Stephen King, threaded throughout stories we find a theme or multiple themes. So what's your thread? What's the theme that you want to convey to your audience? We simply cannot reveal everything about ourselves to one particular audience. Just as an author or journalist must select specific details so that readers understand their purpose without becoming overwhelmed or confused, we too must choose and contextualize our personal information to make it relevant to the occasion and ultimately effective.

Building your theme is an essential characteristic of good storytelling, which involves the ability to engage your audience by placing personal information in context and delivering it with emotional impact. Most of our experiences, our knowledge, our thinking, our ways of knowing, understanding, and living in the world are organized as stories that can be used for good: for teaching, sharing, illuminating, connecting, and for honest, authentic persuasion. If you use your innate storytelling and storylistening skills to build a theme for your portfolio, your ultimate self-presentation will truly resonate with others.

☐ SYMPHONY HELPS US TO SEE RELATIONSHIPS

Entailed within the purpose, outcome, and definition of symphony is the illumination of relationships, connections, and inter-workings that are not always obvious. Symphony requires that we see and imagine in new ways. Pink (2005) describes symphony as an aptitude for "putting the pieces together ... seeing the big picture and, crossing boundaries, being able to combine disparate pieces into an arresting new whole" (p. 66). He also tells us that, "The most creative among us see relationships the rest of us never notice". Anyone can regurgitate chunks of information and parrot findings represented in bullet points on a screen, but what's sought after the most in the workforce and marketplace are those who can recognize subtle patterns and inter-connections, those who are skilled at seeing both the complex nuances and the simplicity that may exist in a specific problem.

Symphony in the world of effective self-presentation does not mean a condensed conveyance of facts, information, or data into meaningless sound bites and moot talking points. Symphony involves using your whole mind – logic, analysis, synthesis, and intuition – to make meaning and sense of ourselves in the world.

Symphony also means seeing and understanding the big picture while determining what is important and what is not before the day of your presentation. It's also about revising what matters and letting go of the rest. Audiences are full of busy, over-extended professionals whose time is at a premium. So make it your business to show them the relationships you most want them to see. A symphonic approach to your promotional campaign involves your ability to bring all of the relevant, focused material together for your audience so that your important messages and objectives are conveyed efficiently and effectively.

☐ EMPATHY HELPS US TO BE HUMAN

Empathy entails imagination, discovering your passion, and seeing things from another's perspective. Empathy means understanding the nonverbal cues of others and being aware of what you are communicating, both verbally and non-verbally. The ability to put yourself in the position of your employer, customer, or audience member is a vital skill that can be learned. One must embrace and practice empathy as part of the integrative thinking, optimism, experimentation, and collaboration qualities one needs to be a good designer.

Empathy allows you, as the presenter, to judge when the audience is "getting it" and reacting to you positively – and when they are not. The empathetic presenter can imagine and understand the factors that may be affecting the audience's reception of their message; and they can then make adjustments based on this reading. You may have had the unfortunate experience of being part of an audience that suffered when a presenter seemed not to empathize with you or anyone else, perhaps even droning on past the allotted time or attention spans, oblivious to the audience's indifferent or even hostile reactions. The presenter who possesses empathy will remain conscious of their audience's wants and needs – including their need to be out of a presentation at a given time.

PLANNING AN EFFECTIVE SELF-PRESENTATION CAMPAIGN

☐ PLAY HELPS US TO EXHIBIT IMPROVISATION

Here I am using the word "play" to refer to determined, exultant, and committed action. Elements of playfulness and humor can take a merely mediocre seminar or presentation into the realm of excellence. Successfully using wit, laughter, lightheartedness, and humor without crossing the line into clownish antics is an incredibly valuable skill to possess as a presenter – a skill that can make your job talk or portfolio presentation really stand out to your audience. According to various studies, individuals who laugh the most and enjoy humor are exceptionally creative and productive; and they are also the happiest and healthiest people.

Effectively incorporating play and humor means honing and using improvisation skills. The ability to improvise can help you react appropriately in the moment and in response to high-pressure situations, such as job interviews or presentations for clients. Mastering the element of play can help you improvise, adapt to any rhetorical situation, and ultimately succeed in your self-marketing endeavors. In work and in life, we all need to play.

☐ MEANING HELPS YOU GO BEYOND

Meaning includes our loftiest, most significant aspirations and actualizations: purpose, transcendence, and spiritual fulfillment. Meaning refers here to going further with your self-presentation than is required – to going beyond the expectations of others and yourself. Exceeding expectations to create meaning often incites opportunities to impact the lives, experiences, and worldviews of those around you – and beyond. Getting in touch with your own inner drive, purpose, and meaning can help you contribute to the meaning collectively created by your community, company, school, etc. If you find you are able to get in touch with this purposeful joy, meaning will be made, and you will have succeeded in going beyond.

"Going beyond" in the specific context of effective self-presentation may also entail generating a different outcome by raising your own expectations. For example, many audiences are so used to uninspired PowerPoint presentations that they've often uncritically accepted it as the normal, mediocre, mind-numbing standard. However, if you strive to exceed prevailing expectations by showing your audience that you've thought about them, done your homework, know your material, and demonstrated how much you appreciate your audience and the opportunity to present yourself and your ideas, then, chances are you'll make an impact. Profound and vital meaning can be created through forging even these small connections. Going beyond to make meaning and purposefully engage even in small, simple ways can be a key to success and fulfillment in your career. ∎

The case studies

WE'VE DESCRIBED, analyzed, and explored the six aptitudes that will help you put together and present the most innovative, impactful, and relevant self-presentation campaign possible. But what do these skills look like when they're implemented? What have others done that has worked? What can we learn from these examples? Rather than presenting you with a case study for each discrete skill, let's look at four case studies that, in various ways, exhibit all of the skills we've just discussed. You will notice that a specific skill may be more prominent in each case study. This is because the designer or creator of the portfolio is using their strongest skill to their best advantage. So take what you are best at and what comes naturally to you and run with it.

CASE STUDY 1

TITLE: UNORTHODOX METHODS
AUTHOR: PROPELLER Z

By employing creative, unorthodox methods for developing their unconventional products, Vienna-based architectural firm propeller Z provides us with an excellent example of adapting to Conceptual Age schemata. propeller Z's ongoing, team-based discourse in project development compels the firm to make each design decision collectively while always checking the proportionality of means. Moreover, this team-based approach to all of their endeavors allows propeller Z products to emerge with a recognizable style infused with the firm's unique brand of humor. The five-person, multidisciplinary organization doesn't take itself too seriously – which is a rare and refreshing professional quality illustrated by their dynamic online portfolio of architectural achievements and marketing collateral.

▶ UNORTHODOX METHODS
PROPELLER Z

One of propeller Z's earliest self-presentation projects was incited by an invitation to participate in Art Traffic–Trafik Art, a 1999 Viennese public-space project/installation. A primary objective of Art Traffic-Trafik Art was to make contemporary art accessible and meaningful to the general public, thus forming a bridge between art and everyday life. propeller Z's philosophy of accessibility and applicability was humorously highlighted by dispensing the art objects via seven vending machines located throughout Vienna. Art-interested buyers had 24-hour access to limited, signed edition contributions from 66 artists and collectives representing the visual arts, architecture, stage design, and new media. The propeller Z team developed their first self-styled Starter Kit™ specifically with vending machine distribution in mind. The team combined a credit card format with the aesthetics of the eraser template (Figure 1) to create a series of cutouts, primarily about the firm's previous exhibition designs.

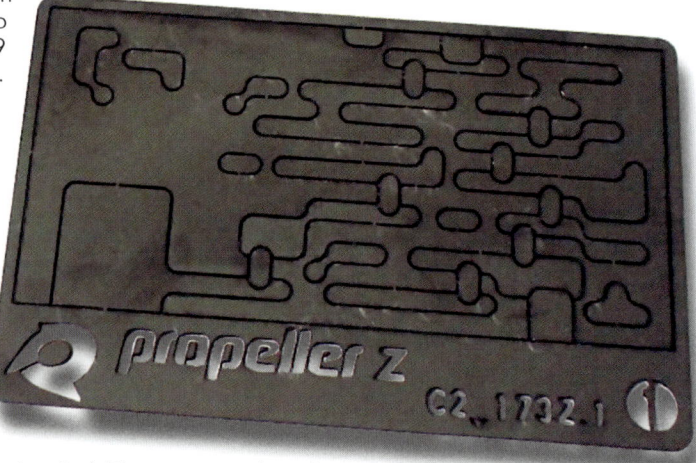

figure **1**

PLANNING AN EFFECTIVE SELF-PRESENTATION CAMPAIGN

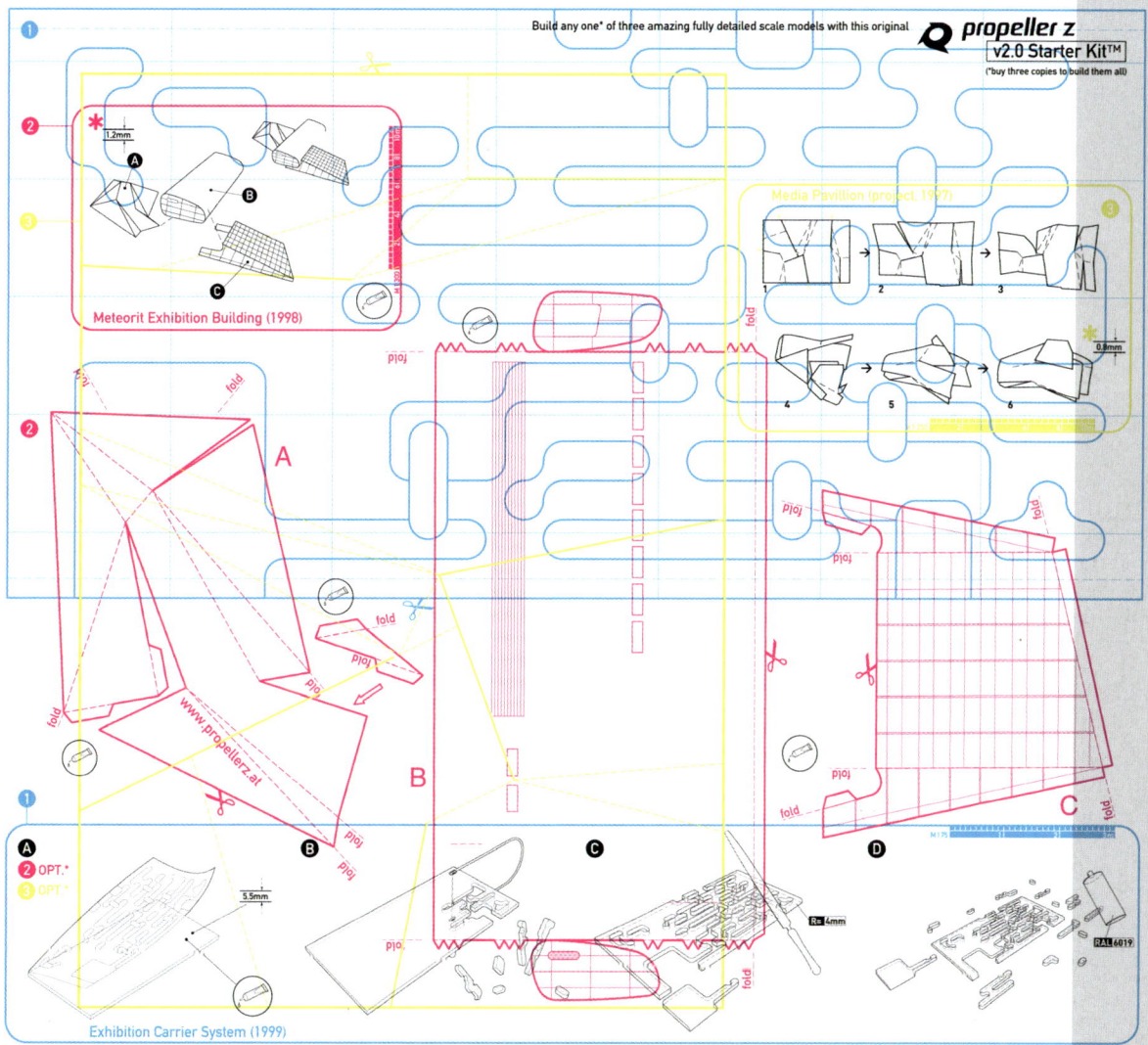

figure **2**

propeller Z's second Starter Kit™ appeared in a December 2000 front-page story in the Austrian daily newspaper, *Der Standard*. The piece featured three different types of projects that buyers could construct as detailed scale models. With a nod to Henri Matisse's gouaches découpés, propeller Z's paper cut-out model was essential to the firm's design-thinking – defined in this specific case as a platform for space, content, material, form, and program research in all fields of two- and three-dimensional design (Figure 2).

PROPELLER Z

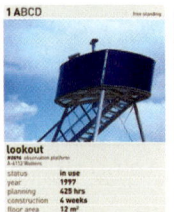

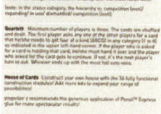

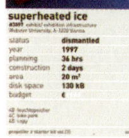

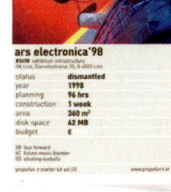

propeller z

The group's third Starter Kit™ – produced for exhibition at the international architectural conference, ArchiLab 2002, in Orleans, France – consisted of 32 playing cards and a 36-piece construction kit. Inspired by Charles and Ray Eames's 1952 "House of Cards", propeller Z's Starter Kit™ was designed as a playful collection of the team's design and architecture projects, from interior proposals to competition submissions (Figure 3). By encouraging users to design their own house of cards, propeller Z's kit overlaid their unique communication/PR portal with a subtle nod to their unique design ethos.

You will probably notice that one of the propeller Z team's greatest, most predominant strengths lies in their ability to incorporate an element of play into their work. They have successfully utilized their propensity for humor and improvisation to distinguish their firm and thrive in a competitive market. What other themes do you see threaded throughout their designs? How are these themes woven together throughout the three projects described above to create propeller Z's unique story? ∎

figure **3**

PLANNING AN EFFECTIVE SELF-PRESENTATION CAMPAIGN

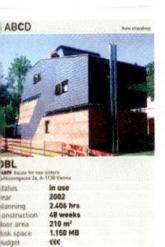

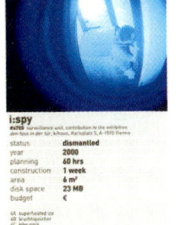

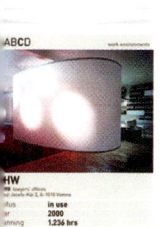

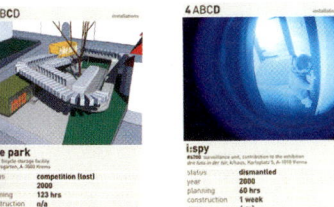

CASE STUDY 2

TITLE: MAPPING A SELF-PRESENTATION STRATEGY
AUTHOR: ALEX HOGREFE

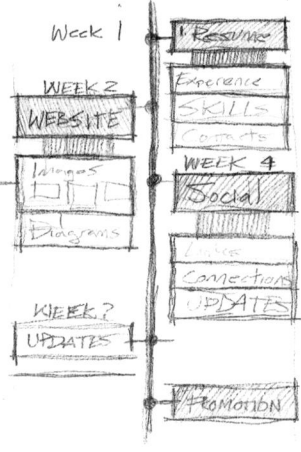

In his essay "Mapping a Self-Presentation Strategy", Boston-based architect Alex Hogrefe offers a straightforward, five-step formula for developing and maintaining a professional digital profile. While Hogrefe begins with the standard CV, he "goes beyond" by offering contemporary design suggestions for ensuring your profile's accessibility on a variety of devices. Hogrefe also presents an array of options for disseminating your CV, including personal websites capable of managing multimedia content. Additionally, Hogrefe offers tips for networking and job hunting, such as: virtual job fairs, online employment databases, and social media sites like LinkedIn and Facebook.

While looking over Alex's thoughtfully planned self-presentation campaign and his suggestions, you may feel like you know Alex. How do the design strategies he uses throughout fashion his own, unique narrative? And how can you encourage employers to get to know you? You may have also noticed that one of Alex's greatest strengths lies in his ability to market himself using various digital and social networking mediums. Which of Alex's marketing strategies can you enact in your own campaign – and what can you take even further – while continuing to recognize and play to your own, individual aptitudes?

One could certainly make the case that Alex went further with his self-presentation campaign than was required. You could also argue that he exceeded the expectations of others – and possibly even his own expectations in the process. Getting in touch with his own inner drive and purpose – with his passion for sharing his knowledge and experience with others – certainly helped Alex transcend the mundane to make meaning.

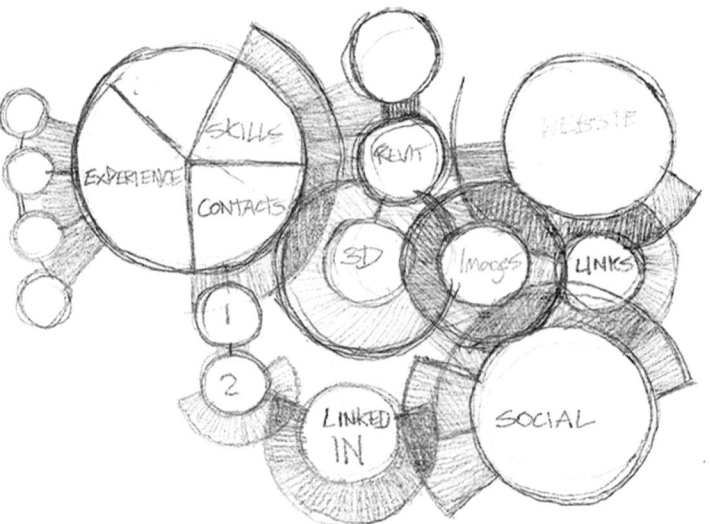

PLANNING AN EFFECTIVE SELF-PRESENTATION CAMPAIGN

▶ MAPPING A SELF-PRESENTATION STRATEGY
ALEX HOGREFE

Self-presentation strategies have become more complex due to the infinite possibilities brought about by the Internet and online social networking. When designing a self-presentation plan, mapping out a logical, progressive system can provide greater control, and establishing clear goals along the way will help avoid what could easily become an overwhelming and confusing entanglement of information.

I have broken down the process I use into five cumulative steps, beginning with the physical/tangible, transitioning to the digital, and ending with the social. The steps are layered by priority, so that the most important items are accomplished early on, avoid the need to have all steps completed before the self-presentation strategies can be implemented.

PLAN

Develop a strategy and set priorities. This means compiling all information into one location and organizing it in a way that any specific piece of information can be accessed easily and quickly when building the résumé.

How will different information be accessed, and how will the different media relate to one another?

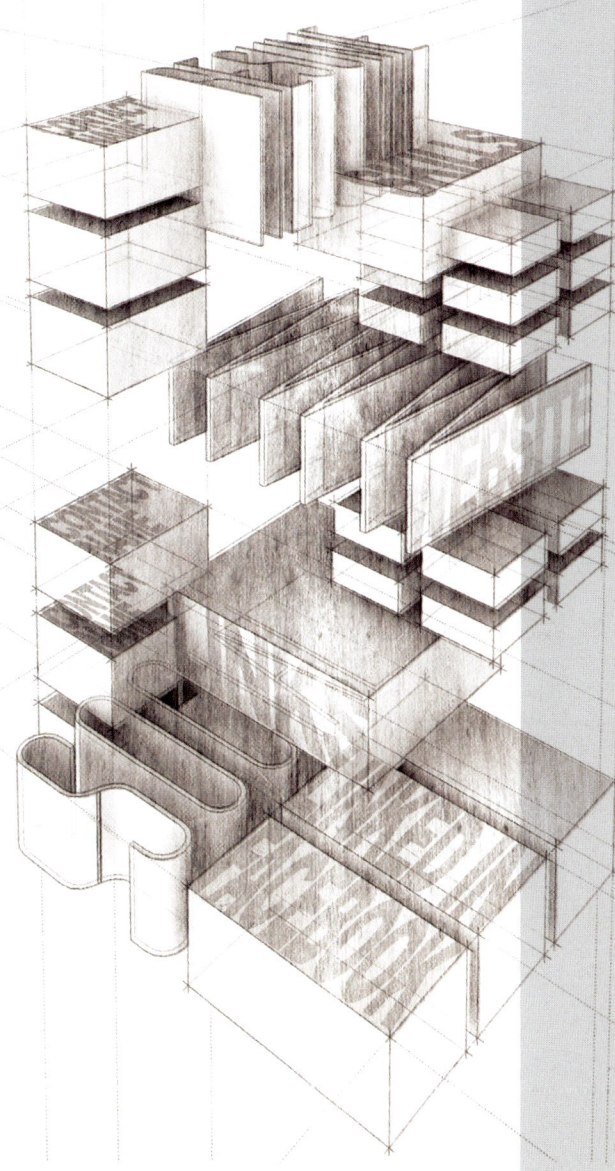

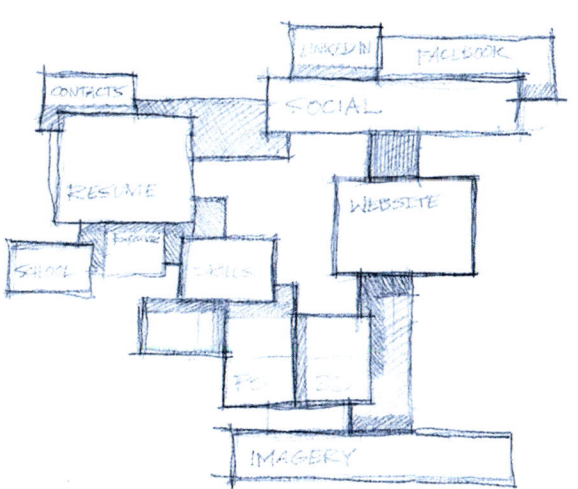

DESIGN

Build a traditional résumé to act as a foundation from which a website and other digital iterations can be launched. Most employers accept the hard copy résumé and many even require it.

Traditional 8.5"x 11". While this is the standard size, how the information is arranged within the margins can be as unique as you want it.

MS Word is not required to build a résumé. I use Photoshop because it allows me greater creative freedom than simple word processing software.

I integrate a time line into my résumé to graphically supplement the text, all the while not detracting from the readability of the document

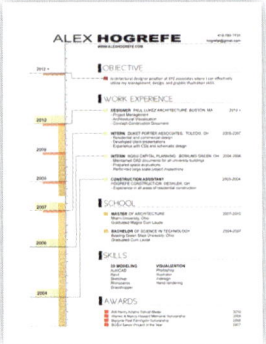

FORMAT

The next step is preparing the résumé to be viewed digitally. Some key questions to consider during the planning phase are: What types of devices will be used to view my résumé? How will orientation and screen size of these different devices influence the design? What types of file formats should be used for these different devices? What is the universal usability of my digital résumé?

JPEG: Universally recognized by most devices and will upload and download more quickly than other formats over the Internet. Ideal for websites.

PDF: Commonly requested format by employers. Accessible on most devices.

MS WORD: Easy copy and paste text but tougher to use on mobile devices.

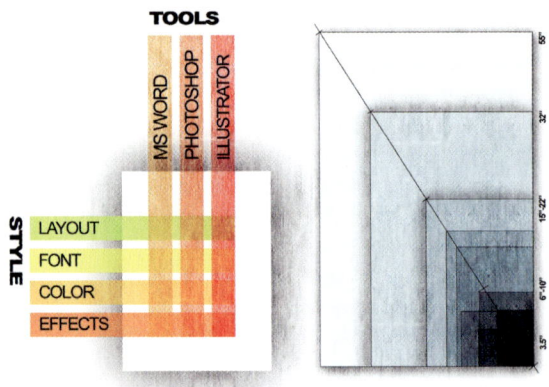

DISTRIBUTE

EMAIL/UPLOAD

The most common way to get your digital information out there is by email. There are some advantages by going this route.

High resolution: What I like about email is that it offers up possibilities of sending high-resolution documents and images instead of being stuck with 72 dpi from online viewing.

Conventional: Most professional environments will accept this way of communication and will already have specific addresses set up. However, almost everybody else will be using this same method making it very easy for your stuff to get "lost" in the pile.

WEB ADDRESS

It is important to take advantage of the Internet and its reach to millions of users. Creating a web address gives you a stronger online presence and provides more opportunities for showing off your unique identity, personality, and skill set. There are two ways to go about getting a web address: create a personal website or use a résumé web hosting service.

PERSONAL WEBSITE

Websites are completely customizable and provide a dynamic experience for users. When I had my résumé on my own site, I created links to my employer's websites as well as to other relevant content on my own site. This allowed interested users to easily access more detailed information.

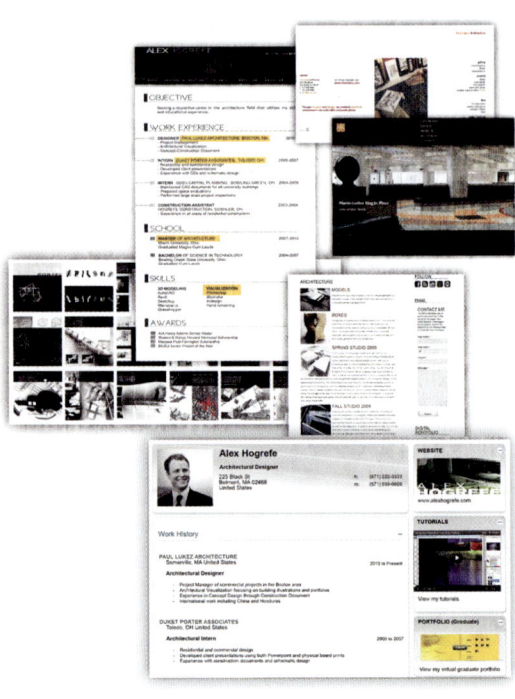

PLANNING AN EFFECTIVE SELF-PRESENTATION CAMPAIGN

RÉSUMÉ WEB HOSTING SERVICE

Finding a good web hosting service can really simplify things. They offer great features such as embedding video, uploading portfolios, and creating links to other important information on the web. A quick Google search revealed many respected résumé hosting services. Best of all, many of them are free.

PROMOTE

POSTINGS

Job postings are everywhere on the web. Knowing where to look can be challenging, although many cities are creating websites that bring the postings to one location. A strong digital résumé will help set your stuff apart from the hundreds of other digital applications.

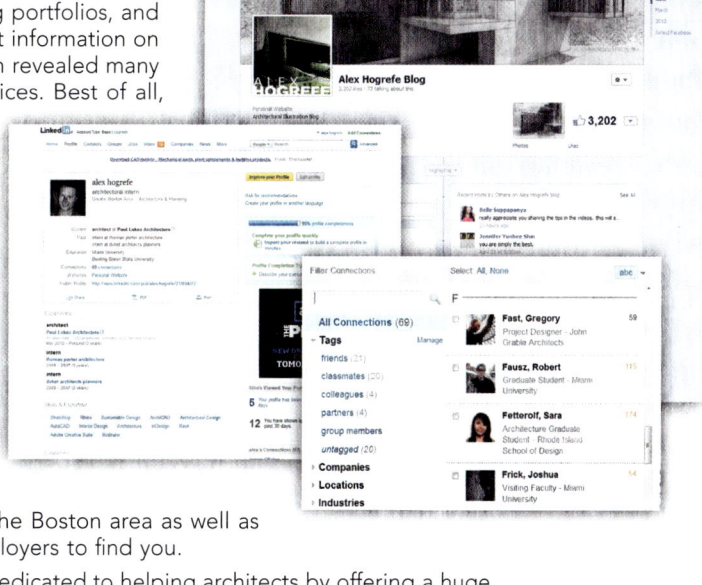

The BSA website is a great resource for searching jobs in the Boston area as well as uploading your résumé for employers to find you.

Websites like Archinect are dedicated to helping architects by offering a huge database of job listings and professional community building opportunities.

VIRTUAL JOB FAIR

Virtual job fairs are quickly taking the place of their face-to-face counterparts. When attending these online events, it's important to have a great set of CV documents ready to go in multiple file formats. Demonstrating proficiency in the digital realm is a huge boost in the virtual environment.

SOCIAL

Possibly one of the most crucial marketing tools is social media. These sites are geared towards connecting people across companies, industries, and locations. Therefore, integrating a résumé package into these sites provides an easy means for anyone to see your stuff.

With LinkedIn, I can easily manage all of my professional connections. I have had a couple of cases where possible employers viewed my LinkedIn profile before contacting me directly to talk.

Facebook is much more informal compared to LinkedIn. However, Facebook offers a larger network and typically closer relationship between users.

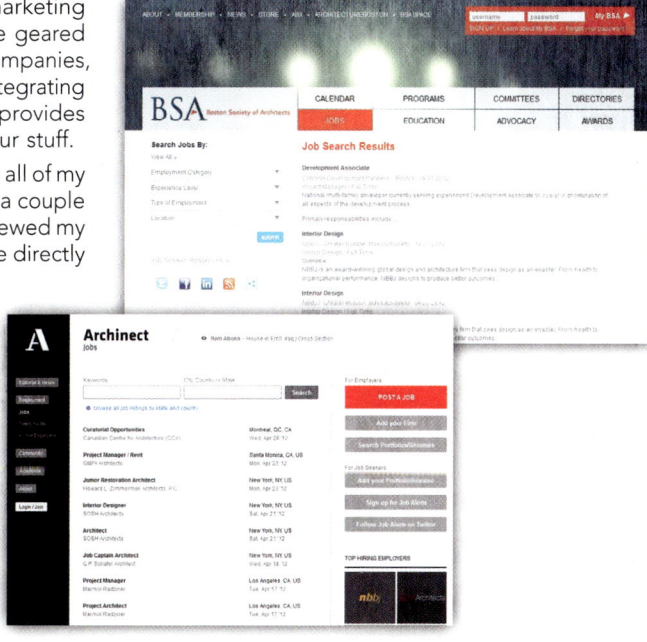

Google Plus is an up-and-coming social network designed to compete directly with Facebook. If you have a Facebook account, it wouldn't hurt to create a Google Plus account as well.

Twitter moves at a much faster pace compared to the other social mediums. Information here can spread very quickly.

1 PLAN

Develop a strategy and set priorities. This means compiling all information into one location and organizing it in a way that any specific piece of information can be accessed easily and quickly when building the résumé.

How will different information be accessed, and how will the different media relate to one another?

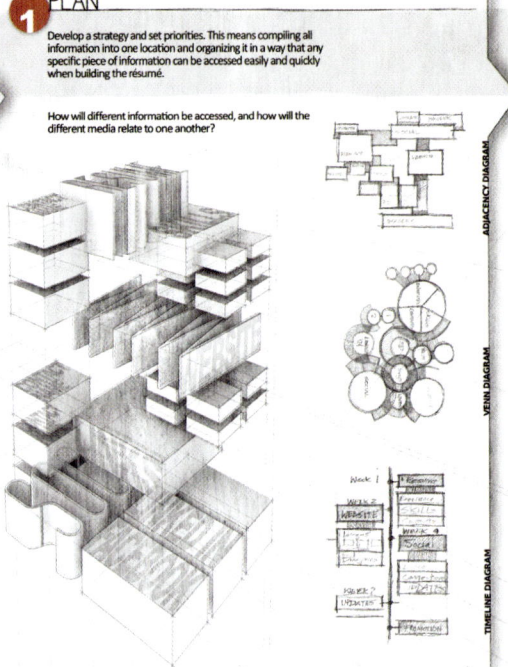

ADJACENCY DIAGRAM

VENN DIAGRAM

TIMELINE DIAGRAM

2 DESIGN

Build a traditional résumé to act as a foundation from which a website and other digital iterations can be launched. Most employers accept the hard copy résumé and many even require it.

TRADITIONAL 8.5"x11" SIZE: While this is the standard size, how the information is arranged within the margins can be as unique as you want it.

MS Word is not required to build a résumé. I use Photoshop because it allows me greater creative freedom than simple word processing software.

I integrate a timeline into my résumé to graphically supplement the text, all the while not detracting from the readability of the document.

TOOLS
- MS WORD
- PHOTOSHOP
- ILLUSTRATOR

STYLE
- LAYOUT
- FONT
- COLOR
- EFFECTS

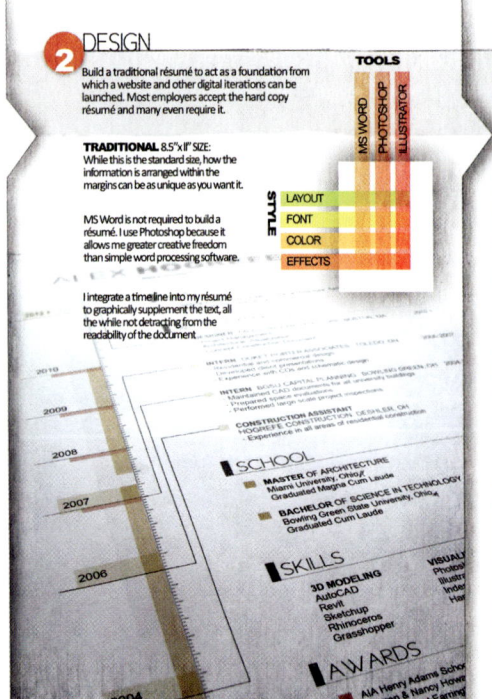

3 FORMAT

The next step is preparing the résumé to be viewed digitally. Some key questions to consider during the planning phase are: What types of devices will be used to view my résumé? How will orientation and screen size of these different devices influence the design? What types of file formats should be used for these difference devices? What is the universal usability of my digital résumé?

SCREEN SIZES

- **55" TELEVISION:** Typical for group viewing from a distance. In these situations, it is important to have a clear, well organized document for easy readability from long distances.
- **15"-22" LAPTOP/DESKTOP:** Currently the most used device/screen size. Larger screens mean attention to detail is key. Higher resolution images are a must.
- **6"-10" TABLET:** Versatile & Intimate: Can adapt to any orientation providing opportunities for creative layouts.
- **3.5" MOBILE:** Small & Intimate: Consider a layout that is clean and simple for easy viewing on small screens.

FILE TYPE:

- **JPEG:** Universally recognized by most devices and will upload and download more quickly than other formats over the Internet. Ideal for websites.
- **PDF:** Commonly requested format by employers. Accessible on most devices.
- **MS WORD:** Easy copy and paste text but tougher to use on mobile devices.

PLANNING AN EFFECTIVE SELF-PRESENTATION CAMPAIGN

4 DISTRIBUTE

4.1 EMAIL/ UPLOAD
The most common way to get your digital information out there is by email. There are some advantages of going this route.

HIGH RESOLUTION: What I like about email is that it offers up possibilities of sending high-resolution documents and images instead of being stuck with 72 dpi from online viewing.

CONVENTIONAL: Most professional environments will accept this way of communication and will already have specific addresses set up. However, most everybody else will be using this same method making it very easy for your stuff to get "lost" in the pile.

4.2 WEB ADDRESS
It is important to take advantage of the Internet and its reach to millions of users. Creating a web address gives you a stronger online presence and provides more opportunities for showing off your unique identity, personality, and skill set. There are two ways to go about getting a web address; create a personal website or use a résumé web hosting service.

1) PERSONAL WEBSITE: Websites are completely customizable and provide a dynamic experience for users. When I had my résumé on my own site, I created links to my employer's websites as well as to other relevant content on my own site. This allowed interested users to easily access more detailed information.

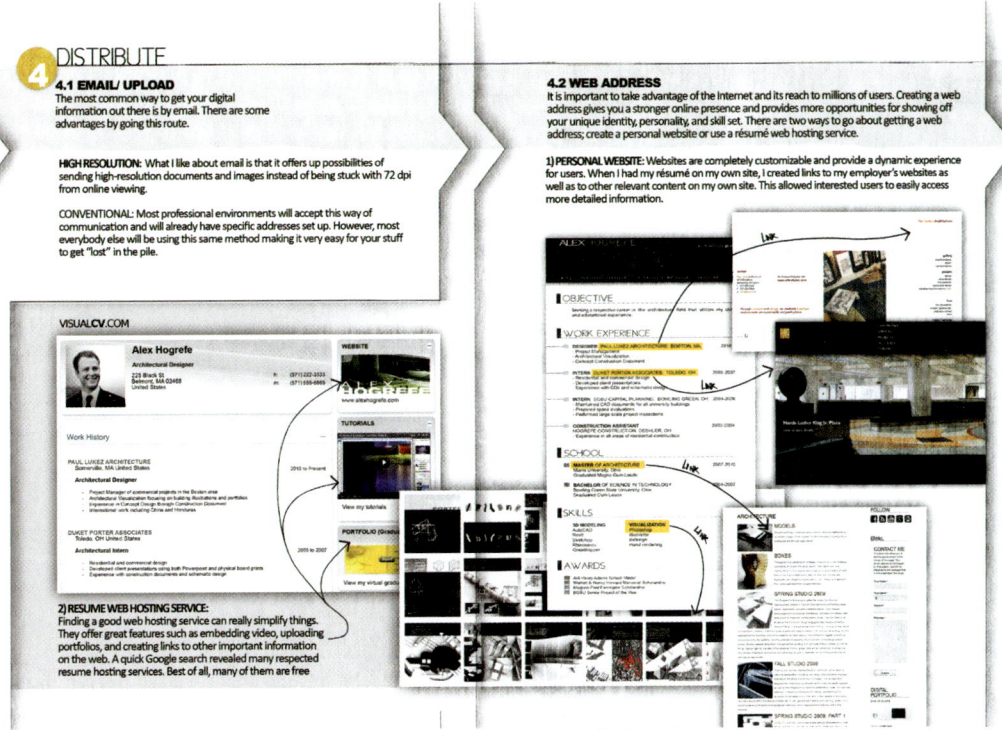

2) RESUME WEB HOSTING SERVICE:
Finding a good web hosting service can really simplify things. They offer great features such as embedding video, uploading portfolios, and creating links to other important information on the web. A quick Google search revealed many respected resume hosting services. Best of all, many of them are free

5 PROMOTE

5.1 POSTINGS
Job postings are everywhere on the web. Knowing where to look can be challenging, although many cities are creating websites that bring the postings to one location. A strong digital resume will help set your stuff apart from the hundreds of other digital applications.

Below, the BSA website is a great resource for searching jobs in the Boston area as well as uploading your résumé for employers to find you.

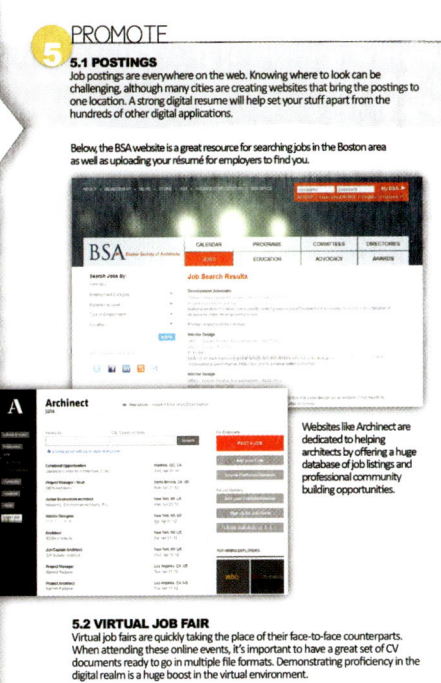

Websites like Archinect are dedicated to helping architects by offering a huge database of job listings and professional community building opportunities.

5.2 VIRTUAL JOB FAIR
Virtual job fairs are quickly taking the place of their face-to-face counterparts. When attending these online events, it's important to have a great set of CV documents ready to go in multiple file formats. Demonstrating proficiency in the digital realm is a huge boost in the virtual environment.

5.3 SOCIAL
Possibly one of the most crucial marketing tools is social media. These sites are geared towards connecting people across companies, industries, and locations. Therefore, integrating a resume package into these sites provides an easy means for anyone to see your stuff.

LinkedIn allows me to easily manage all of my professional connection. I have had a couple of cases where possible employers viewed my LinkedIn profile before contacting me directly to talk.

Facebook is much more informal compared to LinkedIn. However, Facebook offers a vast network and typically closer relationship between users.

Google Plus is an up-and-coming social network designed to compete directly with Facebook. If you have a Facebook account, it wouldn't hurt to create a Google Plus account as well.

Twitter moves at a much faster pace compared to the other social mediums. Information here can spread very quickly

15

CASE STUDY 3

TITLE: PRESENTING, PRESENCING
AUTHOR: NICK AXEL

In his essay "Presenting, Presencing" Madrid-based Nick Axel describes contemporary, professional self-presentation as a multimedia effort encompassing a much larger sphere of activity than the traditional CV and cover letter. While Axel highlights the ways online social networks contribute to broader ways of defining ourselves, he also notes the ways in which such technologies have shifted our concepts and methods of self-actualization. Gone are the traditional, hierarchical protocols of establishing professional identities. In their place, emerging professionals must now carefully navigate a multiplicity of flat, dynamic networks representing both the public and private selves.

Throughout Nick's case study and his portfolio you will see how he brings together ideas, themes, threads, and narratives from different sites, media genres, disciplines, and discourses. He invents his story as well as the purpose, means, and strategies of self-presentation campaigns in new ways. From his work, it is evident that Nick is able to see and imagine in ways that exceed the ordinary and obvious. You will remember that symphony is the elucidation of relationships, connections, and inter-workings that are not always obvious. Seeing symphony is a state of mind in which you use your whole mind. How can seeing an example of symphonic thinking in action help you achieve this state of mind in your own work and self-presentation campaign?

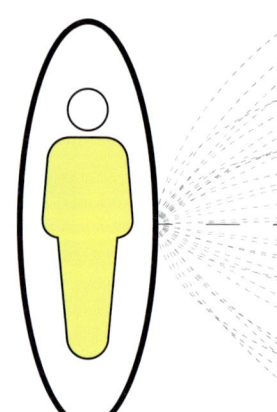

PLANNING AN EFFECTIVE SELF-PRESENTATION CAMPAIGN

▶PRESENTING, PRESENCING
NICK AXEL

The idea of self-presentation is predicated on a situation of presence and the unknown. It is a performance by which you become known to someone that did not know you beforehand. In that sense, self-presentation is an intricate series of actions that results in the formation of an identity in the mind of the person to who you are trying to connect with. We typically associate self-presentation within the labor market and with materials such as a résumé and a motivational letter, but with this potentially wider perspective, I would like to argue that self-presentation is not limited to somebody reading a piece of paper or email, but encompasses a much larger sphere of activity.

That is not to say that self-presentation has nothing to do with these traditional mediums of identification, but if identity is the goal, in our networked culture there are many more ways to establish it, for identity is created through the recognition of presence. With the opportunities for communication that have radically expanded our social and professional realms and are available to us at virtually every location on the globe, it is questionable to maintain the belief that the forms we are used to using are enough.

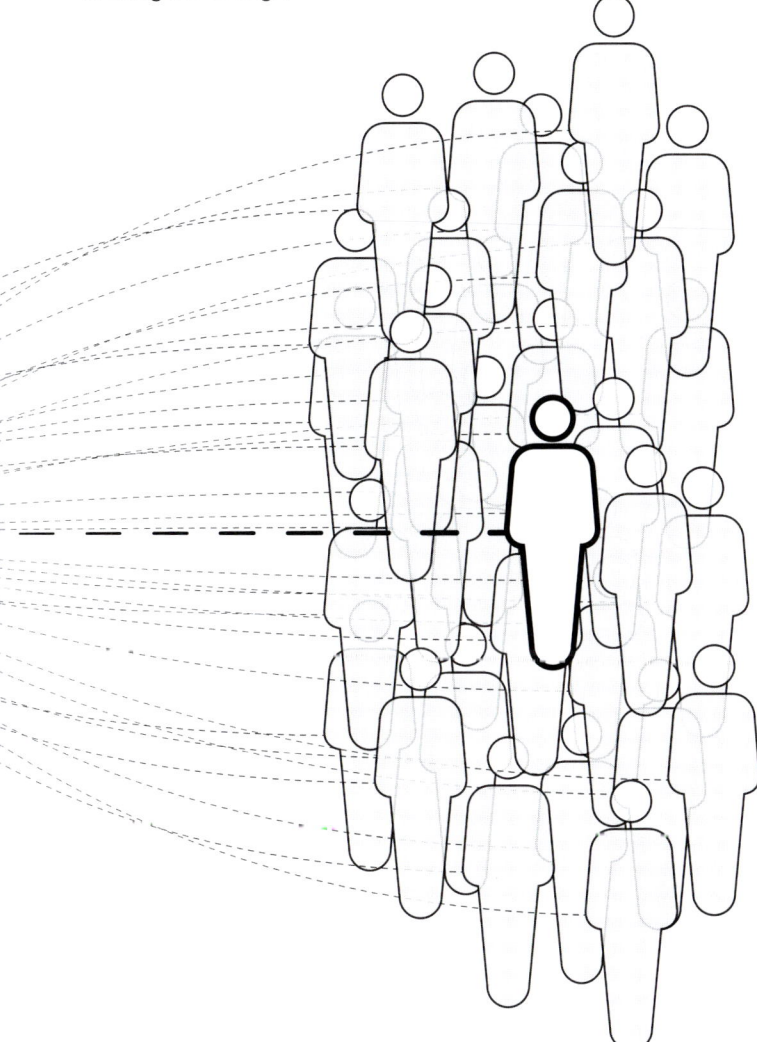

figure **1**
When we present ourselves, we present ourselves to *someone*. It is almost certain that we are not the only ones trying to present ourselves to this specific person. In the eyes of the other, how can we present ourselves in a way that will initiate the formation of an identity in their mind?

In order to properly address this subject, we must start from the top and consider why it is we present ourselves. The CV and cover letter have evolved from a tradition of applying for some sort of professional position. We apply for such things in order to do, learn, and become what we want, but the ability to proceed along these paths of becoming is no longer constrained by this traditional hierarchical protocol. Most strongly exemplified by online communication networks such as Twitter or Facebook, we are more freely able to fulfill these personal desires for development by partaking in a vibrant, flat network of information, communication, and interpersonal relations. These networks not only offer the ability to create a presence for ourselves, but as well to enjoy the fruits of recognizing presence. When we are present, regardless of the place which constitutes it, we grow: we find new things, we meet new people, we come across new opportunities, we test out, discover, and do the things we want.

If and when one's situation comes down to having to apply for a job the general rules may still apply, but the position from which one presents themselves is radically augmented. An expanded presence, one that transcends what the CV says (or what the portfolio looks like), one that is based on active relations and lived memories, can establish a unique recognition in the mind of the potential employer that will set that person apart from the undifferentiated mass of other people who are applying for the same position. Networks provide latent opportunities for your identity to be noticed in a more natural, and perhaps even more honest way. Network presence provides a depth of perspective into the actuality of one's identity, a depth that is only questionably possible to communicate in traditional means. The depth of an independent presence not only communicates one's self more efficiently, but allows for serendipitous relations to be discovered with whom it is you are trying to establish a connection with in the first place.

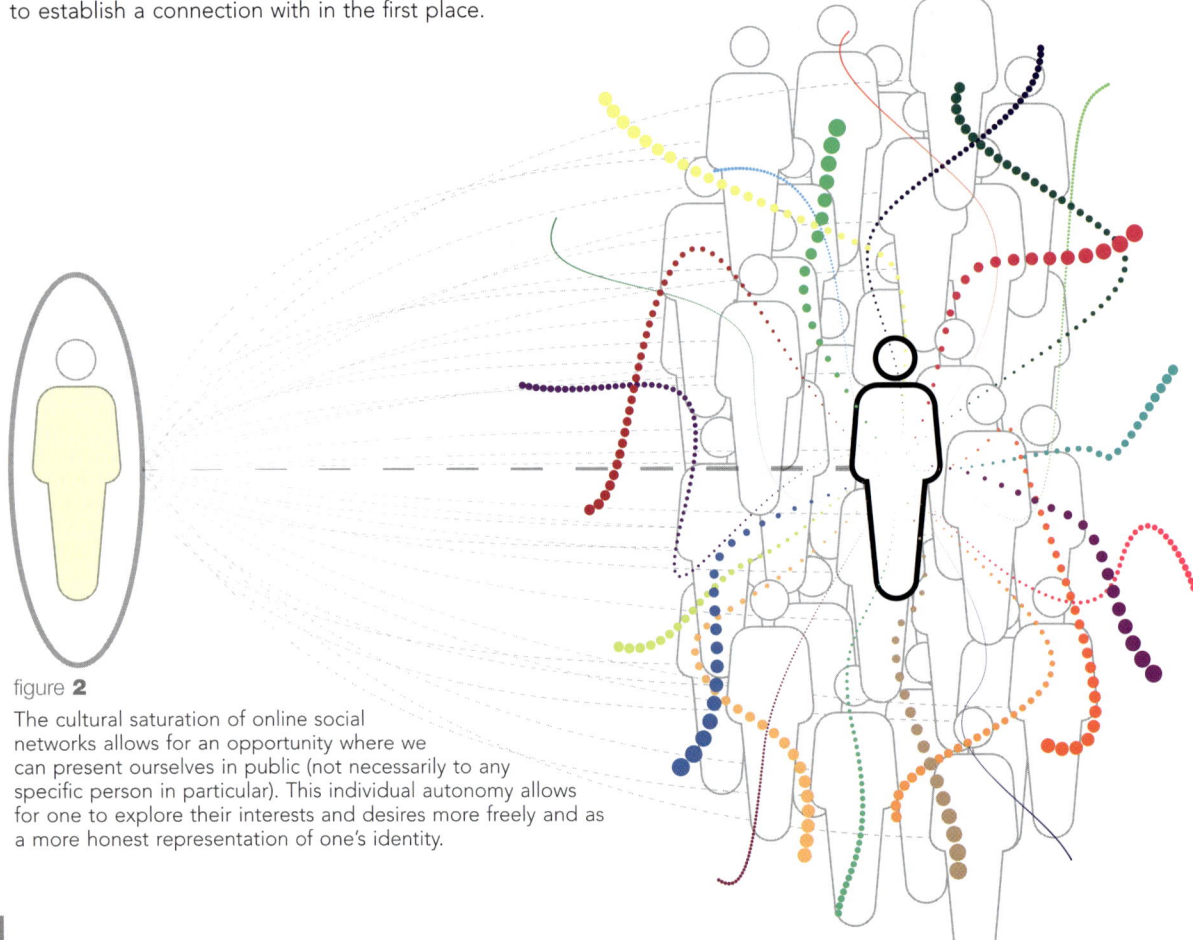

figure **2**

The cultural saturation of online social networks allows for an opportunity where we can present ourselves in public (not necessarily to any specific person in particular). This individual autonomy allows for one to explore their interests and desires more freely and as a more honest representation of one's identity.

PLANNING AN EFFECTIVE SELF-PRESENTATION CAMPAIGN

TRANSCENDING THE "ELEMENTS OF CIRCUMSTANCE"

In traditional western journalism and investigation, the "events of circumstance" define the specific types of information that are required to legitimately know the subject one is dealing with.[1] Having gone through many evolutions over the past two thousand years, these parcels of information have evolved into the categories of *who, what, when, where, why,* and *how*. The main task of our various traditional means to present ourselves is to successfully and efficiently communicate these things about ourselves and our work. Within the hyper-saturated milieu of postmodern identity that we live in, what is more important than any of the specifications listed above is the presence of something that can be further looked at more specifically. Essentially, the *fact that something is* predicates any deeper characteristic for the placement of judgment and value.

The question thus becomes: how can we become recognized (for the person that we are)? To start answering this question begins unfurling an infinite list of possibilities, but the specific potentialities *acted* upon (or not) by each and every one of us are ultimately singular and uniquely identify us. The way we present ourselves in the world ultimately gives a more total definition, demonstrating our perceptions, our interests, our comforts, our desires, and our will. If we only present ourselves to people we want to forge relations with by sending them a CV and motivation letter, what does that say about who we are and what we are hoping to achieve?

That is not to say that the CV and motivation letter have no value; their forms exist as historical protocols that must still be followed. I will therefore discuss their historical and formulaic nature in the relation to the expanded framework of today, and then explicate the performance of various contemporary modes of presentation.

The cover letter is the most explicit way we present ourselves: it is, most basically, a formal introduction. Imbued with the abstract power of language, it has an enormous capacity for the communication of one's identity within the traditional framework of communicating and understanding information. We can use this space to situate ourselves in relation to others, and more importantly, in relation to a larger discourse of architecture that we are attempting to engage with. In this text, it is important to not only express *who* you are and *what* your interests are, but *why* that matters and *how* that relates to your potentials.

The CV is a universal protocol of identification that communicates your previous experiences through which you have become who you are right now: it is a historical and biographic report. As such, it is a language in and of itself that is accompanied by its own internal rules, highlighted by the bureaucratic standardization of the CV within the European Union in 1998 with the Europass system.[2] There is a basic criteria of legibility and fact-based familiarity embedded within the omnipresence of its form. Abstract identifiers such as which university you attended, or what work experience you have had in the past, are intended to signify something specific, and therefore to be understood as clearly as possible.

The signifiers embedded within the CV have come to mean increasingly specific things, particularly in architecture, ranging from aesthetic style to ideological methodology. Universities have been forced by the market to brand themselves and become machines for pedagogical identification. High profile unpaid internships have become a near-required experience in many architectural cultures around the world, providing an opportunity to present one's chosen design sense and ambition through sacrifice and self-marginalization. These means have become so ubiquitous, almost natural, in response to the increasing diversity and cultural saturation of postmodernity. While these represent a possible way to establish professional relations, in our networked culture it is key to recognize that there exist alternative options for identifying one's self that can be more effective than one or two or twelve recognizable and "impressive" items on one's CV.

BECOMING PUBLIC, BECOMING PRESENT

Online social networks have fundamentally altered the significance of self-presentation by constituting a multiplicity of public realms that dynamically interact with each other and laminate themselves on top of our immediate environment, our perceptions, and our being-in-the-world. Those whom we intend to present ourselves to are increasingly involving themselves in these realms not only to present themselves to others, but to become aware of others' presences, making it increasingly imperative to participate in these spheres of activity. With the continual growth and importance of these networks, the online and offline worlds influence each other more than ever, quickly dissolving preconceptions of a difference in value or importance between the two. The enormous potential of online networking is daunting, and its varied theatres for performance are often overlooked or ignored in the face of sheer content. As such, I will seek to reveal the differences between a select few networks, their propensities and consequences for self-presentation.

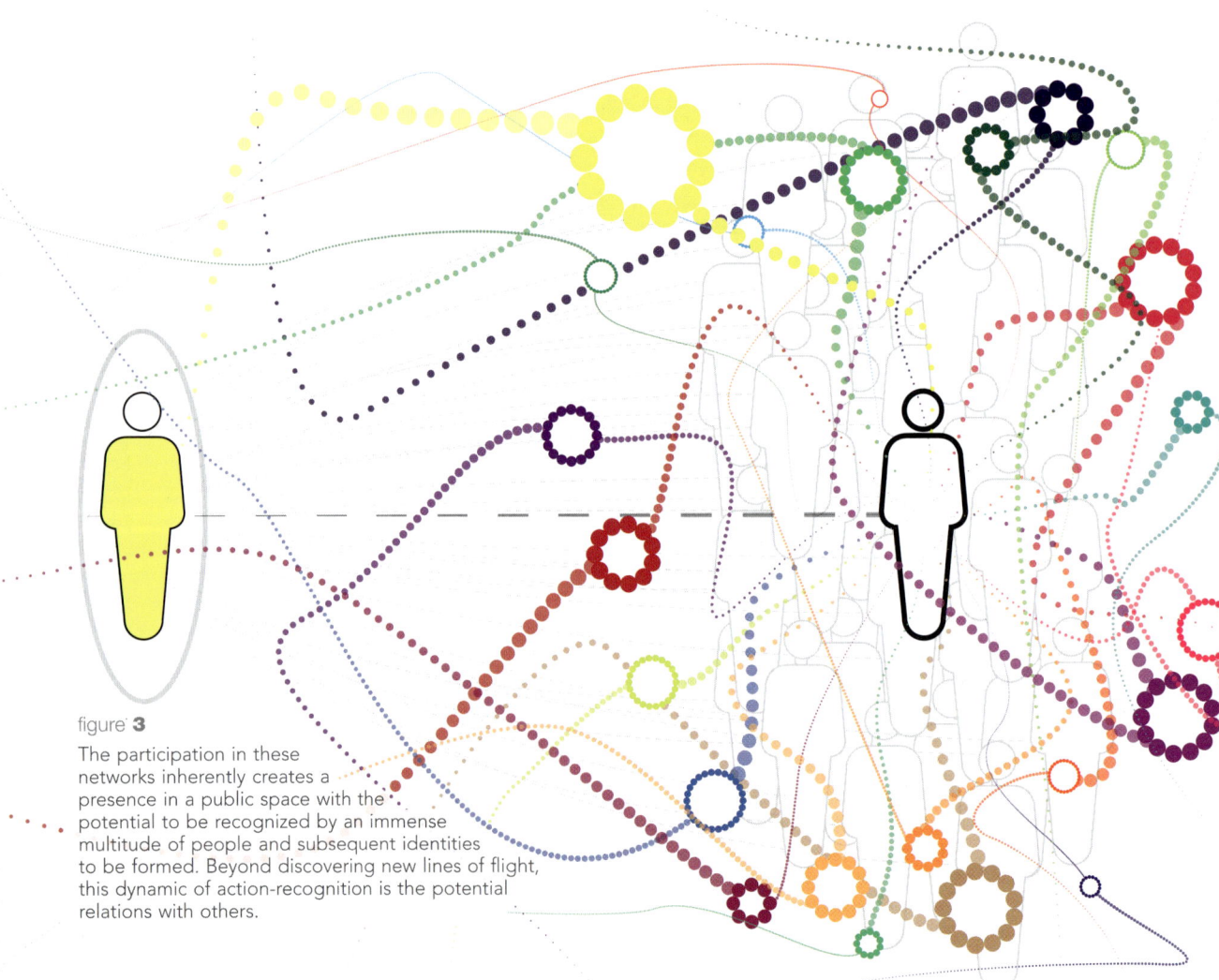

figure 3

The participation in these networks inherently creates a presence in a public space with the potential to be recognized by an immense multitude of people and subsequent identities to be formed. Beyond discovering new lines of flight, this dynamic of action-recognition is the potential relations with others.

PLANNING AN EFFECTIVE SELF-PRESENTATION CAMPAIGN

With nearly one billion active users at the time of this writing, Facebook is, one could say, the largest active public realm in the history of mankind. With the "mission to make the world more open and connected", Facebook undoubtedly achieves what it intends to do. To quote further, "people use Facebook to stay connected with friends and family, to discover what's going on in the world, and to share and express what matters to them."[3] This "personal" statement is revealing of its propensity for self-presentation, further highlighted by a brief recount of its history. Founded at, within, and for Harvard University, Facebook was created in order to give people within the university a way to interact in a more open space, embodying this idealized conception of a university itself, where people come together under a common purpose, and as such are related to each other at the very least, because of that. Facebook quickly spread to universities across the United States and around the globe. In 2005, just one year after its incorporation as a business, Facebook expanded its potential user-base to encompass high-school students, and soon thereafter certain large companies.

In 2006, with over 12 million active users, Facebook made the monumental decision to make its potential user-base open to everyone. This critically meant that the status of a shared affiliation, that which Facebook was created in order to augment and intensify, was no longer necessary. With a basic precondition of internet access and a valid e-mail address, Facebook became a truly public space, unhinging for the first time the limits and potentials of social awareness.

What started as an *explicitly shared symbolic space*[4] quickly turned into a shared space devoid of any symbolic function. While constituting a raw potential for symbolic edification and communal becoming, this paradigmatic transformation is still encumbered by its latent affiliated past; the platform is still fundamentally based on the creation of a profile that surreptitiously reintroduces the private realm along with traditional forms of self-presentation and the "elements of circumstance." While Facebook offers an ideal context for self-presentation, if for nothing more than by pure scale, and as much as Facebook has attempted to alter its framework to mitigate this effect with the introduction of business and professional pages, Facebook is laden with a private disposition that is antithetical to an expanded perspective of self-presentation. By holding onto the distinctive notions of public and private, Facebook creates an internal contradiction that each person must precariously navigate if they are present themselves. While it is open, Facebook is also personal, and it is this dimension that threatens the success of any self-presentation: it is a space where the recognition of an unknown presence may be an undesired activity by those whom we present ourselves to.

It is this act of recognition that can only take place in the public: even the act of opening a post-card constitutes a public space between the writer and the reader. Blogging services provide a substantial alternative of self-presentation to Facebook in multiple regards. Primarily, there is no profile. The identity that is formed by a blog is solely based on what you make it; its presence is actualized solely based on the action which takes place in and on it. Second, as a contemporary interpretation of a log, or journal, a blog is not a static object. It is meant to align more with one's stream of consciousness than with the way one abstractly conceives of themselves. In this sense, a blog can be more radically personal than Facebook. Third, in its traditional form, there is a clear distinction in its form between the creator of the blog and the public body it creates. Fourth, there is no effective network that creates a dynamic interchange of actors within a single space: each blog constitutes its own public space. By mandating autonomy and public presentation, certain pitfalls of Facebook are averted while others are allowed to arise. The notions of one's personal space effectively cannot be violated, as both sides of the blogosphere, awareness and presentation, are entirely based on the agency willfully taken up by individuals. The lack of a physical network that connects blogs together (apart from the specific decision by each blog to affiliate themselves with others in a variety of ways) seems to privilege awareness over presentation by allowing the act of awareness, the consequence of presentation, to go on anonymously, crippling the interactive precondition of presentation itself.

The interaction between who is presenting and who is recognizing is crucial, as only the dynamism of a communicative relationship can produce any production of the desired outcomes for self-presentation. If blogs are accessible yet hierarchical and Facebook is hyper-connected but devoid of any symbolic unification, Twitter is a platform for communication that critically transforms the faults of previous networks by radically emphasizing their beneficial characteristics, making it the ideal realm for contemporary self-presentation. By lacking any sort of "home" and minimizing the significance of a profile to a single sentence and a link to elsewhere, Twitter effectively severs the connection between the public and the private, declaring itself a purely public space. The lack of a profile has a profound effect on the manifestation of presences on Twitter which are subsequently and solely constituted by action which highlights the performative and interactive characteristic of online communication networks. The network of Twitter, that which creates a single public space, is critically unique in relation to the same way in which blogs perform in this way. By channeling all action into one space, sheer content and an extreme flow of information emphasizes the "here and now" by virtually erasing its historical record. This dissolution of the binary structure between "owner" and "visitor" liberates the volition of participants by creating a truly flat space which is impossible to "own", but merely possible to inhabit. This temporal nature is provocative by its very precarity. It is a network entirely constituted by presence, and all there is to do is act.

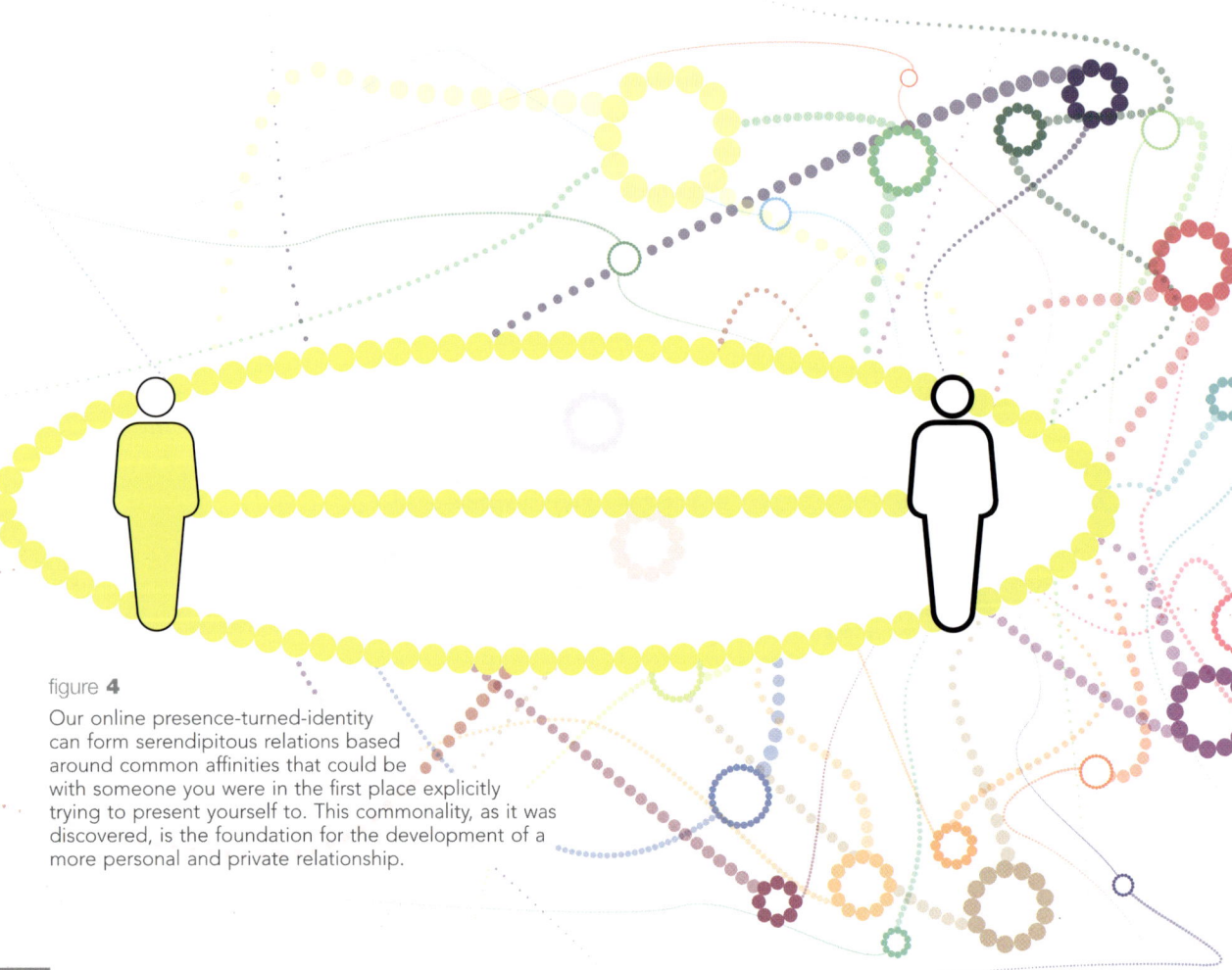

figure **4**

Our online presence-turned-identity can form serendipitous relations based around common affinities that could be with someone you were in the first place explicitly trying to present yourself to. This commonality, as it was discovered, is the foundation for the development of a more personal and private relationship.

This seemingly lack, or empty function, is further emphasized by the superimposition of by an *arbitrary* constraint for expression that effectively provides the symbolic function necessary for a true public realm. The network itself has almost no defining characteristics; in this sense, Twitter is possibly the closest manifestation of Jeremy Bentham's conception that governmental legislation and law should be limited to a "necessary minimum".[5] The transparency of the laws and their totally objective nature grant freedom to whomever chooses to use it (in whatever way they please). Twitter is the contemporary (and digital) manifestation of an agora for the exchange of ideas. It is a public marketplace for information. It is an open and accessible theatre for performance.

While Twitter is an ideal place for the formation of a public identity, it obviates the necessity of a private sphere. The private is not a place for presentation, but representation. A personal website is the contemporary home, and shares many characteristics with the mid-twentieth-century suburban home as an object and means for self-identification. It is the amalgamation of one's varied and dynamic existence represented through aesthetic continuity. It is the place in which everything is collected that one is while demonstrating the extent of one's being. It allows for the greatest degree of design freedom, as opposed to Facebook where their profile (and particularly its projected evolution of the Timeline) serves the same purpose, but constrains aesthetic representation with its rigid structure. The personal website is not inherently connected to anything in particular aside for one's own presence, and as such is the culminating point of a self-charted territory of self-presentation. The personal website effectively liberates the individual with a sense of autonomy to use networks in any which way they please.

The autonomous presence possible to establish within various online networks is an immanent source for the presentation of any self. Networks not only provide a place in which identities can be created, but a place where those identities can connect and form empathetic relations with each other that might not have been possible in any other way. Thanks to the open framework of online platforms such as Twitter, we can make the omnipresence of networks become a network of presences. The network provides us with the opportunity to discover and activate latent collective identities, effectively circumventing traditional means of self-presentation and subverting the hierarchical production of identity.

Notes
1 "Five Ws." Wikipedia. Wikimedia Foundation, 25 Apr. 2012. Web. 29 April 2012. <http://en.wikipedia.org/wiki/Five_Ws>.
2 "The History of Europass." Europass. Web. 29 April 2012. <http://europass.cedefop.europa.eu/en/about/history>.
3 "Fact Sheet." Facebook. Web. 29 April 2012. <http://newsroom.fb.com/content/default.aspx?NewsAreaId=22>.
4 See Chantal Mouffe's conceptual development of agonism and the political necessity for a "shared symbolic space" in Mouffe, Chantal, *On the Political*. London: Routledge, 2005. Print.
5 See Bentham, Jeremy, *An Introduction to the Principles of Morals and Legislation*. 1907. Library of Economics and Liberty. 29 April 2012. <http://www.econlib.org/library/Bentham/bnthPML.html> and Constant, Benjamin. "On the Extension of Political Authority Beyond Its Necessary Minimum, On the Grounds of Utility," in *Principles of Politics Applicable to All Governments*. Ed. Etienne Hofmann. Trans. Dennis O'Keeffe. Indianapolis, IN: Liberty Fund, 2003. Print.

CASE STUDY 4

TITLE: PROMOTION PROPORTIONS
AUTHOR: BRANDON CLIFFORD

New York-based Brandon Clifford's essay, "Promotion Proportions", provides parallel narrative and visual representations of the author's self-promotion processes across three time periods: the professional, student, and academic stages of his life. Clifford measures his marketing endeavors in terms of effort (input) vs. return or loss (output), and offers graphical illustrations of his findings. Surprisingly, Clifford's data suggests an increase in his visibility and demand for services when his focus shifted from application and documentation (publication, competitions, etc.) to networking via everyday activities like teaching, lecturing, and serving on juries. His discovery indicates embedded marketing has been more fruitful for his practice than the use of more conventional and explicit methods.

So it seems that getting out there and building personal and professional relationships face-to-face really does work. What else can we conclude from Brandon's findings? What, specifically, does this tell us about effective self-promotion and personal, professional engagement and marketing? Given what we know about Pink's contention that the impending Conceptual Age will require the ability to truly emphasize, interact, and emotionally engage with other individuals – from employers, to clients, to colleagues and coworkers – in the endeavor to make collective meaning, then are Brandon's findings really all that surprising?

Remember that empathy involves the imagination and the ability to experience the world from another's perspective. Empathy is an extension of self that expands to include others through empathetic thoughts and actions. As we see in Brandon's experience, often the first step to empathy involves a thoughtful, introspective study and working knowledge of self. It involves a looking inward before turning your energy and focus outward.

▶ PROMOTION PROPORTIONS
BRANDON CLIFFORD

INTRODUCTION

Matter Design is a research collaboration between Brandon Clifford and Wes McGee, which focuses on design through advanced fabrication methods. The following diagrams (Figures 1–3) are a retro-analysis of the promotion process at Matter Design across three time periods – Professional, Student, and Academic. These diagrams are not indicative of strictly promotional intent, but rather designed for a comparative and proportional perspective of what it means to promote oneself in a vanguard practice, across a spectrum of contexts and conditions. Each of the three time periods is diagramed in proportion to effort (input) vs. return or loss (output). On the left of each diagram is the perceived effort placed in the following four categories:

- Application – effort spent planning the next career pursuit. For example, as a professional, some time was allocated to applying to graduate schools.
- Documentation – effort spent preparing, organizing, editing, and archiving work in preparation for promotion.
- Release – the act of sending out documentation to various audiences.
- Networking – the act of investing time and service that is not intended for direct promotion, but rather returns indirectly. For example, presenting a paper at a conference may not be explicitly intended for promotion, but it might create a networking potential that later leads to promotion.

Contained within each of these four categories are the proportioned tasks in the form of effort. Each task is then split into the perceived percentage of promotional return vs. loss.

Effort, return, and loss are all proportionately calculated based on an archive of to-do lists as well as documentation of publication. While this is not a scientific method, perception and perspective are at the root of this diagram. Some forms of publication are valued differently depending on perspective (time period). Peer review journals, for example, are perceived as more important in academia than glossy magazines; however, this perception could be inverted if the career trajectory reversed.

PROFESSIONAL

This time period is one where I was working professionally as a project manager at Office dA, Inc. while attempting to start an independent practice. A large proportion of effort was dedicated to documentation of previous design work and building a portfolio designed to open doors in future times. A large portion of this effort is perceived as return because the up-front effort invested in the foundation of this portfolio continues with me as a dynamic artifact. While I continue to build the portfolio, the workload today is much more efficient because the scaffolding is already in place. Some interesting components in this diagram include the amount of time devoted to magazine publication efforts. This time might be misinterpreted as wasted, but rather it is a claim that publication of my work in magazines had little to no impact on the future of my practice. Social media was also a relatively large percentage in comparison to the Student and Academic time periods, though in response to the perceived loss, effort placed on social media dropped significantly to the point where, in the academic period, zero effort was placed in this category.

STUDENT

The student time period is one where I attended graduate school while concurrently maintaining my practice. During this era, a significantly larger portion of time was spent on entering competitions and applying for future jobs in academia. A larger shift was the emphasis placed on editing and contributing to journals, critical essays, and paper publications as opposed to magazines. This time period redirected my focus to extending my efforts to arenas outside the realm of traditional practice, and I focused on academia as the vehicle to make that change.

ACADEMIC

This period is one of an academic researcher and professor. A surprising result from this diagram is the dramatic shift away from application and documentation towards increased networking. Ironically, significantly more work has been produced during this time period, but rather than applying for and pushing material out, more and more requests for publication have been coming in because the majority of effort spent on marketing is embedded in everyday activities like teaching, lecturing, and serving on juries.

PLANNING AN EFFECTIVE SELF-PRESENTATION CAMPAIGN

figure **1** Professional Promo Proportions.

figure **2** Student Promo Proportions.

figure **3** Academic Promo Proportions.

27

CASE STUDY 5

TITLE: HARNESSING THE POWER OF INVENTION
AUTHOR: ALEXIS PEGRAM-PIPER

Alexis Pegram-Piper, a student of Rhetoric who is currently studying Invention for her dissertation, provides a theoretical background on the art of invention and creativity, from ancient Greek traditions to our modern period. She highlights the relevant, practical characteristics and applications of invention, which include: empathy, making important and original connections, introspection, engaging in productive dialogue with others, movement from the conscious to the unconscious, synthesis, and valuing mistakes and dead ends. Piper summarizes and ties the disparate contributions to the book together by pointing out how discovery, as a theme, is woven throughout various contributions. She also demonstrates how essential invention is for launching your own successful self-presentation campaign.

So it seems that getting out there and building personal and professional relationships face-to-face really does work. What else can we conclude from Brandon's findings? What, specifically, does this tell us about effective self-promotion and personal, professional engagement and marketing? Given what we know about Pink's contention that the impending Conceptual Age will require the ability to truly emphasize, interact, and emotionally engage with other individuals – from employers, to clients, to colleagues and coworkers – in the endeavor to make collective meaning, then are Brandon's findings really all that surprising?

Remember that empathy involves the imagination and the ability to experience the world from another's perspective. Empathy is an extension of self that expands to include others through empathetic thoughts and actions. As we see in Brandon's experience, often the first step to empathy involves a thoughtful, introspective study and working knowledge of self. It involves a looking inward before turning your energy and focus outward.

PLANNING AN EFFECTIVE SELF-PRESENTATION CAMPAIGN

▶ HARNESSING THE POWER OF INVENTION
ALEXIS PEGRAM-PIPER

Just as they gave us Philosophy and insights into the importance of self-actualization, the Greeks also gave us Rhetoric. And the first of five arts (or offices) of Rhetoric is Invention. Invention, in this context, involves developing a method (or heuristic) of inquiry. In other words, invention, as an office of Rhetoric, provides us with a way to systematically discover. Understanding and harnessing your capacity to discover, create, and innovate will not only prove invaluable to your future career, but also to an effective self-presentation campaign.

From a Platonic perspective, "Invention is a solitary act in which the individual, drawing upon innate knowledge and mental structures, searches for the truth, using introspective self-examination and heuristic methods of various kinds … Invention is regarded as an unfolding, a manifestation of an individual's ideas, feelings, voice, personality, and patterns of thought" (LeFevre, 1987, p. 1). The Greeks and Romans considered the first office of Rhetoric (Invention) as pertaining almost exclusively to the discovery of logical arguments and available means of persuasion. However, the more contemporary trend in Rhetorical theory has been to broaden the meaning and application of Invention so that the art of Invention is currently tied to creativity and innovation in general. As you think about Pink's six aptitudes and his advice from the introduction to this chapter, as you strive to use your "right-brain" qualities of inventiveness, empathy, joyfulness, and meaning to plan your innovative, thoughtful, and dynamic self-presentation campaign, some background on theories and methods of Invention will serve you well.

The art of Invention has gone by different names throughout history: from discovery, to hypothesis formulation, to creative ability, to critical inquiry, to imagination, to the Muse. In the introduction to this chapter, we told you that the act of design requires a capacity to "freely explore ideas" while harnessing your creative potential to synthesize concepts and perspectives from various disciplines. This is where your imagination, your Muse, your ability to think critically and creatively, or your powers of Invention come in. We learned that, "Symphony requires that we see and imagine in new ways" and "Empathy entails imagination, discovering your passion, and seeing things from another's perspective". Therefore, without the ability to see inter-connections and to systematically discover, to tap into your own method of Invention, you will not have the skills that are essential to the success of your self-presentation campaign. The art of Invention is necessary for making you stand out amongst the crowd and for making your self-presentation materials resonate with your audience.

Whatever name it goes by, Invention is often broken down into various stages. For example, in *Rhetoric: Discovery and Change*, Young, Becker, and Pike divide the method of discovery into four stages: preparation, incubation, illumination, and verification. During the preparation stage "the general movement … is from feeling to conscious analysis as the problem is put into language and explored" (Young et al., 1970, p. 73). Preparation includes engaging in a dialogue with yourself to explore your goals and to discover what the problem or objective exactly is and what your ideas are. The incubation stage entails subconscious activity in which your subliminal intelligence and creativity go to work. You may even take your conscious mind off of the objective and concentrate on other tasks while your ideas stew in your subconscious. After you have researched and studied your subject for a considerable amount of time, and after you have let your subliminal stew simmer, then you (hopefully) will experience the stage of illumination. In this third stage of inquiry "there is an imaginative leap to a possible solution, a hypothesis" (p. 74). In Young et al.'s final stage of inquiry, verification, your hypothesis is tested. As you can see, in its movement towards a final product, idea, or solution the process of inquiry undulates from conscious to subconscious mental activity. Most theorists tend to agree that invention involves movement from conscious, rational reasoning to subconscious intelligence or intuition. In other words, throughout the stages of Invention, there needs to be a fluid dialogue between reason and intuition.

For example, throughout Nick Axel's case study and his portfolio you saw how he brought together ideas, themes, threads, and narratives from different sites, media genres, disciplines, and discourses, thereby synthesizing different perspectives to create something new. Axel is able to access his powers of innovation and invention to communicate his story and professional ethos in new, exciting, and memorable ways. He is also able to synthesize different mediums, discourses, and worldviews by using his whole mind, his right and left brain, his reason and intuition, his conscious and subconscious intellectual capabilities.

Young *et al.* write, "Each of us has a subconscious intelligence, a strong and vital force in our mental life that seems to have a greater capacity than reason for dealing with the complex and the unfamiliar" (p. 74). The act of creating anything original and worthwhile – from a résumé or a professional portfolio to a piece of sculpture or a modern dance routine – demands that we cede some control to the imaginative and the mysterious. And this relinquishing of conscious rationality always involves an element of risk. Therefore, throughout the process of Invention, we need to give ourselves leave to make mistakes. Young, Becker, and Pike remind us that, "We are all reluctant to make errors, but without a willingness to make them, original inquiry is impossible. Invention normally proceeds by a succession of increasingly intelligent mistakes; we learn from them and move ever closer to a solution. If your inquiry is to be independent and original, you must accept the risks involved" (p. 76). Blunders are an important part of the process – and an inevitable part of venturing into intuition, the subconscious, and Invention. As you noticed in the first case study of this chapter, it took a great amount of collective imagination and inventive power for propeller Z to come up with their art-via-vending-machine concept. It was something that had never been done before, so undoubtedly there was a significant element of risk involved, (and there was also undoubtedly blunders and mis-steps along the way) but this act of imagination achieved through the art of Invention was ultimately remarkably successful.

In his essay "How to Keep and Feed a Muse" author Ray Bradbury contends that the subconscious and all of the unique life experiences that are stored there are what sets us apart from each other. Bradbury writes, "The subconscious … is the stuff of originality. For it is in the totality of experience reckoned with, filed, and forgotten, that each man is truly different from all others in the world" (p. 81). The experiences and worldviews that make you a unique individual are perhaps the most vital things you can share with anyone, including prospective employers. These are, in fact, the very essence and reason for communication. Our most vital contributions begin with self-actualization. After first understanding how and why we are unique, we can then assess what we have to contribute. Knowing yourself, realizing your full potential, and getting in touch with your innermost motivations and ultimate purpose are also the first steps in creating meaning for others. In the second case study of this chapter you have seen an excellent example of self-actualization and the communication of a distinct persona in the professional profile of Alex Hogrefe. Hogrefe is able to construct a unique narrative and subsequently create meaning for his audience by first establishing who he is and what he has to contribute.

Hogrefe's contribution to case study two (and all of the case studies presented here) also demonstrates that while Invention and originality may begin with the Self, self-actualization, and an internal dialogue, this is not where the art of Invention ends. Invention is always dependent upon and a product of a sociocultural context. We are incapable of inventing in a vacuum. Or, in the words of Karen LeFevre, "Invention is best understood as a social act, even when the agent is an individual … human agents always act dialectically – in the context of their interconnections with others and the socioculture … the inventor always requires the presence of an 'other'" (LeFevre, 1987, p. x). Invention as a process is impossible without the Social; and invention as a product is pointless without an audience.

However, your distinctive worldview and experiences are not easy concepts to convey. You will run into frustrations and false starts throughout the endeavor. But as you create your professional profile, use reason in your evaluation of the final product, but don't shy away from using your creativity and originality throughout the drafting process – and don't be afraid to make mistakes.

In case study four Brandon Clifford showed us how he discovered that his self-presentation campaign was actually the most effective when he was committed to his work, doing the things he enjoys, and not overtly trying to market himself in more conventional, overly determined ways. Clifford intuited that there are drawbacks to traditional methods of self-presentation, and then he set his reason to work on the problem. Clifford also realized that he and his unique self-presentation campaign were part of a socio-cultural context, and within this context Clifford was not initially getting the reaction from his audience that he anticipated. By maintaining a focus on true, worthwhile objective Clifford was able to see who he is, what he wants, what works as a means to his utmost ends, and what he has to contribute to others who are also presenting themselves in the marketplace.

Although communicating your unique, intuited Self will – more often than not – prove incredibly difficult, it is well worth the effort. Tapping into your own creative abilities, your own inner muse, method of Invention, or process of discovery is also where you will find the most inspiration. It is where your utmost motivations and passions live. Again, we turn to Bradbury who writes, "I believe one thing holds it all together. Everything I've ever done was done with excitement, because I wanted to do it, because I loved doing it. The greatest men in the world for me have changed, but one thing remains always the same: the fever, the ardor, the delight" (Bradbury, 1994, p. 85). He describes his individual process of invention as "The Feeding of the Muse", as "continually running after loves", and as an "ever-roaming curiosity" (p. 85). Hold tight to your passions. Always remember what inspired you to enter your respective field in the first place – and strive to express your passion throughout your self-presentation campaign. Communicating your essential Self will undoubtedly require a method of invention that works for you as well as a great deal of work and a committed, concerted effort.

This love and passion for your ultimate purpose and profession – accessed through the art of continual Invention – is perhaps the most important thing that can be conveyed by your résumé, portfolio, or professional profile. And it is what prospective employers will be inspired by and remember. ■

References

Bradbury, Ray. (1994) *Zen in the Art of Writing: Essays on Creativity*. Santa Barbara, CA: Joshua Odell Editions.
LeFevre, Karen Burke. (1987) *Invention as a Social Act*. Carbondale, IL: Southern Illinois UP.
Pink, Daniel H. (2005) *A Whole New Mind: Moving from the Information Age to the Conceptual Age* (1st edn). New York: Penguin Group.
Young, Richard E., Alton L. Becker, and Kenneth L. Pike. (1970) *Rhetoric: Discovery and Change*. New York: Harcourt Brace Jovanovich.

2

CREATING
A CAREER PLAN

PLANNING A CAREER MEANS KNOWING YOURSELF AND BEING UNDERSTOOD We often learn from our heavily movie-saturated culture – in movie genres from romantic comedies to Disney movies – that dreams are nebulous things that can come true if you wish upon a star, that magic can make your visions come true, and all you need is faith and luck. But perhaps it might not hurt to have some kind of plan. Fulfillment of self and career satisfaction and success are too important to leave to chance. That's why it's so imperative to create a career plan early on. Sure, we all have plans or visions for our lives that can't always be realized, but if we have respect for ourselves and society, we owe it to ourselves and others to develop a feasible and effective career plan.

All personal plans should begin with questions of identity – regardless of whether you are applying for your first job, starting your own enterprise, or finding new clients. These identity-focused questions can include: who am I, what am I capable of, and what do I want? What are my areas of expertise, my weaknesses, aspirations, and goals? By starting with questions that have to do with who we are and what we want, we are establishing an end, a final objective we want to achieve, a self we want to see actualized. By visualizing an end first, we are then able to make concrete plans by deciding what means will help us achieve our specific ends.

Almost 2,500 years ago, the Greek philosopher Socrates told us that, "The unexamined life is not worth living" (Socrates, quoted in Plato's, "Dialogues", *The Apology*, 38a). In order to achieve the greatest fulfillment in the service of the social, one must take a good, hard, unflinching look inward. Socrates believed and taught that the purpose of human life was personal and spiritual growth. Socrates' philosophy can also be summarized as a search for the Self's unique nature and purpose through strategic, purposeful progressions of questions, dialogues, and conceptual thinking. Also according to Socrates, experimentation and risk-taking require the greatest possible self-determination. Self-determination, in turn, requires forms of self-actualization and planning. A knowing, self-actualizing individual is a person who experiences planning as a conscious, carefully cultivated practice that continually develops throughout one's life and career. You will notice in the first case study contributed by Eric Cesal that Cesal knows himself well enough to acknowledge his own diverse interests, unique skill set, and core values – and then Cesal uses these as motivation for forging his own career path and professional experience.

Motivating yourself to pursue and dynamically engage in your own plan of action is possible only through the daily manifestation of your own personal driving factors, including your passion for architecture and design. Harness what motivates you. There is a constant need for high-level craft in the development and communication of architectural and design ideas. Therefore, you must demonstrate your own unique approach to various tasks and themes with a precision of touch; and by touch I mean visual, mental and manual "touch". By strategically inciting one course of action, or by following one particular aspect of your overall vision, you will be able to develop and use your manifesto as a method of belief, a life-strategy, and a motivational tool.

For example, the manifesto or life-guide of an architecture and design professional may read as follows:

- The world is my frame of reference – not myself!
- My architecture and design is unique!
- The architecture and design profession is progressive and bold!
- Architecture and design is a way of life, not just a job!
- This profession is not independent of actions in society!
- My standard is the reality of architecture and design, not other colleagues!
- I use a computer as a tool, but I refuse to be a slave to it!
- I base my work on and I am inspired by originality, substance, boldness, radiance, insight, and personal vision!
- I will not tolerate reproductions, fickleness, lack of effort, or technical superficiality!
- Look to the future!

CREATING A CAREER PLAN

☐ LAUNCH YOUR CAREER

There are three ideal characteristics you can use as guiding factors throughout your career in order to uncover and maintain passion for the profession. These ideals include: curiosity, understanding, and courage.

Curiosity encourages you to ask questions and to constantly search for new approaches and solutions. By analyzing those solutions you strive to understand what is new and unfamiliar. In her contribution to this chapter Vanessa Norwood writes, "I amassed knowledge quickly and quietly … By reading and listening I learnt a new language, that of architecture." Norwood exhibits a unique capacity for curiosity. Her drive to continue learning throughout her career and life has been important for forging a gratifying and successful career.

Through **understanding** and training you develop the talents and skills necessary for success and fulfillment. Throughout this process you are continually strengthening your **courage** to follow through with your convictions and your artistic vision. As you examine the case studies in this chapter, take note of how Eric Cesal uncovered the courage to break with mainstream professional ideologies and the standards of his discipline.

☐ CAREER PLANNING: THE DIY (DO IT YOURSELF) WAY

Career planning is a continuous process that involves perceiving values, identifications, and individual boundaries. An effective career planning campaign is based in a capacity to know yourself – what is important to you, what will fulfill you, what skills you possess, and what skills you would like to acquire. It is imperative to realize your aspirations – as well as your boundaries. The impulse for a career orientation or re-orientation can happen for a number of different reasons. Maintaining a constant, contemplative awareness throughout your decision making process is essential. It is also important to take the necessary time and space to make the best decisions possible.

When you come to a point in your professional life where you find yourself having to make some important career-planning decisions, keep these four phases of career planning in mind:

1. Determine your position.
2. Define your goal(s).
3. Define important milestones.
4. Create a plan of action.

STEP 1 DETERMINE YOUR POSITION

Determining your current position within your life and within your professional development is one of the most important phases of career planning. When you are a tourist in a strange city, the first thing you would probably do is determine your location and your destination on a map. Effective career planning also involves establishing a route; and in order to choose the right road, you need to know your starting point and the eventual destination of your trip. If you have a specific goal in mind, then you can determine the best way to get there. But keep in mind that sometimes the best way is not necessarily the shortest, easiest, most direct, most obvious (as you will see in Eric Cesal's contribution to this chapter), or even the route you may have anticipated (as you will see in Julia Van den Hout's interview, the last case study in this chapter). As both Cesal and Van den Hout's cases make apparent, it is best to find a balance between being motivated by your plan and remaining open to opportunities.

First, take a good, long look at your experiences, which will determine where you stand. Determining your position involves an analysis of the professional goals you have already achieved, as well as an in-depth evaluation of your current skills and competences. What are your strengths and weaknesses? What are you good at and what could you improve on? It may be helpful to create a personality and skills profile during this phase. Figuring out exactly where you are also often entails a mental, verbal, and/or physical articulation of your aspirations, visions, interests and inclinations. As Richard N. Bolles, the author of the best-selling job-hunting book *What Color is Your Parachute?*, so wisely puts it: "Forget about your occupation title and define yourself as a person" (Bolles, 2001).

STEP 2 DEFINE YOUR GOALS

The second phase of career planning includes establishing what possibilities remain open to you. After selecting and limiting your professional possibilities, you can then formulate more concretely the end goal you would like to achieve. But first – before this particular goal can be realized – you must decide on the way, the means, or a specific plan that will prove the most feasible and effective for attaining your goal. "The way" could include continuing your education, a conversation with a superior, a change of scenery, a visit to a foreign country, a new hobby, or a significant change in your personal life.

When reviewing your goals and your means of achieving them, keep the following in mind: possible worst case scenarios pursuing your objective could bring about; a list of people and their resources that could help you in your pursuit; demarcations or boundaries that could prove helpful; as well as your temporal, financial, and energy investment limits. Although we'd like to believe that achieving our given goal is the only eventual outcome that will prove beneficial and satisfactory, sometimes the gain comes in the striving, so it is also important to create a viable exit strategy.

Setting dynamic and beneficial goals involves envisioning where you want to be in a few years. First, evaluate and clarifying your "stretch goals" – these are goals that are reachable only by excessive effort and the extremely fortuitous confluence of circumstances. Or, in other words, "stretch goals" are the goals that seem to be unobtainable with the existing resources available to you. The purpose of establishing stretch goals is to force you to think creatively for solutions to seemingly impossible problems.

STEP 3 DEFINE IMPORTANT MILESTONES

The definition of intermediate destinations is an incredibly important part of achieving large-scale life goals. An integral part of reaching large-scale goals, or "stretch goals", is determining and celebrating smaller, transitional goals. For example, if one of your major goals is to become a partner in a well-known and respected architectural firm, you should define intermediate goals that will help you get incrementally closer to your overall goal. Establishing specific milestones helps to maintain the framework for your goal-attaining process. Marking milestones also helps you to keep your eventual, overall objective in sight.

The bottom line for this phase of career planning is: set achievable intermediate goals (milestones) for yourself that you can evaluate at certain intervals of time. Then, check in to see if you are successfully meeting and using these intermediate destinations so you can correct your milestones or continue sticking to them. Remember that Peter Murray was not born Founder and Chairman of the London Festival of Architecture. He established and achieved numerous, specific milestones along the way.

STEP 4 CREATE A PLAN OF ACTION

Now it is time to make your milestones and career objectives even more concrete. Action planning involves mapping the activities that will bring you closer to the realization of your goals.

A good first step in the action-planning phase could be using the TARGET-competence profile (described in greater detail below). Effective action planning could also involve attending seminars and workshops, or taking the initiative to teach yourself the skills essential to achieving your goal.

You should constantly strive to increase your learning capacity and further develop your skill set – and then talk about it. Successful career planning also depends a great deal on how effectively and strategically you market yourself. Tactical and thoughtfully crafted self-marketing campaigns can convey to your potential employer your self-confidence. But perhaps even more significantly, self-marketing done the right way can also highlight your competencies and experiences.

CREATING A COMPETENCY PROFILE: YOUR TOOLS FOR POSITIONING

Developing a Competency Profile allows you to analyze and document your technical strengths and weaknesses. A Competency Profile can highlight your skills, while also pointing out your greatest strengths and assets. At a later stage in the development of your complete Competency Profile you can compare and contrast your skills profile with the desired requirements of a specific job

There are five basic types of skills that are analyzed in a Competency Profile:

1 EXPERTISE

Starting with the question "So what am I an expert in?" can seem pretty vague – and not to mention intimidating. So, in order to further analyze and define your expertise, it is helpful to ask yourself the following questions:

- What specific technical skills do I have?
- What skills would my colleagues say that I have?
- What would they say is the limit of my skills in a particular area?
- In what areas have I been able to gain work experience?

2 METHODOLOGICAL SKILLS

In determining what methodological skills you possess, you will want to ask yourself: "What rules, practices, or procedures do I enjoy and have a special affinity for carrying out?" For example, do you have excellent organizational or time management skills? Do you have an eye for detail, or do you tend to focus on and be more in tune with larger, structural organizations? Or, perhaps you're familiar with the tools of personal knowledge management?

3 SOCIAL SKILLS

Social competence applies to the areas of teamwork, goal orientation, responsibility, and communication skills. Are you adept at persuasion? Are you good at developing professional relationships with others? Are you good at making peace amongst colleagues? Are you good at motivating others?

4 PERSONAL SKILLS (SELF-COMPETENCE)

Are you able to bring to the table skills such as: self-management, resiliency in the face of obstacles and pressure, or fluency in foreign languages? What unique aptitudes stand out about me as a person?

5 LEADERSHIP

Do you naturally tend to assume a leadership role in social situations? Have you been active in leading groups, or have taken a project management position? How many co-workers were you responsible for?

Below is a table with nine competencies. You can rate yourself in one of five levels in each specific competency, from "Basic" to "Expertise". Basic skills are given a score of 1, and expertise is given a score of 5. You can assess yourself by rating your individual skills. High scores indicate expertise on your core competencies, and low levels can indicate weak points. Move on from your strong points, and focus on your weak points and what you can do to improve them. Now connect your skill levels and you will receive your personal skills profile.

Competencies / skills	Basic Skills				Expertise
Special Expertise	1	2	3	4	5
Negotiating	1	2	3	4	5
Presentation	1	2	3	4	5
Time Management	1	2	3	4	5
Planning	1	2	3	4	5
Collaboration	1	2	3	4	5
Openness for Technology	1	2	3	4	5
Organization	1	2	3	4	5
Leadership	1	2	3	4	5

CREATING A CAREER PLAN

☐ DEVELOPING YOUR PERSONALITY PROFILE

Apart from analyzing your technical skills, there are also individual character and personality traits that need to be understood and utilized for a career of fulfillment and significance. These characteristics can be documented in a personality profile.

Your personality profile can also be developed by using a similar five-step scale and by ranking yourself from "Basic" to "Expertise". A good place to start creating your profile is with the following questions:

- Am I more introverted or extroverted?
- Am I spontaneous or do I feel more comfortable planning?
- Am I comfortable taking risks or do I prefer security?

In addition, you should also think about:

- how you deal with criticism and,
- what motivates you to good performance.

With the creation of your skills and personality profile, you should have a better understanding of your skills and strengths. You know what to work on and what to use to your advantage. In addition, after you have created these two profiles, you will be able to determine your position in relation to others and to your ultimate career objectives. ■

References
Bolles, R. N. (2011) *What Color is Your Parachute?* (40th Anniv. edn). New York: Ten Speed Press.
Plato (2000) *The Apology,* trans. G.M.A. Grube, in *Readings in Ancient Greek Philosophy: from Thales to Aristotle* (2nd edn). Indianapolis: Hackett Publishing Company.

CASE STUDY 1

TITLE: IN DEFENSE OF HAPPY ACCIDENTS
AUTHOR: ERIC CESAL

I humbly submit that a career can no longer be thought of as a set of planned steps, executed faithfully, but must instead be the taking advantage of unforeseen opportunities, while being guided by a set of strong principles. The programmatic approach to life was lost a generation ago, the middle class is dead and life will continue to be faster and more unpredictable. It is now much more common to change careers multiple times over the course of one's life, although clearly no one plans it that way. No one majors in biology with the intention of becoming an architect, but perhaps they should.

I can honestly report that my life so far has been more a series of happy accidents than actual planning, and that whatever I've achieved in architecture came about quite spontaneously. Throughout my life, I have been in the position to respond to certain opportunities, guided by the values of my family and the support of my loved ones. On the shoulders of such things, you typically find that you're never putting very much at risk, even if it seems that way to the world around you.

I give thanks daily that I was never granted the life I had planned, as none of the planned versions of my life had me here, at this moment, on my thirty-fifth birthday, sitting in a smoky Japanese karaoke bar with five stools and three guests, listening to an obviously depressed Japanese salaryman belt out "Bridge Over Troubled Water" while trying to meet my second extension on the writing of this chapter. Life in architecture can take you to interesting places, if you let it. In this case, I traveled from Port au Prince, Haiti to Sendai, Japan, to assist the Sendai office of Architecture for Humanity in long-range strategy for Tsunami recovery. I took a brief break from that to write this, because I figured it would be better to tell my own story before someone told it for me.

I have been a writer all my life and have had the opportunity, blessing and occasional shame to look back on the writings of my younger self and reflect on their wisdom and their naiveté in equal measure. Certain things are clear.

As I read the writings of my 16-year-old self, it's clear that that man (boy) knew everything about the world. There's no doubt or qualification in the writing. He (I) was certain of what he was going to do with the world, what kind of woman he was going to marry, how he would raise his kids, and where he would live.

As I read the writings of my 18-year-old self, who was at that time reading the writings of my 16-year-old self, it's clear that the elder didn't admire the younger. My 18-year-old self thought my 16-year-old self to be a blazing idiot and impossibly naive. However, my 18-year-old self could then report, *with confidence*, that he finally knew what he was going to do with the world, what kind of woman he was going to marry, how he would raise his kids, and where he would live.

This cycle repeated as I read the writings of my 25-year-old self, who looking back, thought both the prior authors were morons, and yet reflected with the same confidence as they had, that he finally knew what he was going to do with the world, what kind of woman he was going to marry, how he would raise his kids, and where he would live.

Now, at 35, I can finally look back and report with utter confidence that all these prior versions of myself were significantly wiser, smarter, and more honest than I am now, with the exception that I have finally learned to act in the world with a measure of humility and to surrender myself before the unconquerable complexity of life, architecture, and all the rest. What will follow is a tale of acquiescence, and will hopefully inspire the reader to slough off grand plans and stick to core values. They will serve you much better in the end.

My early professional years were unremarkable, inasmuch as I never did anything that would appear in a magazine, or rubbed shoulders with anyone famous, or worried much about either of these things. I mention it, not because it bothered me (or bothers me now), but because these conditions seem to be the benchmarks against which young architects chart the progress of their careers. They are bizarre metrics against which to judge oneself, and I think are ultimately destructive for the profession. They impress on young minds the idea that there's a narrow band of meaningful architects and architecture afoot, and the rest of the profession is where you end up if you lack sufficient talent and ambition. Certainly, some architects are better than others. And young architects should seek to place themselves in the company of the best mentors that they can. But the idea that one can leech some cultural capital by a physical presence in the office of someone famous is shallow, at best. At worst it sets before young architects the idea that it's better to be a modelmaker in the office of someone famous then it's to work for someone anonymous and actually learn how to be an architect.

In my early professional years I *learned*. I learned a lot. About the basic functionalities of architecture – how to draw, how to write, how to present. How to work with a group, how to lead, and when to follow. It is probably fortuitous that I was relatively un-preoccupied with my 'career' (whatever the hell that is) during these years because it allowed me to learn openly, without pretension and angst. Learning how to write a good specification is not something young architects dream about doing, but it is nonetheless an important part of practice, and learning how to do it well is a critical milestone.

If there is one discontentment that is recorded in my writings and my memory, it was a sense of dissatisfaction with the authority of an architect. Not my own authority, per se, because I was old enough to realize that I was young enough to not have earned that much authority. But in looking at the way my peers and superiors interacted with those of other professions (contractors, construction managers, project managers, clients, officials, *et al*.) it seemed as if the architect was in a position of lowly authority, and that that authority was being eroded constantly, even within the short, five year period of my practice. It seemed as if the positions and opinions of an architect never landed with much oomph, and that his arguments never carried much weight.

This rising discontentment coincided with my encroaching thirties, and the realization that graduate school was looming. I *had* to return to graduate school – I had put it off for quite some time and the path to licensure ran straight through the academy. At the time, I resented this fact. I felt that graduate school would be a disruption to the comfortable life that I had crafted. I had a nice apartment, a beautiful partner, and a standing within my firm that was difficult to look away from. I did not at the time believe that I had figured out architecture, but I had at some level figured out life, or some dimension of it. My life, at the time, worked. I was content with all dimensions of my life, except for that one mentioned above, and it was difficult to contemplate stepping away. However, towards the back of my mind a suspicion was beginning to boil. I began to suspect that what I had hewed out of life was, in actuality, a child's idea of what it means to be successful. It had all the trappings of a comfortable middle class existence which had been impressed upon me when I was six and had somehow become frozen in my mind. My comfort with that life began to thaw and the pillars of my life began to unravel. Some, I had a hand in, others, not so much. I did eventually leave that life, with very little in hand, except for a sense of purpose and determination to find for myself a new mode of practice – a new way to define architecture and how to do it. For anyone who has ever had an *itch*, I'm sure you can understand what it means to step away from comfort and into ambition.

It is perhaps fortuitous that I never found a way around the graduate school obstacle. In contemplating my return to graduate school, I figured that the only way that I could stomach such a transition was to structure it around the discontent that I was nurturing towards the profession. An education that would merely accelerate me along that path that I was traveling seemed to be a waste of time, money and energy. I didn't need any help to continue along the path that I was heading. If I was going to go, I would have to figure out something transcendent out of the experience. I thought, at the time, that I would rather mutate the conventional meaning of the word "architect" and do what I wanted to do, than to succeed farther and farther on a path that seemed to be heading towards obscurity, impotence, and discontent. The idea of becoming a "successful" architect seemed to be more and more comical. To become a successful architect merely meant being the best at a profession that was increasingly marginalized and subordinated.

At the time, I believed that the key to avoiding this trap was a higher understanding of these peripheral occupations. I use the term "peripheral" with a bit of my tongue in my cheek, of course, because to them, it was architecture that was peripheral. Nonetheless, it occurred to me that if these other professions were to be our eventual masters, I would learn to defend our work in their language. I had seen enough of the world to understand that there were some players who could never be convinced by anything other than a spreadsheet, or a schedule, and learning how to talk with those tools would be essential to whatever I wanted to do in architecture. If the key to legitimating an architectural ambition was to learn how to read, write, and speak in finance, then I would do so. Similarly, with construction and construction management, I would learn their ethics, their motives, and their lingo as a sort of subversive counter-intelligence program.

This confused nearly everyone I spoke to about it. Whenever I told people that I intended to return to school and get a Masters in Architecture and an M.B.A., the very typical reaction was a long, confused pause, followed by *"So ... you want to be a developer?"* I had to explain that no, I did not want to be a developer. I merely wanted to be able to stand toe to toe with such characters and argue for an architectural agenda in multiple languages, and not rely on rendering skills to convince a stalwart developer that he was actually going to make his hurdle rate. The reactions were at times visceral and even mean – a fact I attributed to a long-standing tradition within architecture that to engage something *outside* of architecture was a betrayal of its values. That the first guy to leave the studio was always the one who cared the least, and here I was, leaving the studio before I even got there, in a way. I was confessing, even before admission, that there were things outside of "architecture" that interested me and would compete for my attention. I was therefore confessing a lack of complete dedication, or, I imagined that that was the way that it seemed.

I had trouble convincing people of the honesty of my intentions. Architecture was my first and only love, and I could never see myself leaving her. But understanding these other things seemed to be the key to advancing architecture (my own, at least). My process for identifying graduate schools was fairly systematic. I made a list of all the schools I could think of with top architecture schools and cross-referenced them with schools I knew to have good business schools. I only applied to schools that had both. I was acutely aware that the educational program that I was pursuing was unusual. I had committed to getting two Masters degrees and was plotting my third. I knew that cooperation of the faculty would be essential to getting through it, and if it was something where I was going to have to fight every semester, the program would likely fall apart. For that reason, I invested in a multi-state trip to visit every school I was applying to, in advance of filing my actual applications. The results were telling. At almost every school, my plans were greeted with furrowed brows and puzzled looks. Even after explaining myself, I could read the thought bubbles over the heads of various deans and admissions officers:

"Why would you want to do that?" I heard repeatedly that doing an M.B.A. would be a distraction from getting a Masters in Architecture and vice versa. Interestingly, even schools that publicly advertised joint M.B.A/M.Arch programs seemed to have no idea what I was talking about. It seemed a complete anathema within the siloed halls of academia.

The one exception was Washington University in St. Louis, which up until then had been a dark-horse candidate for me. I had occasion to meet with Peter MacKeith, who was then Associate Dean of the architecture school whose basic position was that it sounded like a cool idea and I should come to WashU and try it. This was something of a relief for me, since every school I had visited prior to that was either cool or outright dismissive of the idea and I was beginning to question my plan a bit. However, the discovery of at least one person who believed in my idea was at the time enough to sally forth. It taught me another lesson about architecture, practice and life inasmuch as I found that it's better to have one or two friends who really believe in your ideas than it is to have a chorus of phlegmatic supporters. If your ideas gain wide, quick, and easy support, it likely means that you are just thinking generic thoughts.

Not that there's anything redemptive about thinking different. More often than not, having a different opinion means that you're being stubborn or contrary or may even just don't know what the hell you're talking about. Hence, the importance of good friends with whom you can check in once in a while.

I was aided in graduate school by some serendipitous scheduling. In business school, my courses were primarily in finance, which tended to occur in the morning, sometimes starting as early as 7am. In architecture school, the crux of my program was in the afternoons (studio, naturally) and construction management school met at night. I would then work through the night on whatever was pressing and tried to sleep every Tuesday. The respective deans of these programs were fairly generous in terms of allowing me to cross-register for different programs and I owe a debt to a bevy of advisors, deans, and counselors who worked with me to pull off three masters degrees at the same time. It was a busy time in my life, but the structure of the program was also strangely self-refreshing. It was hard to get bored or frustrated. Whenever I was stuck at anything, I always understood that within a few hours, I would be in a different program, tackling different problems, and among different friends. The fact that I was stepping out of studio, both mentally and physically, on a daily basis was critical to my own development and how I would come to see architecture.

The most powerful memories, which themselves seeded *Down Detour Road* (2010) were of the opposing cultures at these three different institutions. Because of the close and constant opportunities for cross-cultural comparison, and my own difficulties in finding identity during this period of my life, it became easier and easier to understand graduate school as a process of culturalization, rather than technical education. I did receive a fair amount of technical education, and so I know how to draw a wall section as well as I know how to do a free-cash flow analysis, but my lasting impressions were of culture. Specifically, that architecture school fosters a culture where larval architects learn to devalue themselves, each other, and the profession as a whole. What amazed me was how proud and self-satisfied were the students in the other disciplines. They believed that they were being taught something valuable, and that the professions that they were entering into contributed a valuable service to society and that they should be paid accordingly. There was of course a competitiveness in these other programs. Students wanted to be the best in class and get the awards, just as in architecture. The distinction however, was that they maintained a reverence for the thing itself. The act of "business" or "construction management" inasmuch as you can define that, was a useful thing. I would of course try to do it better than you, but did not approach that competition as a zero-sum game.

Architecture school, by contrast, taught a different ethos. It taught, indirectly, that architecture, as an idea, was not worth that much. The path of the generic architect was one of disenfranchisement, obscurity, relative poverty, and disappointment. Therefore, the only way to have a meaningful life was to distance oneself from the bland architecture of the day and separate oneself from one's peers. There was no attempt to elevate or even legitimize architecture as a whole. The act of design, and the service of architecture must necessarily be devalued, if one was to legitimize one's own architecture.

This was a difficult thing to digest from the desolate landscape of a studio desk, because of the other major difference between architectural education and the rest. The one that everyone readily condemns but everyone seems powerless to address: isolation. No other program requires of its students a physical isolationism quite the way architectural school does. Whatever is formally communicated to students during their schooling, a culture of masochism rules, where the student who stays the latest is perceived as being the most committed. It was always a source of great sadness to see young undergraduates bragging and competing over who had gone the longest without sleep, as if it were a competition. I bought into it as well, though, and kept both a refrigerator and a George Foreman grill at my desk so I could minimize any extraneous trips to my apartment for "food" and other luxuries. I spent plenty of nights at the studio, awake, asleep, but usually somewhere in between.

Beyond the obvious physical, developmental, and psychological effects of this behavior, the cumulative effects on the profession are much more damaging inasmuch as it leaves young architects culturally isolated from the world it is ostensibly being asked to serve. Going to university is the unifying cultural experience of all professionals, everywhere. It is probably the only experience shared by a civil engineer in India and a psychologist in Wisconsin. Architecture, however, removes its young from this unifying cultural experience in favor of an experience only universal among architects (studio culture). The inevitable result is a profession with a communication problem. Architects know little of how to convince non-architects of their value, and those outside of the profession are little inclined to search for architecture's value of their own accord. Every profession has their lingo and their technical speak, but no other discipline teaches you that speak against a backdrop of complete isolation.

As I saw all of this come into focus, I was busy trying to blend into three different cultures (but never at the same time) pass three sets of exams and spend time with three separate groups of friends (who never seemed to have anything to say to one another). It all cumulated in an epic disappointment and heartbreak which was adequately discussed in *Down Detour Road* so I won't discuss it in detail here. It did, however, sharply reaffirm my belief that architecture was in the midst of a value and self-esteem crisis that was masquerading as an employment crisis. That the search for work was really a minor thing, and that the search for purpose and identity would be the great architectural journey of our time.

These maturing thoughts and the disintegrating economy launched a period of my life: twelve months of dejection, reflection and writing that produced a book that would ironically leave me more lost but more inspired than at any other point of my life. Its writing would challenge those things that I had always understood about architecture and its publication would put me in an awkward position of being a lighthouse for a bunch of young, lost architects. I say "awkward" because by the time people started reading *Down Detour Road*, I had already fled the country in some attempt to make real the hope that I had dug out of the recession.

In January 2010, my little manifesto was done, but not finished, and I shuddered with thoughts that I had suddenly become a theorist. Although the book would not hit the shelves for another 10 months, I was restless. "Theorist" was a word I had always treated with disdain, probably for no other reason than my having come from an egalitarian/puritan/earthy family of immigrants and farmers. The idea of someone making a living by postulating seemed pompous.

I struggled quite a bit, at that time, with how the publication of the book would alter the path of my career and the risk that it would pigeonhole me into some dreary faculty position. I could see myself, sitting behind a desk piled high with papers which I would get teaching assistants to read, adjusting over-sized eyeglasses and pulling on my beard and thinking big, puffy thoughts about architecture. It didn't seem like a bad life, per se, but I was concerned that it seemed to be creeping up around me in a way that I couldn't entirely predict or control. I was thirty-two, and was not ready to have my life settled.

There was always the same criticism of the theoretical class: that they would write some brilliant masterpiece of words and diagrams that would somehow never really translate into buildings. This seemed to be a lingering criticism of scholars like Robert Venturi and Christopher Alexander, and although I would never count myself in that company, it nonetheless concerned me that someday I would be subject to the same criticism. I needed to practice. Not just any architecture, but *my* architecture. I needed a way to know, for myself, that what I was writing about was possible.

For those who are a little lost, serendipity may seem a little like fate. I don't believe in either, but at some point the tea leaves line up with the coffee grounds and you learn to trust in the universe a little bit. As such, a few weeks after I had sent off the final manuscript for *Down Detour Road* (2010), I received a curious call from Architecture for Humanity, asking me whether I would consider moving to Haiti for two years to establish and lead their response to what was increasingly understood as the largest and worst disaster of modern times. I would have to be on the ground in three weeks' time. Haiti, even before the earthquake, was known as a place of violence and extreme poverty, and now could add total physical destruction to its list of woes. Shortly thereafter, it would add cholera and kidnapping.

It seemed appropriate, however, on several levels. First, it was not my first brush with disaster. I had previously worked with Architecture for Humanity on two separate occasions during their Katrina response, and had a deep affection for the organization and the work that it did. More to the point, though, I had just written a book, the main conclusion of which was that humanitarian architecture was the last, best hope for our profession. It argued that if architecture was to survive, it had to actively make an attempt to deal with the world's worst problems. It seemed at some level that I was being given an opportunity to put my money where my mouth was, and test out the ideas of *Down Detour Road in situ*.

Beyond the current facts of that particular crisis, and my contemporaneous crisis of faith, service had always been a part of my thinking, back before Katrina and even my involvement with architecture, so it seemed a natural extension of my belief system – both its private and public aspects. Haiti was, at some level, what I had been waiting for. It shames me to say that 250,000 people had to lose their lives in order for me to find purpose in mine. Nonetheless, the facts bore out this truth and I made preparations for my move.

All this deliberation happened within the span of a short conversation, and I gave a conditional yes to their request, under the auspices that I had to check with friends and loved ones, and had some existing commitments to tie off. However, looking back, I don't think that there was any way that I would not have come to Haiti. It was a matter of principle. A principle on which we do not act is a meaningless thing, like a design that does not get built. It was the next logical step in my life, although could not have been planned that way, any more than could have the publishing of *Down Detour Road*.

The particulars of my move to Haiti are too extended to cover in this format. However, suffice to say that it was panicked, terrifying, and ultimately redemptive. Disaster would be the oven to bake certain principles of architecture and find out whether my words would translate into action. I left St. Louis on March 1, 2010 with 95 lb of gear on my back on the first commercial flight into Port au Prince after the airport reopened. I had only the faintest idea of what the next two years would bring. No one could have known. I was farther and farther from the architect I had planned to be, but was getting closer and closer to the architect that the world needed me to be.

It may seem strange to argue that disaster is an appropriate crucible in which to place the profession of architecture. That the urgent, mortal needs of disaster survivors must necessarily stand in contradiction to the loftier goals of spirit, culture and development that most architects would lobby for. This thinking, however, relies on old modes of thought both in architecture and in international disaster response. We are increasingly aware that the key to preventing disaster is development, as the root cause of all disaster is not nature but poverty. Conventional thinking has held that the needs of disaster victims (at least the ones that we are prepared to address) are limited to base biological needs like food, shelter, and sanitation. Increasingly, however, we are coming to understand that it is just as important to address the needs of the spirit: emotional and psychological security, hope, respect, dignity, and the means to self-actualization. To neglect these needs leaves communities in a trap of desperation and poverty, which in turn leaves them exposed to future disasters.

This is the ethos that drives Architecture for Humanity's work in Haiti. It is the idea that an architect has a place in poverty reduction and can through his work be a driver of social equity. Design and construction, when guided by this principle, bring about more than four walls and a roof. They can bring about real growth and change.

I wish I could affirm for the reader that I have a plan of some sort that will guide the next steps. However, I don't really make plans anymore as much as I respond to conditions. I've learned to trust enough in my values and principles to know that at the end of the day, I won't do anything for which I might hate myself later. In terms of my relationship with architecture, I can lean heavily on the knowledge that architecture is, and has always been, whatever we say it is. The opportunity to define architecture lies in the hands of every generation, and anyone who tells you that architecture is something immutable and predefined is probably trying to sell you a book.

I would encourage any young architects or architecture students reading this tome to shake off all small plans and timid steps. Shake off the big plans, too, for that matter. Think broadly about architecture and one's life, and understand these things in terms of key principles – not licenses, brands, portfolios, technologies, images, and other such superficialities. In the end, small decisions made in service of great principles will yield more.

References
Cesal, E. J. (2010) *Down Detour Road: An Architect in Search of Practice.* Cambridge, MA: The MIT Press.

CASE STUDY 2

TITLE: THE MEDIUM IS IN THE MESSAGE
AUTHOR: PETER MURRAY

When I was at school and contemplating a career I was undecided. I had wanted to be an architect from the age of nine having watched my father at home supplement his meagre public sector salary by drawing up plans for local builders. The evening meal cleared, he would set up his board, tee square, bow pens, stencils and anglepoise on the kitchen table and draw away happily into the small hours. At breakfast the next morning I would wonder at the finished elevations and then a year or so later he would point out the completed building as he drove me to school. His particular fascination was small country churches; no weekend trip was complete without a stop to inspect some interesting example of Romanesque or Gothic, to walk, whispering, down the musty nave, point out medieval masons' marks and rail against insensitive nineteenth century intrusions.

Then, as a teenager, editing the school magazine kindled an interest in writing and I investigated a career in journalism. I was swayed to take up architecture by a Christmas lecture given for young people by the charismatic architectural historian, Tom Burrough, who taught at the Royal West of England Academy School of Architecture (RWA). I remember little about the lecture other than its transformative power and I am frequently reminded of it today when I lecture to young people and see the impact that one can have on such an audience.

I therefore decided to study architecture at the RWA and soon became involved in student activism and publishing. My first venture into publishing was a stencilled broadsheet protesting about aspects of the course at Bristol. This led me to join the British Architecture Students Association which provided a wider market for my publishing exploits and in 1963, with Dean Sherwin, I published *Megascope* magazine, reflecting the discontent among many students about their dreary courses, stuck in a Modernist rut. We were inspired by Archigram and the idea of a world driven by new technologies where the detailing of Gemini space capsule was of far greater significance than the Ville Radieuse. We led protests about the dead hand of new architecture and publicly burnt an effigy of the Robinson Building, Bristol's then tallest building, much to the annoyance of older students who vainly attempted to extinguish the pyre.

My extra curricular activities made me very unpopular with the professorial staff at Bristol and at the end of my third year I decided to move to the Architectural Association in London. Soon after arriving there in 1966 I met Geoffrey Smyth with whom I shared similar architectural and publishing interests and we put together *Clip-Kit* magazine. It was focused on new ideas and technology, car manufacturing, the space race, adaptability and change; our mentor was Cedric Price. *Clip-Kit* was literally a plastic clip, subscribers would be sent the magazine in monthly installments and then place them in the clip. I was also at the time editing the *Architects' Journal* student section; however, when I used one of the pages to advertise my own new magazine, I was fired.

CREATING A CAREER PLAN 2

Producing *Megascope* and *Clip-Kit* provided useful insights into the freedoms, both in design and access, of offset litho printing – a technological advance which would soon revolutionise the magazine publishing business. It was also useful experience in understanding some of the fundamentals of running a magazine – creating the concept, controlling costs, obtaining financial support and/or selling advertisements, and organising distribution. Only when you have these basics in place can you start writing, for without them your precious baby will only survive a few months.

In my vacation I got a job with *Nova*, then a new and radical magazine for women. The art editor knew of *Clip-Kit* and gave me a job laying out pages. I then started writing a regular design column, a job I continued to do into my final year as I, unsuccessfully, tried to complete my thesis. Attracted by what I saw as the glamorous life of magazines I abandoned my architectural training for a career in the fourth estate.

Soon after leaving the AA I joined *Architectural Design* (AD) magazine, then edited by Monica Pidgeon, in a period when it was very concerned with environmental issues, energy conservation and alternative lifestyles. As a result I went on a fact finding trip to California visiting hippy communes and recycling plants as well as interviewing architects. To pay for the trip I sold the interviews – including the first for a British magazine with Frank Gehry – to *Building Design* newspaper. When I returned, they commissioned me to do weekly interviews with leading architects. Luckily our hours at AD were from 11am till 6pm allowing time in the early part of the morning for freelance work.

When *Building Design* was looking for a new editor in 1973 they invited me to take on the job which I did for 5 years – a period of time which for me provided an ideal cycle, long enough to do something positive but not too long to get bored and stale.

In the late 1970s the *Royal Institute of British Architects Journal* was losing a lot of money and the institute was considering selling it to another publisher. I had the temerity to suggest that if they got the editorial right and ran the business side more effectively there was no reason why they should not keep it in-house and make a profit; so they gave me the job of managing director and editor. In three years, in the deepest recession the profession has seen in recent years (worse than now), we managed to make the magazine profitable. At the same time I had learnt the basics of running a magazine, understanding the world of advertising and production, so at the end of five years I felt it was time to start my own magazine. Sadly, within a few years the *RIBA Journal* was losing money again and was then sold off; it was an interesting lesson in the difficulties institutions have in dealing with commercial realities.

In 1983 with Deyan Sudjic, now Director of the Design Museum in London, and the graphic designer Simon Esterson, I put together a team to produce *Blueprint* magazine. As we had very little money it was organised as a collective and we produced the magazine for the first 18 months at weekends for no pay. Our aim was to "discuss issues of architecture and design that is comprehensible and accessible to the professional and laymen alike." Although our circulation never got above 12,000 copies in my time as publisher, thus having a fairly limited "public" audience, it was read by other journalists and programme producers who picked up on stories and personalities and spread the word in other media.

Deyan and I were invited by the Royal Academy to organise the exhibition "New Architecture – the work of Rogers, Foster, Stirling" in 1986. This was at an important juncture for British architecture. The criticism of the architectural profession by the Prince of Wales had some momentum among the populace and there was a real danger that neo classicism would become the standard fare of new development. The exhibition was highly successful and put across another view of architecture and balanced the debate. It also convinced me of the power of the exhibition as a medium. Despite the fact that an architectural show is often but a proxy for the real thing, used in the right way, with the attendant support of media coverage and catalogues, it can communicate a message with tremendous impact.

Blueprint had an influence way beyond that which its circulation might suggest and inspired magazines like *Wallpaper* and *Icon*. But the recession of the early 1990s was too tough; *Blueprint* lost half its readers and advertising, and was haemorrhaging cash. We were forced to sell it in 1995. We had only managed to keep going so long because we had set up a separate design studio designing brochures for developers and architects about their work.

This happened through two routes: Lord Palumbo had commissioned James Stirling to design 1 Poultry in the City of London, but Stirling drawings were designed for an architectural audience: his plans, renderings and worms eye axonometric were not understood by the potential occupiers of the building. Stirling refused to do any other drawings. Palumbo in frustration asked Simon Esterson to come up with a brochure that properly communicated the benefits of the building.

At the same time the developer Stuart Lipton, a keen reader of the magazine, was building the massive Broadgate complex in the City. He did not like the conventional designs of property agents and he also invited the *Blueprint* team to design newsletters and brochures. We based the marketing strategies on detailed research carried out by DEGW into occupier needs and integrated it with Esterson's clear graphic style. It revolutionised the way property was communicated and soon developers were queuing up for a Wordsearch brochure. The profits from this enterprise subsidised *Blueprint* during the recession, until the bank manager decided enough was enough.

I then set out to build up Wordsearch as a specialised branding and marketing agency working with developers and architects. Broadgate was at the centre of our workload and we produced most of its communications for a period of 25 years. We also grew the business internationally with work in Europe, Russia and the Far East. Today projects include Taipei 101, KPF's International Commercial Center in Hong Kong, Gensler's Shanghai Tower, Foster's Masdar City in Abu Dhabi, Renzo Piano's Shard in London and 1 World Trade Center and Hudson Yards in New York.

In 2002 while at the Venice Biennale I had the idea of putting on a London biennial show, but one that would be very different. While Venice is a great location for such an event, the Biennale had few links with the city – architects flew in and then flew out without engaging with the place, except to enjoy its cuisine and ambience. I thought that a festival that engaged with local communities and local issues could make productive use of bringing together such a bunch of architects.

The Clerkenwell Architecture Biennale was launched in 2004 as a one-off. We expected it to attract only a few architects, but some 15,000 people turned up to the opening event – where we grassed over a street to show how easily it could be turned into a new public space – and over the ensuing fortnight the exhibitions, lectures and tours were packed out. We realised we had a formula that had legs. In later years we changed the name to the London Festival of Architecture, to give it wider geographical appeal and it is now probably the largest event of its kind in the world and in 2012 it became an annual, rather than biennial event.

The Building Centre in Store Street, off London's Tottenham Court Road, was once the Architectural Association's product sample store. Over the years it grew into a major exhibition centre for building products aimed both at the public and professional. However the impact of the internet meant that the demand for a physical exhibition had diminished. One day the Chairman of the Centre took me out to lunch and asked for ideas for the use of the display space. A year earlier I had put on an exhibition entitled "New City Architecture" with Nick McKeogh and suggested that the Building Centre should put on a permanent show of New London Architecture (NLA) – all architects in London, as well as other professionals, are interested in what is going on in the capital, and this would surely draw in the crowds.

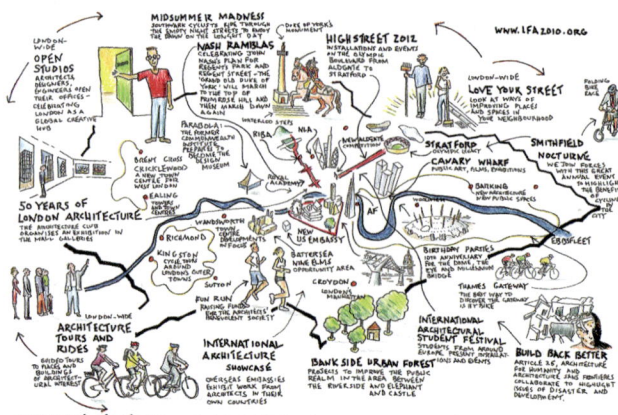

CREATING A CAREER PLAN 2

And so it proved. The NLA brought new life into the Building Centre and has developed into a significant focus for debate and discussion about issues related to architecture, planning and development in London with a permanent display centred around a 1:1500 scale model of central London, a programme of exhibitions, seminars, think tanks and publications that inform the future of the metropolis, including the *New London Quarterly*.

I have always believed that if you manage a business properly, it gives you greater freedom to carry out the real purpose of that business – whether it be publishing or architecture. I was therefore pleased to receive an invitation from Javier Quintana de Uña, Dean of the IE School of Architecture in Madrid, to teach students on the Masters Degree in Architectural Management and Design about how to communicate. In my career I have seen too many talented designers fail to reach their full potential and too many great buildings remain of the drawing board because of their authors' inability to get their message across.

In 2011 I published my first novel *A Passion to Build* about two architects and their lifetime of competition to win the big projects and awards, a sort of modern day Fountainhead. To do this I set up Clip-Kit Ltd, a digital publishing company. I called it Clip-Kit as a reference to my early publishing days which were made possible by the development of offset litho printing technology which hugely widened accessibility to media. I wished to make the point that the internet has done the same, but to an even greater degree. The book includes many of the lessons I think architects need to learn about the art of communications – delivered in an entertaining fashion.

What lessons does this short résumé of a career in communication provide to architects and those wishing to promulgate architectural ideas? The main lesson I take from my time dealing with architects over a complete career is that those who have understood the significance of being able to communicate to a wide audience have been more successful than those who failed to see communications as a key part of their practice.

Architects are often too concerned with peer approval. Look at most practices' website and you will see that they always talk about themselves from an internal perspective, they rarely mention the benefits that the client or user might reap from working with them.

Marketing and communication are important tools in guiding the future and development of a practice. Architects can choose what sort of work they want to do, unlike the days when marketing was seen as "touting" and new practices put up their brass plate and then had to wait for the work to come in. Now they can go out and get it.

I would advise all architects to get good training in presentation techniques. Very often clients choose their architects for reasons other than the pure quality of the designs on the table.

Architects make too great a use of "archispeak" – an opaque language that is often not even fully understood by their peers, let alone the outside world. They need to pay more attention to their audience. Always ask "Who is my audience?" before writing, or saying, a word.

References
Murray, P. (2011) *A Passion to Build*. Amazon Digital Services, Inc.

CASE STUDY 3

TITLE: SELF-PRESENTATION: THINGS I HAVE LEARNT, THINGS I AM LEARNING AND SOME THINGS I MAY NEVER GET
AUTHOR: VANESSA NORWOOD

"Your career will ever only make sense looking back, never forwards."

Shumon Basar

Education cannot prepare you for the real world. When you've decided to take your degree in Visual and Performing Arts one increases that risk to a forgone conclusion. My chosen study did however leave me with a rich set of references drawn from the world of cinema, arts, theatre and music. I know my Andrei Tarkovskys from my Werner Herzogs, my Richard Longs from Robert Wilsons and a well-placed reference is a useful tool. But having a serious allergy to mime (I go all white and chalky) my career as a performance artist was always going to be short lived. I needed to somehow plot a career fresh from a study environment that rendered one passionate but ill-equipped to steer that passion into a job. I was lucky that serendipity led me in a straight line (that became an arc) to the Architectural Association, onwards to architects' offices, an architectural communications company and back to the AA.

    I have to confess to not having a CV but rather a list of projects and past employees. Within that list, under subheadings and bullet points alongside sketches, doodles and photographs are the details that form the trajectory of my career.

    When I first came to the AA I worked in the Photo Library, which proved the best place to get a crash course in architecture. I sat with a copy of the *Penguin Dictionary of Architecture* on my desk and would surreptitiously turn the pages to look up things that I was unsure of. Thus I learnt that Vitruvious was a Roman writer and architect and not a volcano. I amassed knowledge quickly and quietly. Certainly not becoming an expert, but not a novice either. By reading and listening I learnt a new language, that of architecture.

    At Wordsearch I worked for Peter Murray, author of the previous case study, and he was a great influence. Employed as a project manager for several years, I oversaw many interesting projects from Battersea Power Station to Paternoster Square. Influences are not quantified, written down and added to your CV, nor do they get sent to you in an email for you to ponder. They are not always instantly identifiable but will have an effect on your career for years to come. At Wordsearch, I learnt many things about the process of design. There can be a good way of working, or a reaction to something that clearly isn't working. I remember sitting in on a design discussion with Peter who was presented by one (freelance) designer with a spread of photographs of a square building that the designer had seen fit to place in bubbles which floated freely across the page. While Peter's expression said it all, he politely asked why the images were in circles. The designer had no excuse and the photographs were duly placed on the page in a far more fitting linear form. That day I understood how important it is to respect the beauty in the simplicity of a project. There is a very fine line between clarity and interference.

Another valuable lesson I learnt at Wordsearch in my role as a project manager was keeping quiet in meetings, listening to what people have to say first, carefully considering your reply. For someone who likes to talk incessantly, this was a very important skill to master. Project management is like therapy. Only there are multiple patients around the table, all with their particular point to consider.

After Wordsearch I went on to work for two architectural practices of different sizes but both possessing a passion for architecture; Lifschutz Davidson and dRMM.

Although not trained in architecture I was beginning to understand the language more. Having collected a metaphorical notebook full of interesting words I was now able to speak in fairly competent sentences. I was starting to see the world through an architectural lens.

All the time I was meeting interesting people who orbit the architectural world, and I was forming an inner diagram of knowledge and connections.

At both practices I learnt a huge amount about the final representation of built work and what makes a good image. I started to recognise the importance of a beautiful photograph to tell the story of a project. I learnt about presenting work; the mechanics of choosing and sending images that represent your work, being thoughtful about how to show the work, the best frame. I learnt the hard way not to leave it to chance through the publication of an image with the fingers holding the model still visible in the frame.

The Architectural Association is an intense hub of activity. More ideas, conversations and projects are crammed per square foot into the Georgian buildings that make up its home, than imaginable. Many new things are learnt, accepted and then, after some time, revisited and more new things are learnt from seeing them in a new light. This is challenging. Usually in one's career, a steady build-up of information occurs, where knowledge is amassed and you become an "expert". Exhibitions are more often than not different every time, with a new set of demands and challenges; like the architect who asked us to build him an invisible house (Figure 1) or the practice that turned the AA Gallery into a Japanese bathhouse (Figure 2).

figure **1**

Pascal Schöning: Cinematic Architecture, AA Gallery 11/9/2005 – 9/11/2005. Photo by Quintin Lake

The exhibition installation takes the form of a cinematic house, constructed of glass and a sequence of projections. The house aims to create a sense of liberation and openness through dematerialising solid space, playing on our experience of home and cities. The resulting technical and poetic synergy captivates and inspires while reminding us that emotion can be a most potent building material.

The work of Pascal Schöning's Diploma Unit 3 defined this cinematic and narrative condition and marries it with spatial and technical requirements in order to create architecture.
By their very nature the only way to communicate these time-based proposals is through film or the sequential pages in a book – in itself an exciting process for building space.

There are differences to learn; like those between curating shows and organising them. With curating, you get to be the author, to be visible in a way that you should resist doing if you are organising on behalf of someone else. Curating a show can be the most amazing opportunity to gather together great works.

Autoprogettazione Revisited a show celebrating a project by Italian legend Enzo Mari allowed us to invite a selection of artists to revisit and respond to Mari's existing work. The show resulted in new pieces especially commissioned by Phyllida Barlow, Martino Gamper and Graham Hudson amongst others.

Inviting artists to show and then watching them work can be an amazingly instructive opportunity to learn about constructing an exhibition. The Russian artists Olga and Alexander Florensky, *Moveable Bestiary* show at the AA was one of the best. The Russians have a saying that roughly translates as "Oily Oil" which means that something is overdone, too much. To avoid oily oil they cleared the gallery space totally and then introduced work piece by piece. Their art is truly quirky so it was interesting to see that there was so much method to a look that resembled madness.

When you look back, there are fine threads that can be traced through your career. People, interests, questions that can continue to hold a fascination for years. It is important to recognise and nurture them. A love of photography sparked at art college turns into an appreciation of good photography that becomes an understanding deep enough to be able to ask interesting questions of the subject and reframe it in new and interesting ways. The photography exhibition we curated as a department at the AA, *Reading Landscape* (Figure 3) collected a body of work that did not show any built environment at all. The works were all nominally landscape, although in all the pictures the landscape was manipulated or revealed in such a way that the photographer was somehow present (although unseen) in the frame. The exhibition included work by some of the finest contemporary photographers around.

figure **2**

KDa at the Bath House, AA School, London, February, 2005. Photo by Sue Barr

Klein Dytham modelled the show on a Japanese bathhouse, complete with white tiling and authentic taps, reception desk, an ambient soundtrack of a real bathhouse and curtain dividers.

Klein Dytham hit on this idea because the AA's gallery, divided into two identical halves with a central entrance, reminded them of the men's and women's sides of a Japanese bathhouse. Klein, whose wickedly dry sense of humour counters Dytham's joviality, describes it off-handedly as "just some eye-candy". But while there is little more to it than meets the eye, the attention to detail and the development of the concept ensures that the effect is more than the sum of its parts.

CREATING A CAREER PLAN 2

57

My recent work as co-curator of the British Pavilion for the 13th Venice Architecture Biennale has taught me that all the experience in the world can never totally prepare you for the rush of a huge project executed in very little time. *Venice Takeaway* is a project that turned all conceived ideas about an exhibition to be shown in a national pavilion on its head. Rather than showing architecture from the UK we sent 10 teams made up of architects, writers and curators around the world to bring back ideas with the aim of provoking debate on changing British architecture. When other design teams in other countries were already finessing the drawings of their installations to be shown in their own pavilions our "explorers" were gathering material in various parts of the globe to become the raw material for the *Venice Takeaway* show. This created a huge, daunting and amazing challenge for curators, designers and participants. I believe the show will bring real changes to the way we think about architecture in the UK.

Your career is the passing of years used to build up to a bank of knowledge. Spend that time looking at the world as much work as you can; build yourself a personal visual encyclopaedia to be drawn on. Keep your eyes open. So there are definitely things I have learnt and I am still learning too many things to list. As for the things I suspect are beyond me I shall keep them to myself, only adding the importance of accentuating the positive. Keep calm; enjoy the strange mixture of purposeful decision and arbitrary chance that is called your career. ■

figure **3**
Reading Landscape: Contemporary Landscape
Photography, AA Gallery, 15/10/2010 – 10/11/2010. Photo by Sue Barr

Reading Landscape presents a selection of contemporary photographers who work in the realm of the uninhabited. The photographers on show read rather than record landscape and their authorial presence is often felt in the images – a set of photographic lights, a flare thrown into the night sky, dust gathered in the studio. Some of the photographs articulate the unease we feel when confronted with rural landscape, denying us the comfort we find in the density of the built environment.

Other photographs show landscapes that we may take for granted, whose history belies a less sanguine past. Originating in the early seventeenth century, the word landscape was initially a painters' term describing natural scenery; only 300 years later did it come to refer to the land itself. *Reading Landscape* explores this gap between the real and the revealed: the space between, where our dreams and fears reside.

CREATING A CAREER PLAN 2

CASE STUDY 4

TITLE: MULTIPLE PATHS: CURATORIAL FELLOW, CO-FOUNDER AND EDITOR OF CLOG
AUTHOR: JULIA VAN DEN HOUT

DID YOU SET OUT TO BE A COMMUNICATIONS AND PRESS MANAGER?
Being the press manager at Steven Holl Architects (SHA) is something that happened unexpectedly for me. I have an art history and urban design/architecture background, and was asked to fill this role in the office without much previous experience.

CAN YOU ELABORATE ON YOUR BACKGROUND A LITTLE? FOR EXAMPLE, DO YOU COME FROM A DESIGN FAMILY?
I come from an academic background. I am originally from Amsterdam, the Netherlands. Both my parents were professors at the University of Amsterdam before relocating to Chicago in 2000. Since then, they have both been professors at the University of Chicago.

Neither of my parents are in design fields, but both are in linguistics. Due to their fields, travel has always been important in my family, and with our travels came frequent exposure to different museums and cultures. I believe that is the combination that led me to my interests in architecture and art.

CAN YOU TELL US ABOUT YOUR A&D CURATORIAL INTERNSHIP AT THE ART INSTITUTE? WERE YOU AT SCHOOL IN CHICAGO?
I spent four years in Chicago and then moved to New York to attend New York University. During my time at NYU, I always spent the summer months in Chicago. These were usually filled with summer jobs at the University of Chicago. However, when I was certain of my interests in architecture and urban design, I decided to use the summer break to gain more experience in that field, especially searching for the intersection between art and architecture. I applied for an internship with the Art Institute and was very fortunate to work in the A&D department. It was a time that the department was preparing for their move into the larger galleries of the Renzo Piano-designed wing. The department was working extensively on new acquisitions and simultaneously working on an exhibition about the British firm, Graphic Thought Facility. It was this show that I mainly worked on, but seeing also the further development of the department was invaluable.

CAN YOU GIVE US A BRIEF CHRONOLOGY OF YOUR ACTIVITIES SINCE YOU GRADUATED FROM SCHOOL?
I started working at SHA immediately after completing my degree.

HOW EXACTLY DID THE JOB AT STEVEN HOLL ARCHITECTS COME ABOUT? PERSONAL RECOMMENDATION?

Much like the position at the Art Institute, the job at SHA was one I simply applied to. After applying to several gallery jobs, and not yet being offered a job, I decided to take a chance on the position at SHA, and was both surprised and thrilled to be asked to come by for an interview. I met with the Communications Manager and Managing Associate in early April 2008 and had a second meeting a week later with Steven Holl and Chris McVoy. I was quickly offered the job officially and started the same day I finished my last exam at NYU!

APPROACHING YOUR FIRST JOB AFTER GRADUATION, WHAT WERE THE LEADING SKILLS YOU PLANNED TO OFFER A PROSPECTIVE EMPLOYER? WRITER? DESIGNER?

I saw my strength coming from my wide range of experiences, from museums to galleries, from art to architecture. My range of interests was what I thought was my greatest asset.

HOW LONG HAVE YOU BEEN COMMUNICATIONS AND PRESS MANAGER AT STEVEN HOLL ARCHITECTS?

I have been here since May 2008, almost four years.

WHAT DOES A COMMUNICATIONS AND PRESS MANAGER DO?

The press manager aims to promote the work of the office. This is a two-part role, with both a passive side and an active side. I process all the incoming publication requests that come to our office, whether this is from people who would like to interview Steven Holl, publish one of our projects in a magazine or in a book, or show our work in an exhibition. The active side of this position means finding magazines and books to publish our work, drafting our press material – from press releases to assembling press kits to keeping our website/Facebook and Twitter up to date.

CAN YOU GIVE US AN IDEA OF WHAT A TYPICAL DAY AT WORK IS LIKE?

I start my morning by reviewing the press requests that we have received over night. Publication requests are sent either by email to the office's general inbox, directly to my email address, or are gathered through the website where anyone can request a press kit. When I have responded to all incoming emails, I set to work on finding new press opportunities for the office – working on gathering new materials, coordinating with editors, scheduling photography of our projects, etc.

PLEASE DESCRIBE THE TYPICAL CONTENTS OF A PRESS KIT

Our typical press kits include watercolors by Steven Holl, plans/sections/elevations, diagrams where appropriate, and photos or renderings – depending on whether the project is in design or completed.

WHAT ROLE DO SOCIAL MEDIA PLAY IN PROMOTING STEVEN HOLL'S ARCHITECTURE?

With the increase of social media and the use of the Internet to promote work, we have started to think of the best way to represent our work in various formats. We have a Facebook page and a Twitter account for the office. While this is a valid way of promoting work, we have decided to try to use these formats as a unique element in the presentation of the work. We see it as a valuable opportunity to give a behind-the-scenes look at our process and office. The construction process is always very insightful and we like that online media allow the opportunity to show photos from our construction site as well.

We now also have the opportunity to show our work in new ways. We work with several fantastic photographers, but increasingly feel the desire to also show an experiential aspect of the work. Video is allowing us this opportunity. This is a mode of representation that we will be using more often in lectures, exhibitions, and on our website.

WHAT HAS BEEN YOUR GREATEST CHALLENGE AS A PRESS MANAGER AT STEVEN HOLL ARCHITECTS?

The greatest challenge is coordinating opening events, a process that starts months before the completion of a building, and coordinating major stories. These days, more and more magazines ask for exclusives, and this is most often difficult to accommodate.

CAN YOU DESCRIBE THE WORKING PROCESS AT STEVEN HOLL ARCHITECTS?

All projects are started by Steven Holl. The process of painting a watercolor allows him to explore form, color, light, and texture in fluid and instinctual motions, producing a design that is deeply inspired by a site or context. While this is not the end of his involvement in the projects – he is actively engaged in all stages of design and construction – the design is brought to the larger office after this initial conception.

An architectural team works on drawings and building models, while I work on editing the descriptive text of the design concept. These phases in the design process form the first foundation to the public life of each project. The renderings, photos of the models, and text-based materials will all eventually become part of what we prepare for publication. Preparing a project for publication means distilling the concept to a digestible amount of information, explained properly and clearly in its most simple, yet visually rich form. It has to convey what the essence of a project is in words and in images and be able to communicate that idea to anyone new to the project.

Because of the design process of all of our projects, we have standard elements that comprise a press package. We include concept watercolors, concept text, a fact sheet, credit sheet, floor plans and sections, and images.

For our use within the office, we also have extensive watercolor and model archives that are used by all architects to refer to materials they need.

CAN YOU IDENTIFY A SIGNIFICANT EVENT OR SERIES OF EVENTS THAT LED YOU TO YOUR CURRENT JOB?

While I came to this office unexpectedly (I had envisioned working in more of a gallery or museum context), my interest in architecture has been strong for quite some years. Important to my decision to accept this position was previous work experience at the Art Institute in Chicago. I have never wanted to become an architect, but have long been interested in the way architecture is discussed and presented.

DID YOU HAVE A MAIN FOCUS OF STUDY AS AN UNDERGRADUATE? WHAT WAS YOUR DEGREE?

My degree is a bachelor's degree in Art History with a minor in Urban Design and Architecture. After a few years of taking various classical art history courses, I became interested increasingly in graphic design. I ended my studies with a written Honors Thesis about Hendrik Werkman, an intriguing Dutch printer/graphic designer who worked from the 1920s until his death in 1945. My research led me to a great study of the avant-garde movements in Europe of that time, such as De Stijl, Dada, and Futurism.

CREATING A CAREER PLAN 2

YOU ENVISIONED WORKING IN A GALLERY OR MUSEUM CONTEXT, IN WHAT CAPACITY – WRITER? EDUCATOR? DESIGNER?

I originally envisioned working in a gallery setting in an administrative position. I spent most of my years at NYU also working a few hours a week in galleries in Chelsea. Despite my interest in architecture, I assumed that working in a gallery was the natural next position for me after finishing school.

IS THERE A BOOK, PAINTING OR BUILDING THAT INSPIRES YOU?

I find many of Steven Holl's buildings, particularly when light and color play a central role, very inspiring. They create beautifully serene and spiritual places. For me, the work of Peter Zumthor has a similar quality. Works such as his Thermal Baths in Vals and his Saint Benedict Chapel on top of the mountain in Sumvitg are beautiful in their loyalty to material, detail, and quality of sound and light. ■

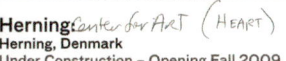

3

THE ABCs
OF CV RÉSUMÉ

DIFFERENT RÉSUMÉ FORMATS In the United States professionals present their experience and skills in a résumé. In the United Kingdom and throughout Europe the same document is called a Curriculum Vitae, or CV for short. In the United States and Canada a CV is associated with academia and is far more comprehensive and detailed than a résumé, which is used primarily for recruitment purposes. Of course there are deviations of résumés and CVs based on country-specific working cultures; for example, the Europass, which has led to an attempt by the European Parliament and European Commission to develop a standardized CV in 2004. The Europass CV (http://europass.cedefop.europa.eu/en/home) was designed to help employers overcome linguistic barriers while comparing, as quickly and easily as possible, prospective employees applying for positions throughout Europe. The Europass documents also recognize non-accredited learning and work experience.

A CV or a résumé can be organized and formatted in a number of different ways. The most common method of organization is the chronological résumé, which list jobs in reverse chronological order, starting with your current or most recent position. Most applicants use this format and employers typically prefer it because it's easy to see what jobs the applicant has held and when. A chronologically organized résumé or CV provides continuity while also presenting your employment experiences as a ladder to future success. In addition, if you have been working for a number of well-known companies, reverse chronological order is the format best suited to highlight those work experiences.

However, the chronological résumé often proves problematic if you have gaps in your résumé, frequent relocations, professional re-orientations, career changes, or if you have minimal experience. Under these circumstances, it is better to create a functional or skills-based résumé. In a functional résumé, different categories of experience, training, or special skills are strategically arranged. Therefore, this approach is particularly suitable for re-starters – for example, if you had to take a leave of absence or if you have experienced a re-orientation or gap in your career. In addition, if you have no formal training in a profession, you can use the skills section to arouse the curiosity of your prospective employer and to draw their focus away from your lack of experience.

Another option is a hybrid-résumé, which is a mixture of the two résumé formats just discussed. The hybrid-résumé is organized by your specific priorities, and by your particular objectives for each position. The following overview is intended to serve as a guideline showing you what elements are considered essential as a standard part of the résumé and what should be excluded, depending on the country you are seeking employment in.

In the UK the essentials of any résumé are as follows:
- Personal details (name, address, phone number, email)
- Career statement (optional)
- Education/school (degrees with date and accurate description)
- Professional or work experience (in reverse chronological order, time and exact dates, and a brief description)
- Language and computer skills.

In the United States, the standard information that should be included on a résumé is as follows:
- Personal details (name, address, phone number, email)
- Career statement (optional)
- Education/school (degrees with date and accurate description)
- Professional or work experience (in reverse chronological order, time and exact dates, and a brief description)
- Computer skills
- Certificates and licenses
- Professional memberships (optional)
- Honors awards (optional)
- Do not include personal data or interests (including marital or parental status) – and do not include a photo!

THE ABCs OF CV RÉSUMÉ

☐ YOUR CV IS YOUR FIRST IMPRESSION

You never get a second chance to make a first impression; and your CV or résumé is the first impression you make on your potential future employer. Therefore, it is important to carefully consider what effect you want to achieve with your CV. For example, do you want to leave a serious and modest or an artistic and original impression? Because it is such an important first impression, contemplating and crafting the tone of your résumé is the first step towards a successful job hunt.

The purpose of a CV or résumé is to showcase your experience and skills – as well as your individuality and creativity – as effectively as possible. In this sense your objective will be to create a CV unlike any other. If you are transitioning from academics to the professional world, you will need to showcase your abilities, rather than your limited professional experiences. The creation of your résumé, therefore, often becomes an incredibly strategic undertaking, and the more you study it the more résumé writing becomes a discourse in itself. Format, image size and placement in relation to text, paper choice, number of pages, and font are all choices that affect the overall impact and success of your final product.

The traditional CV form and format fits into a standardized, corporately sanctioned way of doing things. Following traditions, yet managing to express yourself within those traditions, shows impressive levels of initiative and professionalism. It demonstrates that you can fit into a larger company structure while cooperating effectively and productively with others. However, it is also important to distinguish yours from the other résumés in the same large stack. Even such things as a small change in paper size, for example, can set you apart from the pool of candidates and incite employers to take a second, closer look at your application materials. In my experience, the most unique and intricately crafted CVs are the ones that make it through the first cuts and get passed throughout the office.

As you read through Chapter 3 take note of the example résumés in Jordan J. Lloyd's contribution. In particular, notice how the "Poor Résumé" example – or the example of what not to do – is not interesting, unique, or intricately crafted (page 80). By comparison, the positive résumé examples illustrating for you what you should do are distinct and visually appealing while also remaining simple, straightforward, and easily accessible at a cursory glance.

As you survey Bill Mackey's contribution to this chapter, observe how he adeptly navigates the fine line between adhering to standard, professional expectations for résumé content and his own original visual narration of his accomplishments and experiences. What impression do you think he makes with his unique résumé? Also notice how he includes all of the pertinent and essential information while also breaking with traditions to create his own interpretation of a résumé – a résumé that successfully creates an interesting and distinctive sense of continuity.

☐ STANDARD CV ETIQUETTE: THE GROUND RULES ACCORDING TO A CAREER PROFESSIONAL

- A paper copy is almost always preferable, and it is even better if you can deliver it by hand.
- Make sure the print quality is the best possible, not pixelated or blurry.
- Always include a cover letter making your CV relevant to the company and the specific position you are applying for (avoid generalizations).
- The envelope should fit the size of the paper.
- Your address should be printed, rather than handwritten.
- Spell check, spell check, spell check!
- Call the company in advance to find out who, specifically, to address your CV and cover letter to.
- Call in the following week to make sure your application materials were received.

☐ NOT TOO MUCH AND NOT TOO LITTLE

Within the architectural and design profession the images and examples of work you show will be more important than anything else, so you should always try to present your CV/résumé with visual examples of your work. With that being said, there is no concrete consensus about how long a CV/résumé should be. Therefore, length is at your discretion; however, make sure that all of the necessary and impactful information is presented concisely. A single page is too concise, and over four pages is too long. A CV should be short and to the point; it should not be a mini portfolio of your work.

When it comes to résumés, less is more. Your central idea or theme should be recognizable at a glance – therefore, avoid clutter. HR directors and hiring managers simply don't have time to pour over the hundreds of résumés that land on their desk, so it's a matter of making it as easy as possible for someone to put your résumé on the "yes" pile. The goal is to make your CV as concise and to the point as possible. You want your prospective employer to view it as a taster rather than a comprehensive catalogue. If you have questions and would like feedback on résumé length or content after you submit your résumé – or even after an interview – it could be helpful and beneficial to contact someone at the hiring company for their comments.

THE ABCs OF CV RÉSUMÉ

☐ TARGETING YOUR CV

If you asked the HR Manager of a large firm – a manager who receives and analyzes résumés every day – to give you constructive feedback on your résumé you might be surprised that the manager probably wouldn't be able to offer specific comments on format, design, or layout. What the HR Manager would be able to tell you is what they first look for in a résumé. And their list would look something like this:

- your professional level (for example, in the UK Part 1/ 2 Assistant, Architect etc.);
- how many years of experience you have;
- what software you can use and how well.

Now that you have this information, you can use it to reorganize your résumé – and highlight what is the most important and expedient information.

☐ SIX KEY CHARACTERISTICS OF AN EFFECTIVE CV/RÉSUMÉ

Whether you're a new graduate looking for your first position, or whether you're only seeking a summer job, the time to send your résumé is as fast as possible. Therefore, here are some characteristics of a good résumé that you should keep in mind.

- **Be concise**

The purpose of your résumé is to incite the interest of a potential employer, to call attention to your qualities and your skills. The person screening your résumé probably has over 200 others to read; therefore, it will benefit you if that screener can identify, as quickly as possible, the element that distinguishes you. So keep it short and simple and to the point. If your résumé is concise and strategic enough that it sets you apart quickly, you will be sure to get an interview.

- **Be accurate and specific**

In the résumé and professional worlds, "specific" goes hand-in-hand with "concise". The fact that your résumé should be short and to the point does not mean it should be vague in any way. Your CV or résumé should not omit any important information, nor should it embellish any material or experiences. Your representation of your professional self via your résumé should be absolutely accurate.

- **Be clear, coherent, and comprehensible**

In your quest for brevity, you should not sacrifice clarity or organization. The final draft of your CV should be clear, legible, and divided into several parts for easy reading. A well-presented and well-ordered professional document reflects an orderly and conscientious personality. For this reason, your résumé can be divided into several different categories: education, languages spoken, employment experience, career objective, etc. These categories should be organized strategically, for maximum effect. Depending on the skills you are looking to emphasize or develop and the type of position you want, you should choose to highlight specific employment experiences and skills by strategically placing them.

It is also worthwhile to note that you should never send the same résumé or cover letter to different companies. Rather, each CV and cover letter must be tailored and re-worked for each position.

- **Be persuasive**

The best way to nab your dream job is to create a résumé that will make a profound positive impact on the hiring manager. Therefore, it is advisable to call attention to a catch phrase, highlight your desired career objective, or emphasize the area in which you want to work. Remember that your résumé or CV is the first step in selling yourself. Prospective employers need to be persuaded to buy. Convince them that they need you. Convince them that what you bring to the table is indispensable.

- **Be professional**

Also keep in mind that – while you certainly want to stand out – you also want to be taken seriously. An overly complicated layout or using word processing tricks that make reading more difficult should be avoided. You need to walk the tightrope between fresh and original and freaky and ridiculous. Avoid the gratuitous use of font and paper colors. A good rule of thumb to follow throughout the résumé creating and submitting process (and life) is: stay classy and somewhat sober.

- **Be comprehensive**

You should strive to make your résumé as complete as possible and appropriate. Do not forget to include such crucial information as name, education, qualifications, and professional experience. When submitting a résumé in European countries, pertinent interests should also be included because they can allow your prospective employer to understand your personality, energy, motivations, and your ability to get involved in a project. In the United States, this section can be omitted.

You can now use these six specific characteristics as a checklist for evaluating your résumé or CV. Remember that your résumé's purpose is to open doors to interviews, so careful, considerate creation of that résumé is essential for planning and living your most rewarding and enriching career path.

As you peruse this chapter, remark how the pointclouds (the 3D graphical files used to model the shape or structure of solid surface geometries) in Lillie Liu's contribution would certainly persuade prospective employers or clients to open their doors to her and her colleagues. By illustrating how Flotsam transformed their research data into dynamic, nonlinear, interactive, and multimedia web content, Liu offers a concise, comprehensive, unique, professional, and persuasive showcase of her work.

☐ YOUR LETTER OF RECOMMENDATION

If you've picked up this book, you have probably completed – or are near to completing – your degree and looking to enter the workforce. However, you have also undoubtedly realized at this point that it takes time to build a positive reputation and earn respect in the professional world. One of the ways to overcome your lack of experience and reputation is making your application more personal by submitting a letter of recommendation along with your cover letter and CV. A letter of recommendation is a way to add to build your qualifications while also differentiating yourself from the other candidates.

- Who should you ask for a letter of recommendation?

If at all possible, it would be ideal if you could ask a prestigious professor known beyond your university for a letter of recommendation. However, if such a professor does not know you personally, the letter will lack authenticity and will not reflect your true qualities. Instead, choose the professor or instructor who knows you best, or perhaps an advisor with whom you worked with closely throughout your studies. Sometimes, it is possible that you have worked more closely and spent more time with a teaching assistant (TA). If so, you can ask them to write your letter and your professor may agree to sign it.

Another person who may write a letter of recommendation for you is your tutor. The advantage of asking your tutor is that they have seen your work and they will probably be able to comment on how you operate in a professional environment. Your tutor or even your supervisor has also followed your work and has seen your progress. More than likely they will also be able to write a letter that is personal, authentic, and meaningful.

Although it can be awkward if you are leaving your current position, you can also ask your employer for a letter of recommendation. There are several situations in which your employer can make your letter of recommendation relevant. For example, if you did well at your job, or if you were employed throughout your studies, and now you are looking to move on after graduation. It would also be appropriate to ask for a letter of recommendation from your employer if you were hired on a fixed term contract. In these instances and others it is appropriate and beneficial to request a letter of recommendation from your employer. You can even request a letter of dismissal if you parted with your employer on amicable terms and if they are willing to speak well of your work.

☐ FINDING A JOB THROUGH YOUR NETWORK

A network is all of the people you know: family, friends, family friends, acquaintances, former colleagues, former classmates, etc. If you were to make a list of people you know, you would soon realize that it is very long – probably longer than you would have expected. This is your network, both "professional" and "personal". But don't worry if you think your network isn't as extensive as other people's – it's quality over quantity when it comes to networks.

Your individual network is an intricate tapestry that is woven gradually over time and it has multiple functions: finding places to go on vacation, finding an apartment, finding the best childcare, the best restaurants – and the best career opportunities. According to articles published in professional journals, 94 percent of people who successfully find a job do so because they are able to tap into their professional network.

☐ HOW TO BUILD A NETWORK

Remember that for it to be effective, your network must be comprised of individuals from diverse backgrounds to give you the widest possible perspective. Cast the widest net possible. To make the most out of the network you already have in place, you should give priority to contacts who have direct links with industry professionals, with people whose interests, knowledge, and expertise could be of use to you. If you already have a job, remember that it is always good to network within the company where you work. Build good relationships with your boss, your colleagues, and people who work in other departments.

If you are still in college and actively pursuing your degree, make an effort to be social; don't shut yourself up in your dorm. It is important that you create contacts and interact with other students, academics, and professionals. Learn as much as you can – from your courses and from people. In addition to being social, professionals agree that it is a good idea to create a blog, visit forums, join mailing lists, and chat to create a specialized network. Remember that the Internet offers extraordinary and historically unprecedented opportunities for networking.

Also keep in mind that, like good roads and infrastructure, networks and personal connections need to be maintained. With the ubiquity of cell phones, social networking sites, email, and other technologies it is easier than ever to maintain relationships. Be polite, show respect, and keep in touch. If you lay the groundwork and then maintain it, it will not be difficult to make productive, beneficial, career-building connections.

THE ABCs OF CV RÉSUMÉ

☐ INITIAL INTERACTIONS WITH PROSPECTIVE EMPLOYERS

With diploma in hand, you have finally landed your first interview. But even with your hard-won education, it will prove advantageous to spend some time learning about how to interact with recruiters and interviewers. Here are some tips that can help you to secure an interview and a position while distinguishing yourself from other candidates.

LESSON 1: BE YOURSELF

If you want to stand out amongst the pool of candidates, avoid formatted answers. In this chapter you will not find canned responses to possible interview questions. Stick with your own vocabulary and your own ideas. Be polite and professional while maintaining your own individuality and your own way of speaking. Keep in mind that you are interacting with recruiters, HR specialists, and managers who probably conduct countless interviews. What they want is originality and personality.

LESSON 2: LEARN TO IMPROVISE

One of the greatest challenges of any interview is the fact that you can never be sure what questions will be asked. That is why the ability to improvise is such an essential skill. Stay calm and collected and respond to every question to the best of your ability. Draw from your knowledge and experience. And don't panic if developing your response takes a moment. Pauses are part of the interview process. In addition, keep in mind that an interviewer may ask you an unusual or difficult question just to gage your reaction and to see how you handle a challenging situation.

If you are afraid of not knowing what to say or of completely botching it and saying the wrong thing, train yourself. The best way to practice is to ask a friend, colleague, or relative to play the role of the recruiter or hiring manager while conducting a mock interview. Repeat the mock interview exercise until you feel comfortable and confident. The goal is not to create a pre-scripted dialogue but to feel comfortable with improvising responses and to think about certain aspects of the interview that you had not considered.

LESSON 3: KNOW WHO YOU ARE DEALING WITH

Never go into an interview blind. Do your research and uncover as much pertinent information about the company and your interviewers as possible. Scoping out the company's website is a good place to start. Seeking out and talking to someone who has worked or is working for the company is also a good idea.

It is also incredibly important to acquaint yourself with the philosophy or the mission statement of the company you are being interviewed by. In addition, be prepared to discuss the services and products the company offers. Often it is even appropriate to request to meet your future colleagues. All of these preparations show that you are genuinely interested in working for this company in particular and becoming part of their team.

LESSON 4: TRANSFORM YOUR WEAKNESSES INTO STRENGTHS

Of course, throughout the interview process you should make every effort to show how highly motivated you are while highlighting your best qualities as frequently as possible. However, if you are directly asked about your potential weaknesses, a good way to address them is to turn them into strengths, into positives. For example, you can turn your youth and relative lack of experience into vitality, innovation, and fresh thinking. Consider your weaknesses and strengths in advance and know how to talk about them because these are topics that are often discussed in interviews.

LESSON 5: CHILL OUT

It's often difficult when confronted with a big interview to avoid a trembling voice, nervous gestures, or sweaty palms. However, you must learn to control your nervous energy and stress to avoid appearing overly anxious or stressed out. You should strive to appear calm, collected, and confident. Adopting a comfortable position and consciously taking deep, controlled breaths can help you keep your cool.

It is also a good idea to take time before the interview to find and practice getting to the interview location. There is no need to create additional, unnecessary stress by arriving at the last minute – or worse, arriving late.

WHAT YOU SHOULD DO AFTER THE INTERVIEW

You have already achieved two important steps: you sent out a good application and you interviewed successfully. Now you must be patient while waiting to hear back from your prospective employer. However, there are some important things you can focus on in the meantime.

- **Document your interview experience**

Immediately after the interview, record your impressions. Write down whatever comes to mind. Start with the positive, with what went well, and then work your way to what you can improve on. Write down the questions you found especially challenging, and the responses that you are the most proud of. Reflect back on your attitude, how you responded to particular questions, what your reactions and the reactions of your interviewers were, and how you felt throughout the interview. Record your thoughts and impressions even if you thought the interview did not go well. You can also make a list of the advantages and disadvantages of the position and the company. These records will be of use to you if you are called in for a second interview, if you enter negotiations to accept the position, or if you need to continue interviewing for other positions.

- **Write a thank you note**

After the interview, you can follow up by writing a message of thanks to the recruiter, hiring manager, or interview committee. Often a hand written, delivered message is best, but an email is also appropriate as well as practical. Your thank you note should be short and sincere and devoid of arguments for your unique fit or qualifications. The purpose of a thank you note is to remind the company of your professionalism and your continued interest and enthusiasm for the position.

- **Maintain contact**

Even if you feel like you have done enough already and the ball is now in the interviewer's court, there are still some favorable actions you can take. If you were savvy enough to ask at the end of the interview how long it will take before you receive an answer, do not contact the interviewer before that scheduled date. However, if that duration of time has passed, take the initiative to call.

When and if you do call or receive a post-interview follow-up call, be prepared. Take notes and draft your questions and responses. Even if the interviewer is late in getting back to you, always remain professional and courteous. If you have other offers and interviews, you can certainly disclose this information; however, be very careful not to offer any ultimatums. Convey your continued enthusiasm for the company and the position without pressuring the individuals you want to hire you.

PREPARING FOR A NEGATIVE POST-INTERVIEW OUTCOME

Unless you are extraordinarily lucky, you will not get every job you interview for. Therefore, you should prepare yourself for the inevitable rejection. If you receive a negative response, remain courteous despite your disappointment. State that you remain interested in the company and available. Keep in mind that, for any number of reasons, it may not work out with the candidate who was initially chosen. It is therefore important to stay on good terms with the company or organization and the individuals who do the hiring.

Above all, do not take rejection too personally. You do not know what goes on behind closed doors and you don't know the real reason you were turned down for the position and someone else was chosen over you. An initial rejection does not mean that you are not an excellent candidate or that you did not interview well.

It may also be appropriate and helpful to ask the recruiter about their impressions of your interview – what went well and what didn't go so well. Ask for advice on what you can do better at your next interview. While it is almost never pleasant to hear a rejection, take and learn what you can from the interview experience and remember that there may be a different career path for you to take.

CASE STUDY 1

TITLE: NON-RÉSUMÉ
AUTHOR: JORDAN J. LLOYD

WHY DO I NEED A RÉSUMÉ?

Common wisdom will tell you that a résumé, also known as a curriculum vitae, is an integral part of getting yourself on the career ladder, probably a job in the architectural profession. I am hoping that by the time you've reached this page, you have been offered wildly diverse and possibly more effective ways to get ahead and lead a remarkable life in whatever path you choose. Counterintuitively, one could argue that a résumé is a medium that actually communicates the complete opposite of how you choose to project yourself to a potential employer or collaborator. Your intention is most probably to come across as a passionate and versatile person who has taken on a load of extra-curricular activities; but the reality is that everyone else is doing the same thing. So how do you make sure you get noticed? There are several points to consider.

BE INTERESTING

The most successful candidates are the ones who come across as highly skilled and extremely interesting. Why? It is because they are focused on, and have deep knowledge of, a specific topic.[1] With that demonstration of deep knowledge is the implicit skills, applied intelligence and dedication needed to become an interesting person.

WHAT ARE YOU COMMUNICATING, AND TO WHOM?

Ask two questions here: 'What message am I sending out?' and 'Is this the most effective and appropriate way of demonstrating my skills?' Sending poems about yourself on small scrolls encapsulated in a block of wood, although unusual, won't be taken seriously by most people; but an intricately made wooden box with attention to joints and finishings may be the most effective way to apply for a craft-based career. Whatever medium you deliver to your intended audience, make sure you understand who you are sending it to: is it a commercial architecture firm, or a not-for-profit NGO operating in disaster zones? Or are you applying to consumer technology companies like Apple or Microsoft?

HIERARCHY

Think about the order in which text or visual information is received. Analysing any major newspaper is a great exercise in understanding information hierarchy. Make sure you have something that can be easily read by anyone, especially if the communication is unsolicited.

THE BEST RÉSUMÉ IS NO RÉSUMÉ

A very effective way to stand out is to send out a single project, where you have been responsible for the vast majority (or all) of the work and demonstrate a deep knowledge of a field or context; this could be an illustrated project with contextual and detailed information (or in one particular case, a thesis dissertation) – and stick your contact details in at the end. That's it. Be concise, but very specific with the details.

The suggestions that follow are composites of real résumés, culminating in the single project 'non-résumé', and some parting words of advice.

DON'T BE DECEPTIVE

Despite the all-too-common mistakes of the poor résumé or the visual rash, perhaps the most misleading of résumés are the ones that are well presented, but actually feature the work of others and not the applicant. An amazing rendering of a large commercial project in a recent graduate's portfolio will most certainly raise suspicion, so make sure you acknowledge collaborators and emphasise your own input. It's OK to include a small thumbnail of a professional rendering you didn't do, but make sure it is credited and follow it up with detailed drawings of the aspects of the project you specifically worked on, even if it is the car parking layout for sub level 4. Be prepared to talk about your involvement at length with your audience.

DESIGN YOUR DELIVERY METHOD

Make sure your delivery mechanism is appropriate and convenient. Sending a large case full of intricate drawings by courier is inconvenient and will take up space in an office (and soon, the bin). Sending a hardbound portfolio with a double page spread featuring only a small heading screams 'wasteful' and 'pretentious', and is therefore inappropriate. Even if you send the much more convenient A4 PDF attached to your covering letter (see below), make sure your file size is small enough to not crash your recipient's email application.

THE COVERING LETTER . . .

Or more likely, the covering email. Attach the same amount of reverence to an email as you would to an unsolicited letter. Be succinct, mention the work of the recipient and your interest in working with them, and make sure relevant information is included. Demonstrate initiative by finding out the name of the person who deals with applications: 'Dear Sirs', or 'To Whom it May Concern' hardly makes the best first impression.

Above all, make sure your covering email is going to the right person and triple check the spelling of their name. Customise your email: it's probably best not to declare you are a huge fan of 'Zaha Hadid's work' unless you are applying for a job at Zaha Hadid's office.

DOUBLE CHECK

Names, spelling and grammar. There's no excuse.

. . . LASTLY

Think twice before deciding to deliver your message unsolicited and in person. Disregard this advice if you have been specifically instructed to visit your recipient, but it has been known for well-meaning graduates to literally gatecrash client meetings, demonstrating the most effective way to ensure the application is rejected immediately.

- Be interesting and specific, and you can't go wrong.

Note
[1]For a more detailed explanation and further reading, check out Cal Newport's excellent blog Study Hacks: http://bit.ly/KZwwtm
Study Hacks
http://calnewport.com/blog/ Cal Newport has been working on identifying the traits of career success for many years, and has written several books on the subject. Essential reading.
Down Detour Road
By Eric Cesal, published by The MIT Press. The one book every graduate needs to read and study in detail. Cesal has managed to write a concise overview of the state of the architectural profession in 2012 in an easy-to-understand language.
Basics Design 02: Layout
By Gavin Ambrose, and Paul Harris, published by AVA Publishing.
A comprehensive introduction to laying out material visually, complete with technical terms. This book covers fundamental principles of how to create effective visual communications for your projects.
The Visual Display of Quantitative Information
By Edward Tufte, published by Graphics Pr.
There are a number of fantastic contemporary books and websites that explore information graphics and data visualisation; but none can beat the original. Tufte explains with copious illustrations effective methods of communicating complex information visually.

Poor résumé

Most résumés are vague, boring and yield no useful information, or important information is hidden away in a wall of dense text no one will read.

Intention "Motivated and interesting."

Impression "Tedious."

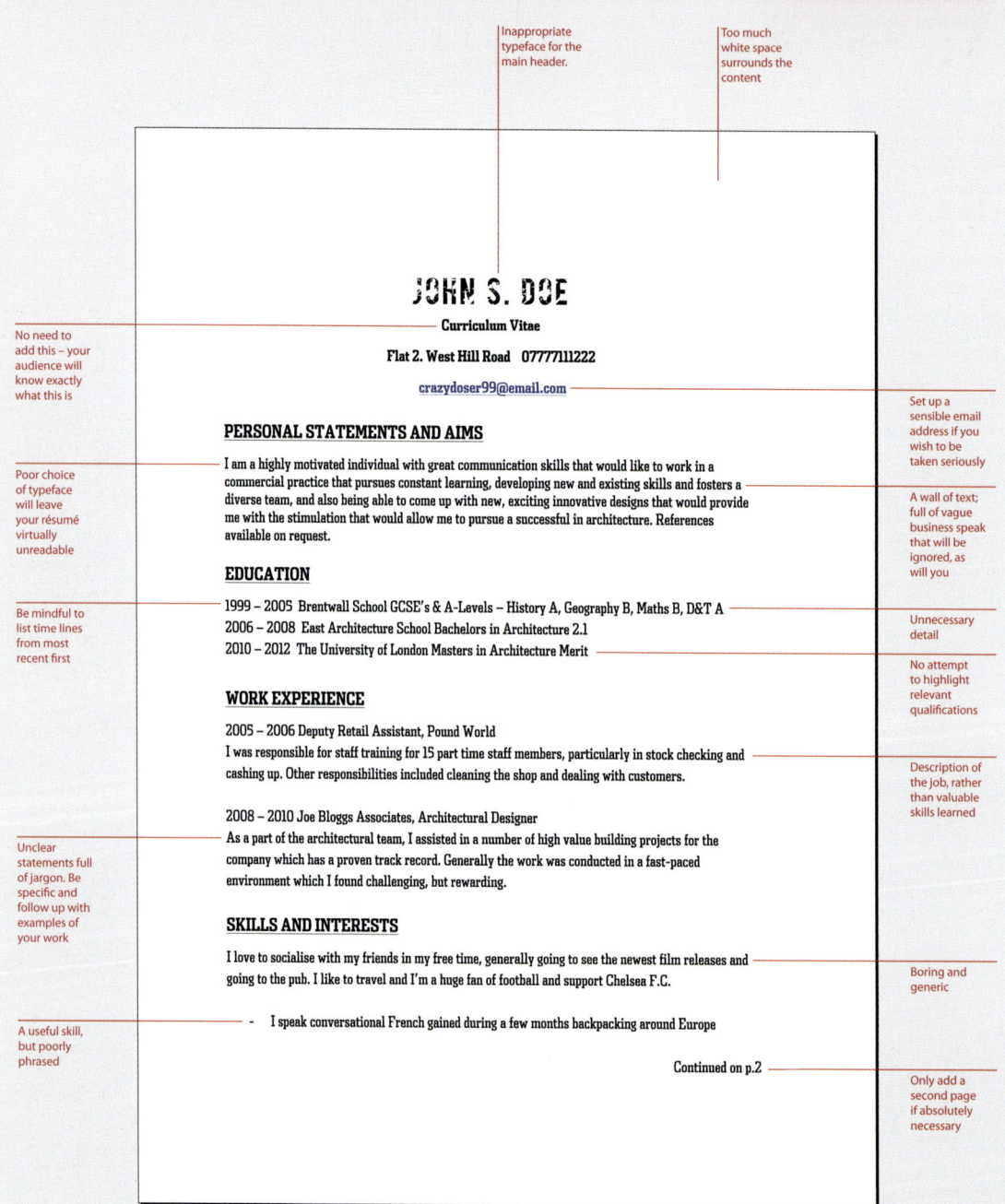

Composite example sourced from several real résumés

THE ABCs OF CV RÉSUMÉ 3

Simple text

For basic information, choosing a format like A4 or Letter is useful when you need to print on the fly, in the likely scenario of your target audience printing it out themselves. You have about six seconds to make an impression, so list key information on one page, and keep headings left aligned and bold for easy scanning.

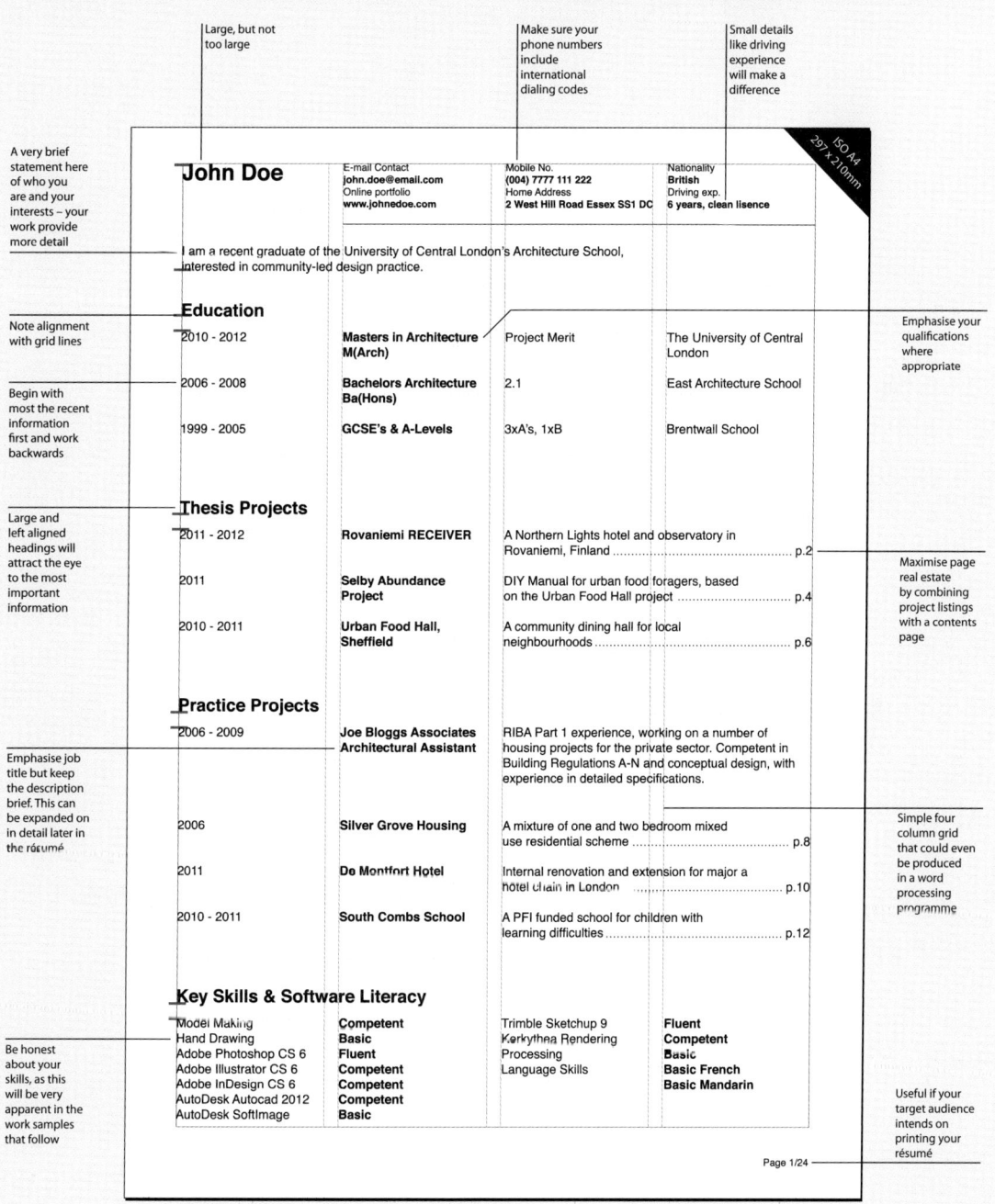

Large, but not too large

Make sure your phone numbers include international dialing codes

Small details like driving experience will make a difference

A very brief statement here of who you are and your interests – your work provide more detail

Note alignment with grid lines

Begin with most the recent information first and work backwards

Large and left aligned headings will attract the eye to the most important information

Emphasise job title but keep the description brief. This can be expanded on in detail later in the résumé

Be honest about your skills, as this will be very apparent in the work samples that follow

Emphasise your qualifications where appropriate

Maximise page real estate by combining project listings with a contents page

Simple four column grid that could even be produced in a word processing programme

Useful if your target audience intends on printing your résumé

John Doe

ISO A4 297 x 210mm

E-mail Contact
john.doe@email.com
Online portfolio
www.johnedoe.com

Mobile No.
(004) 7777 111 222
Home Address
2 West Hill Road Essex SS1 DC

Nationality
British
Driving exp.
6 years, clean lisence

I am a recent graduate of the University of Central London's Architecture School, interested in community-led design practice.

Education

2010 - 2012	**Masters in Architecture M(Arch)**	Project Merit	The University of Central London
2006 - 2008	**Bachelors Architecture Ba(Hons)**	2.1	East Architecture School
1999 - 2005	**GCSE's & A-Levels**	3xA's, 1xB	Brentwall School

Thesis Projects

2011 - 2012	**Rovaniemi RECEIVER**	A Northern Lights hotel and observatory in Rovaniemi, Finland p.2	
2011	**Selby Abundance Project**	DIY Manual for urban food foragers, based on the Urban Food Hall project p.4	
2010 - 2011	**Urban Food Hall, Sheffield**	A community dining hall for local neighbourhoods p.6	

Practice Projects

2006 - 2009	**Joe Bloggs Associates Architectural Assistant**	RIBA Part 1 experience, working on a number of housing projects for the private sector. Competent in Building Regulations A-N and conceptual design, with experience in detailed specifications.	
2006	**Silver Grove Housing**	A mixture of one and two bedroom mixed use residential scheme p.8	
2011	**De Montfort Hotel**	Internal renovation and extension for major a hotel chain in London p.10	
2010 - 2011	**South Combs School**	A PFI funded school for children with learning difficulties p.12	

Key Skills & Software Literacy

Model Making	**Competent**	Trimble Sketchup 9	**Fluent**
Hand Drawing	**Basic**	Kerkythea Rendering	**Competent**
Adobe Photoshop CS 6	**Fluent**	Processing	**Basic**
Adobe Illustrator CS 6	**Competent**	Language Skills	**Basic French**
Adobe InDesign CS 6	**Competent**		**Basic Mandarin**
AutoDesk Autocad 2012	**Competent**		
AutoDesk SoftImage	**Basic**		

Page 1/24

Visual rash

There is a particularly unfortunate trend for résumés to feature many distracting and unnecessary elements in their composition. Too many styles and effects equals an incomprehensible mess.

Intention
"Dynamic, software genius."

Impression
"Visually illiterate."

Uninspiring title that dominates the most important part of the page

Background collage is distracting and adds nothing to the composition

Large wall of text no one will read

Titles and captions should be consistent and in the background

Poor choice of contrasting colours creates a complicated and confusing composition

Colour blocks often take up valuable page space, so be aware of what it will be used for

Be mindful of what information to include. Do not add unnecessary information as 'filler'

Just one good image will convey the essential ethos of the project, so choose well

Project Reims Quartier Terroir (cannibalised!), J. Lloyd with Sarah Hunt, 2011
Layout composite based on several real examples

THE ABCs
OF CV RÉSUMÉ **3**

Simple, illustrated

The nature of architecture and design will inevitably mean that you will include some visual examples of your work. Edit your images to show a range of skills and keep your project details concise for maximum impact.

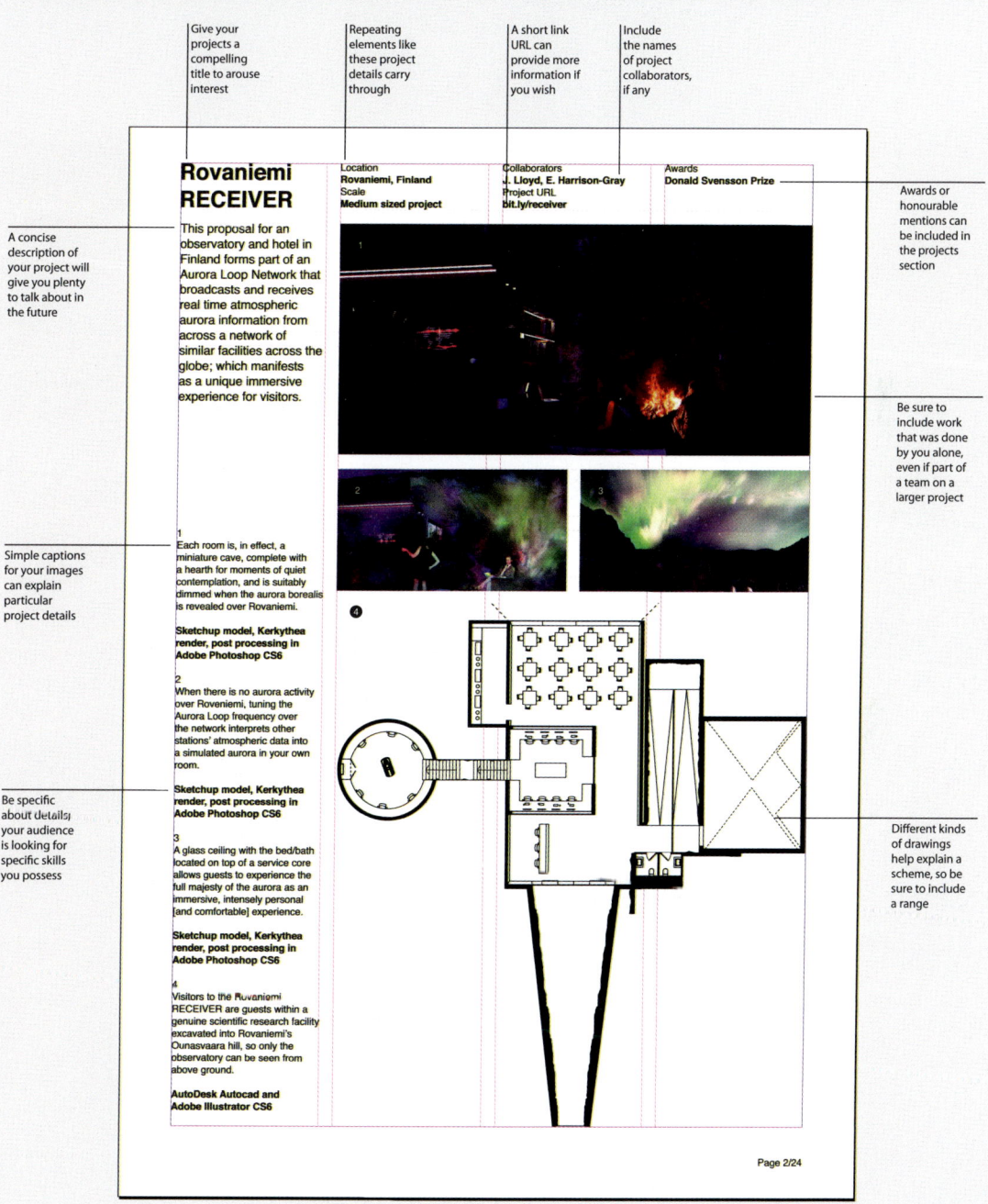

Give your projects a compelling title to arouse interest

Repeating elements like these project details carry through

A short link URL can provide more information if you wish

Include the names of project collaborators, if any

A concise description of your project will give you plenty to talk about in the future

Simple captions for your images can explain particular project details

Be specific about details your audience is looking for specific skills you possess

Awards or honourable mentions can be included in the projects section

Be sure to include work that was done by you alone, even if part of a team on a larger project

Different kinds of drawings help explain a scheme, so be sure to include a range

Project Rovaniemi RECEIVER, J. Lloyd with E. Harrison-Gray, 2012

Information graphic

On the whole, information graphics should be very carefully considered before inclusion, but for added impact, you may consider devices like Ritwik Dey's excellent LifeMap or research clustering which can help your audience to quickly identify your interests within a wider knowledge base.

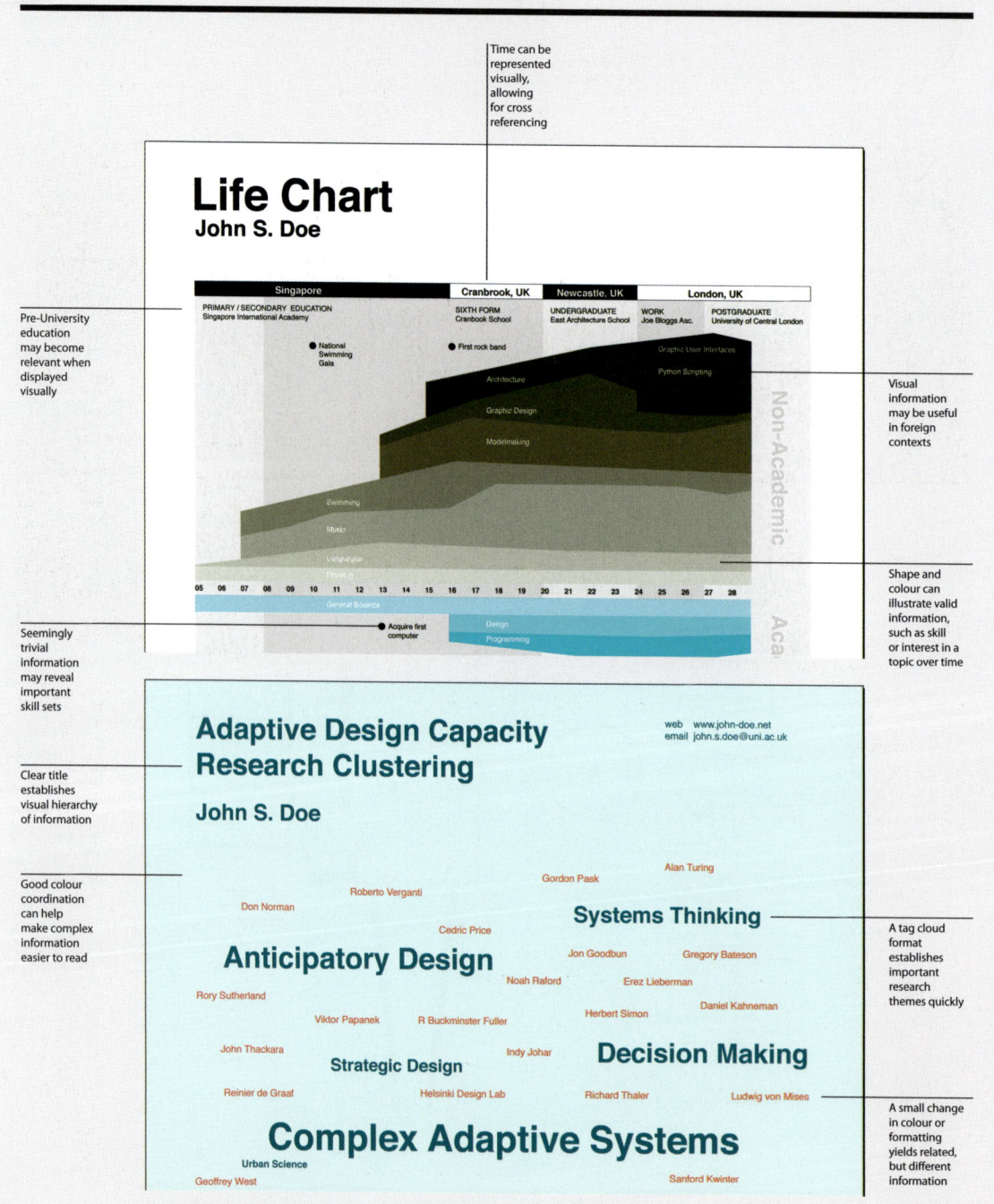

Top — Redrawn from Life Map by Ritwik Dey, 2005. See the (much better) original at www.ritwikdey.com
Bottom — A tag cloud-esque clustering quickly identifies your areas of interest and points of reference

THE ABCs OF CV RÉSUMÉ 3

Single project

Arguably the most effective approach would be to send a single detailed project that has been tailored specifically to your audience, utilising one or several of the approaches on the previous pages, whilst avoiding common mistakes.

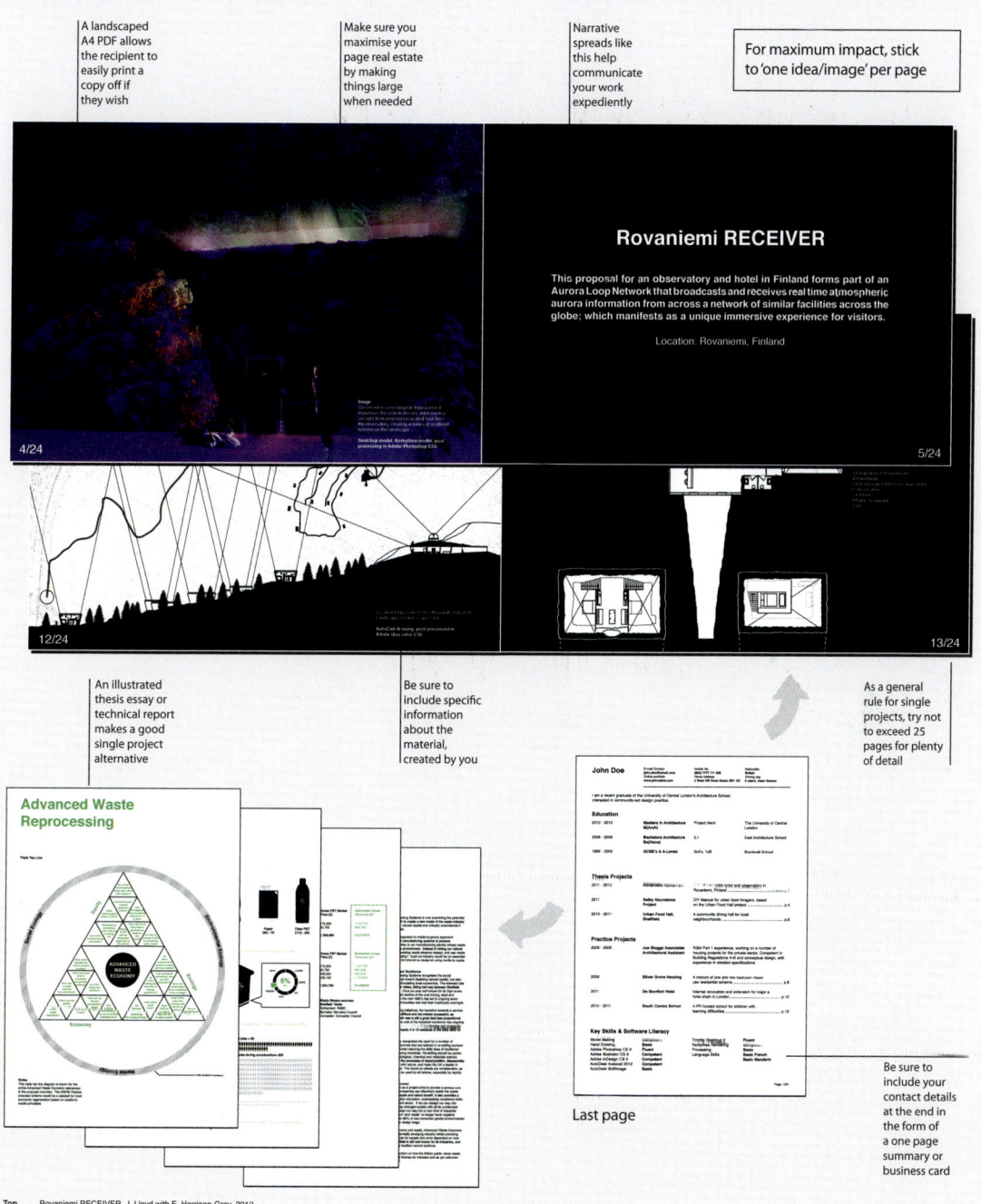

A landscaped A4 PDF allows the recipient to easily print a copy off if they wish

Make sure you maximise your page real estate by making things large when needed

Narrative spreads like this help communicate your work expediently

For maximum impact, stick to 'one idea/image' per page

An illustrated thesis essay or technical report makes a good single project alternative

Be sure to include specific information about the material, created by you

As a general rule for single projects, try not to exceed 25 pages for plenty of detail

Be sure to include your contact details at the end in the form of a one page summary or business card

Top   Rovaniemi RECEIVER, J. Lloyd with E. Harrison-Gray, 2012
Bottom Advanced Waste Economy, J. Lloyd, Studio 2, 2009

CASE STUDY 2

TITLE: INTERPRETATION OF A RÉSUMÉ
AUTHOR: BILL MACKEY

PRESENTATIONS (PUBLIC)

2011 **"You Can Have Your Cake and Eat It Too, v.2,"**
American Institute of Architects Southern Arizona Chapter, Tucson AZ

2011 **"Exhibitions,"**
Light it Up, Phoenix AZ

2011 **"You Can Have Your Cake and Eat It Too, v.2,"**
TEDx Talk, Tucson AZ

2011 **"Food Paper and Alcohol,"**
Conference on the Constructed Environment, Chicago IL

2011 **"Food Paper and Alcohol,"**
American Institute of Architects Southern Arizona Chapter, Architecture Week, Tucson AZ

2011 **"Distribute This!"**
American Institute of Architects Southern Arizona Chapter, Slide Slam, Tucson AZ

2011 **"Food Paper and Alcohol,"**
Arizona Historic Preservation Conference, Tucson AZ

2011 **"You Can Have Your Cake and Eat It Too, v.2,"**
The Graham Foundation, Chicago IL

2010 **"You Can Have Your Cake and Eat It Too, v.2,"**
University of Arizona Honors College, Tucson AZ

2010 **"Perception, Marketing, and Infrastructure,"**
American Institute of Architects Southern Arizona Chapter, Tucson AZ

2010 **"As long as we can afford it, we don't care what you do,"**
Museum of Contemporary Art, Tucson AZ

2010 **"Architecture without Program,"**
University of Arizona Department of Geography, Colloquim, Tucson AZ

2010 **"Downtown Master Plans,"**
American Planning Association, Tucson AZ

2010 **"Downtown Master Plans,"**
City of Tucson Landscape Advisory Committee, Tucson AZ

2010 **"Downtown Master Plans,"**
American Institute of Architects Southern Arizona Chapter, Tucson AZ

2010 **"Downtown Master Plans,"**
Arizona Historic Preservation Conference, Flagstaff AZ

2010 **"Convenience Stores,"**
Arizona Historic Preservation Conference, Flagstaff AZ

2009 **"Maps, Signs, and Collage,"**
The Union Gallery at the University of Arizona, Tucson AZ

2009	**"Art and the Built Environment,"** *College of Architecture, University of Arizona, Tucson AZ*
2009	**"Art and the Built Environment,"** *College of Geography, University of Arizona, Tucson AZ*
2009	**"Overlay Maps,"** *Arizona Historic Preservation Conference, Phoenix AZ*
2009	**"More Maps,"** *ignite TUCSON!, Tucson AZ*
2009	**"Regulatory Signs,"** *ignite TUCSON!, Tucson AZ*
2008	**"Automobiles, Convenience Stores, and Commercials,"** *Museum of Contemporary Art, Tucson AZ*
2008	**"Maps,"** *you are here, the journal of creative geography, 10 year Anniversary Celebration, Tucson AZ*
2008	**"Maps,"** *ignite TUCSON!, Tucson, AZ*
2008	**"Culture and Collage,"** *Inside/Out Poetry Class, Pima County Juvenile Detention Facility, Tucson AZ*
2007	**"Chicken or the Egg,"** *Museum of Contemporary Art, Tucson AZ*
2007	**"The Human Figure in Architectural Design and Drawing,"** *College of Architecture, University of Arizona, Tucson AZ*
2005	**"Experiencing Tucson at 30 Amps,"** *Museum of Contemporary Art, Tucson AZ*
2005	**"New Construction in Historic Neighborhoods,"** *Arizona Historic Preservation Conference, Tucson AZ*
2003	**"Congress Street Redevelopment,"** *Congress Street Community Development, Tucson AZ*
2002/03	**"Cohousing in America,"** *College of Architecture, University of Arizona, Tucson AZ*

PUBLIC SERVICE

2011	**Trainer, "Trim Your Energy Waistline,"** *Metropolitan Energy Commission*
2009/11	**Commissioner,** *Tucson/Pima County Historic Commission*
2007–	**Member,** *Design Co*op Tucson, Arizona*
2010	**Facilitator/Educator,** *West University Neighborhood Association Design Charette, Tucson AZ*
2010	**Tour of the Future,** *Design Co*op and City High student workshops*
2010	**Architect in Residence,** *Museum of Contemporary Art, Tucson AZ*
2009	**Participant,** *Livable Communities, Tucson AZ*
2009	**Committee Member,** *Senior Capstone Project – Margaret Kane, College of Architecture, University of Arizona*
2009	**Public Art/Public Space,** *Design Co*op and City High student workshops*

2008	**Mapping Downtown,** *Design Co*op and City High student workshops*	
2007	**Block Play,** *Design Co*op and City High student workshop*	
2007	**Block Play,** *Design Co*op and Imago Dei student workshop*	
2007	**Block Play,** *Design Co*op and General Public workshop*	
2004/05	**Commissioner,** *Tucson/Pima County Historic Commission*	
2004/05	**Chair,** *Plans Review Subcommittee, Tucson/Pima County Historic Commission*	
2002/05	**Committee Member,** *Pima County/Tucson Women's Commission*	
2004	**Committee Member,** *Primavera Foundation, Tucson AZ*	
2004	**Committee Member,** *Senior Capstone Project – Erik Petersen, College of Architecture, University of Arizona*	
2003	**Committee Member,** *Senior Capstone Project – Chris Thompson, College of Architecture, University of Arizona*	
2002/08	**Guest Reviewer,** *College of Architecture, University of Arizona*	
1999/02	**Member,** *Santa Cruz River Alliance, Tucson AZ*	
1995/97	**Architect,** *Sam Hughes Water Tower Restoration Project, Sam Hughes Neighborhood, Tucson AZ*	
1994/95	**Historical Research,** *Stone Avenue Temple Project, Tucson AZ*	

HONORS, AWARDS AND GRANTS

2012	Kresge Arts In Tucson II P.L.A.C.E. Initiative Project Grant for the project, Worker Transit Authority
2011	AzSLA Honor Award, Women's Plaza of Honor, University of Arizona, Tucson AZ
2010	Metropolitan Pima Alliance, Common Ground Award for Historic Preservation/Revitalization, OCA-Tucson
2010	Graham Foundation for the Advanced Studies in Fine Arts, publication award, Field Guides and Checklists Series
2010	Home of the Year, 825 North Norton, Southern Arizona American Institute of Architects
2010	Honorable Mention, 825 North Norton, AIA Western Home/*Sunset* Magazine Design Awards
2010	Grand Award, Outdoor Spaces, *Custom Home* Magazine, Play Yard
2009	Creative Capital Professional Development Workshop, Tucson AZ
2009	Tucson Pima Arts Council, Artist Roster for Public Art
2009	Merit Award, Outdoor Spaces, *Custom Home* Magazine, Moltz Landscape
2009	Structural Design and Innovation, American Concrete Institute (Arizona Chapter), Moltz Landscape

2007	Green Case Study School, Arizona Department of Environmental Quality, Davidson Elementary School
2006	Tucson Pima Arts Council Mini-Grant
2006	Preservation Award, Tucson Pima County Historic Commission, Individual Recognition
2004	Grant Funding, Arizona State Heritage Fund, Arizona State Parks, Royal Johnson House
2004	Preservation Award, Tucson Pima County Historic Commission, Royal Johnson House
2004	"Building from the Best of Tucson" Award, Sonoran Institute, 261 North Court Avenue
2003	Grant Funding, City of Tucson "Back to Basics," Rialto Building
2002	Grant Funding, Arizona State Heritage Fund, Arizona State Parks, Royal Johnson House
2001	Historic Preservation Award, State of Arizona, 261 North Court Avenue
2001	"Preservation Award, Tucson Pima County Historic Commission, 261 North Court Avenue
1995	Design Award, 1st Place, Pima Community College Gateway Competition, Tucson AZ

TEXT RÉSUMÉ, PAGE 1 OF 3, 2012. BILL MACKEY OF WORKER, INC.

This is the STANDARD résumé. Much of the formatting is based on a template used by faculty at the School of Architecture, University of Arizona. Categories include *Presentations, Public Service, Honors/Awards/Grants, Selected Architectural Projects and Research, Bibliography, Publications and Illustrations, Exhibitions, Education, License and Architectural Practice, Academic Experience*. These categories can shift position depending on the intended audience (i.e., for résumés intended for an art-based grant, Exhibitions is located at the top of the résumé). This résumé shows NO RELATION between the work indicated in the résumé – it is left up to the audience to make any connection between the various categories.

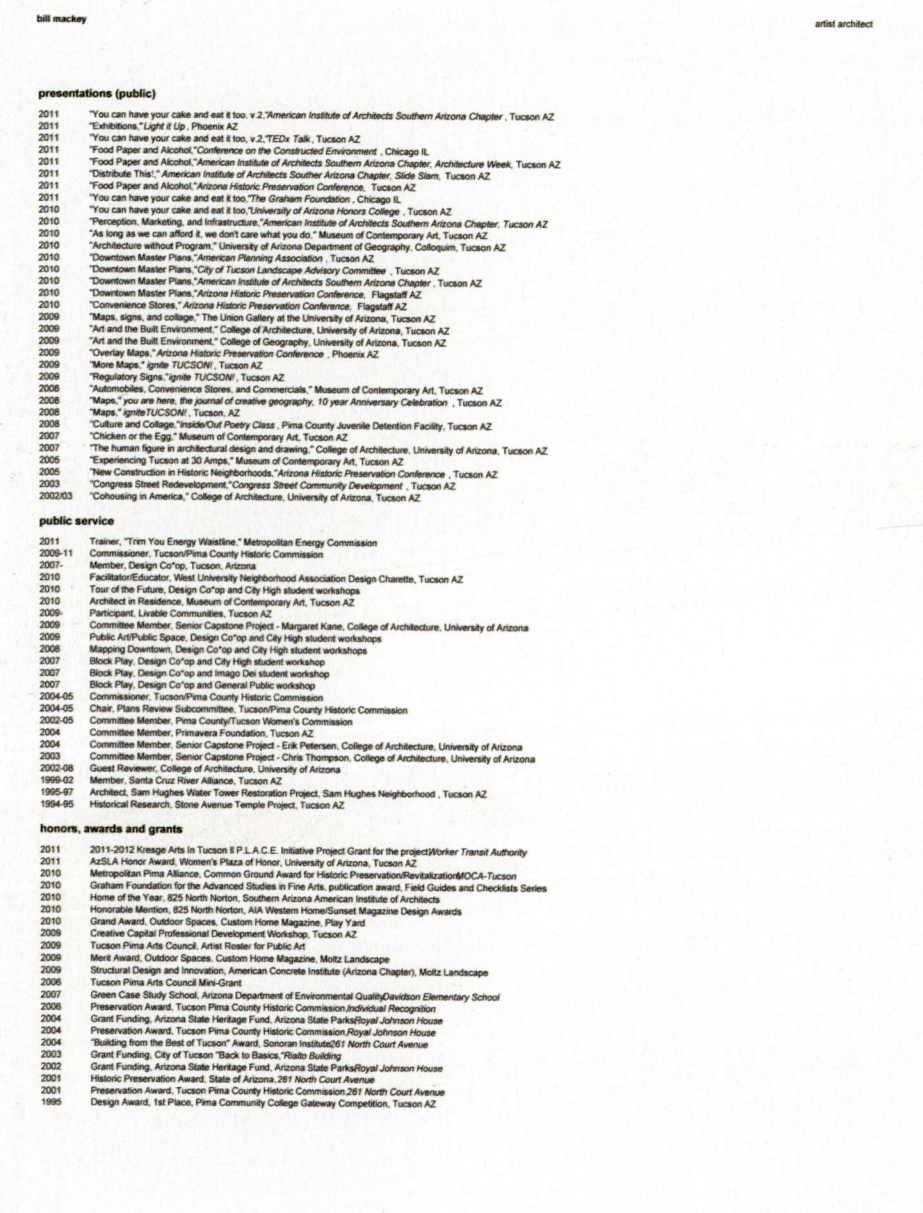

GRAPHIC RÉSUMÉ, BILL MACKEY OF WORKER, INC.

This is a graphic résumé. The intent of this résumé is to indicate the interconnectedness of all of the work of Worker, Inc. The categories do follow some of the standards used in basic résumés, but it also places emphasis on the types of work produced by the company. Categories include *Architecture, MOCA-Tucson, Education, Public Service, Reviews, Academic Experience, Awards, Publications and Illustrations, Overlay Maps, Collage, and the Neighborhood Residents Resources Ethnography Studies Unit*. With this résumé, no strong hierarchy is displayed, for everything has equal weight and value within the company. Updating the résumé is not easy.

THE ABCs OF CV RÉSUMÉ 3

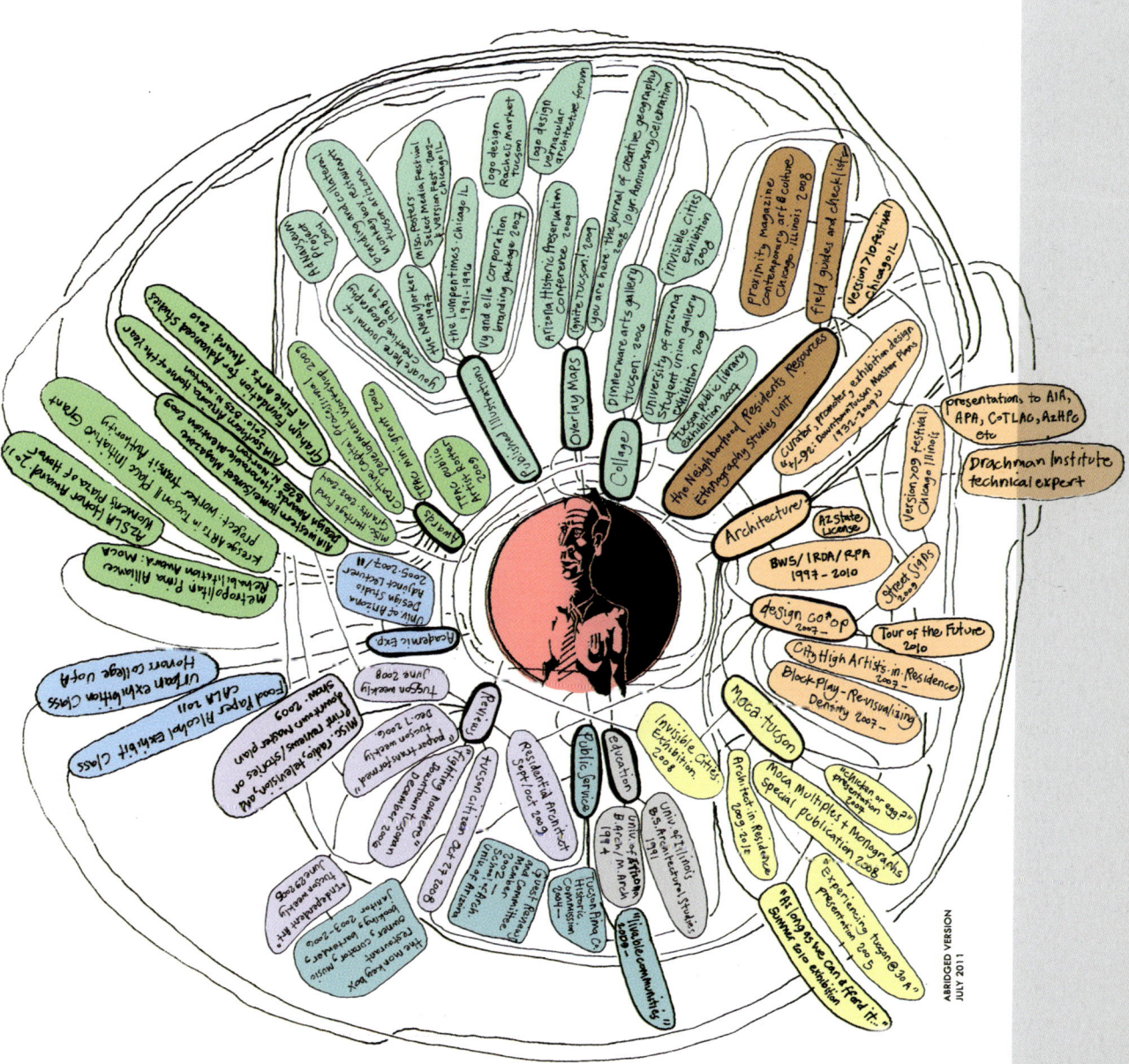

THE URBAN CHECKLIST AND ITS RELATION TO WORKER, INC., 2012

Diagram indicates the relationship of one product to other work of Worker, Inc., showing how the purchase of two nature checklists at a gift shop can lead to grant awards, architectural projects, teaching positions, and an actual planning project with a municipality. The lines between the various bubbles stress the interconnectedness between the work.

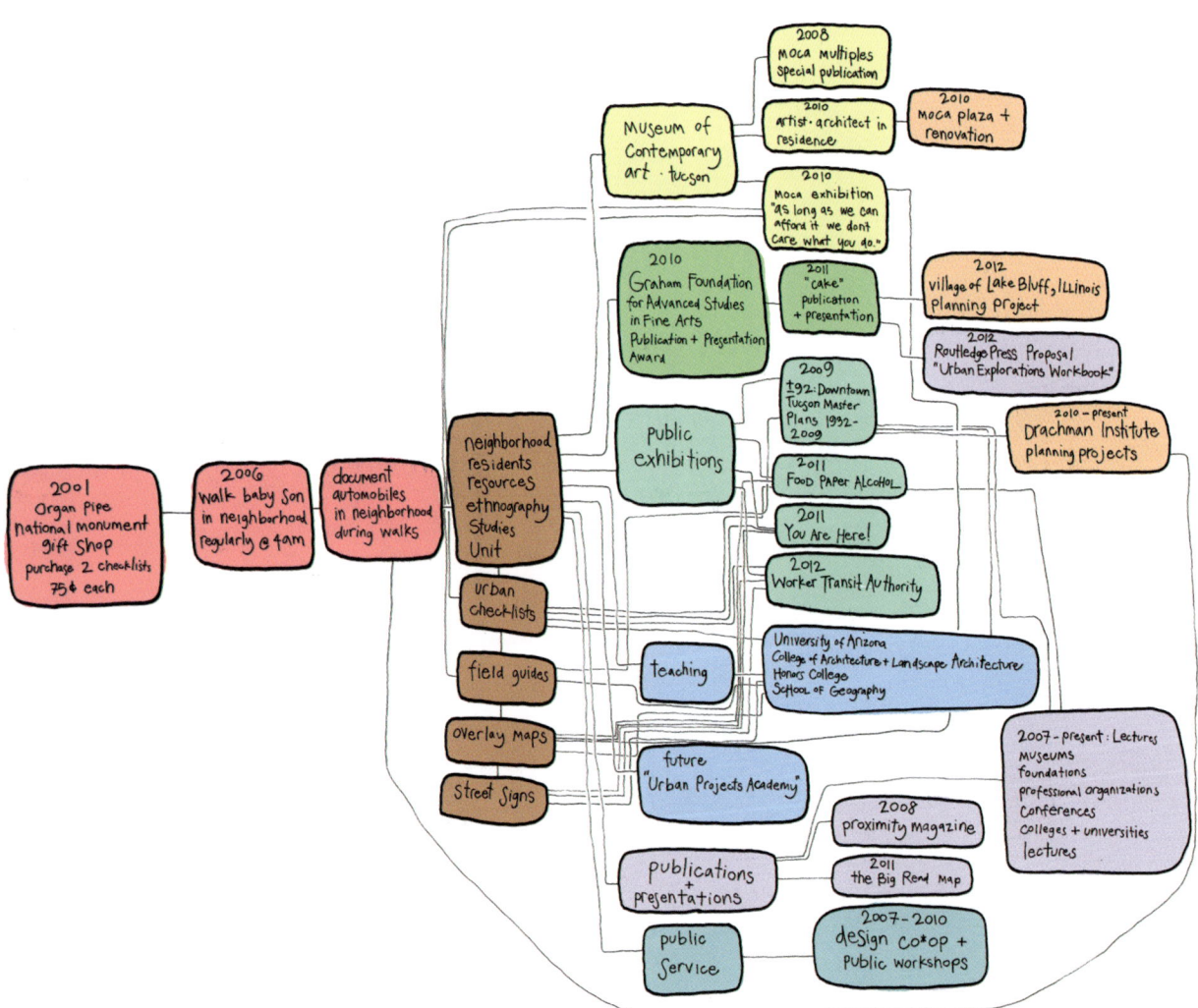

THE ABCs OF CV RÉSUMÉ 3

WORK IS MONEY, EXPERIENCE, AND PASSION, 2012

Diagram indicates the variety of "work positions" held by Bill Mackey of Worker, Inc. The element of time is introduced in this diagram to show a slow confluence of the work (passion) done on the bottom half and the work (experience/money) done on the top half into the middle (extreme passion/zero to very little money). The lines indicate the support between the various bubbles – in the beginning there was a clear distinction between the top and bottom halves without much connection to the middle. As time progresses, Worker, Inc. hopes to merge the top, middle, and bottom into a cohesive organization that specializes in the convergence of art and planning. ■

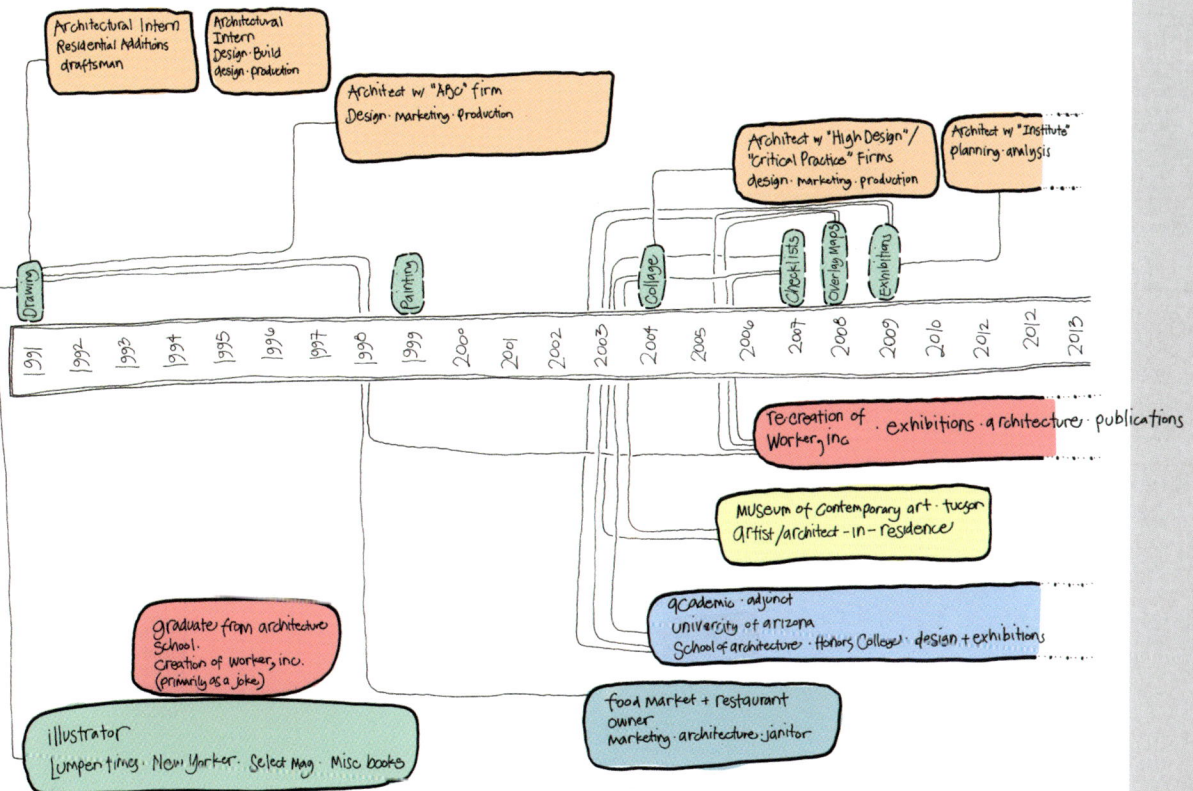

CASE STUDY 3

TITLE: A RÉSUMÉ TRANSFORMED FROM BOOK TO WEB
AUTHOR: LILLIE LIU

CLOUDS

clouds (pointclouds) is a thesis project developed by **Flotsam**, a team of young architects who collaborated during their graduate studies at the Architectural Association's Design Research Laboratory. During an 18-month period of research and design, Flotsam developed a machinic design methodology to utilize and interpret point clouds. The technique is driven by continuously modified scripting and offers an interactive and adaptive design process. The point clouds, generated by strange attractors, are a set of points that surface after many iterations and are plotted from different algorithmic formulas. As the logic of strange attractors becomes translated through Flotsam's tool, this technique not only produces spaces with varied degrees of porosity, but also allows for vertical and horizontal interweaving of private and shared spaces in a building, generating new potential ways of connectivity.

Fortunately today, many offices and clients around the world share an interest in computational design or products of computational design. These ideas no longer exist solely in our imaginations or on paper, but are becoming built projects – sometimes faster than we anticipate. In the professional world, we don't always have time to develop design tools as we have in academic settings – yet the sensibility that is gained from such a project carries through in our design processes.

What we gain is an adeptness to develop architecture using inspiration that is not only intriguing in form but has an underlying logic and system to it. To explore how this logic can be applied to architecture – whether it be spatial organization, circulation, or materiality is a unique skill set that takes full advantage of digital tools available to us today. Furthermore these techniques seek to re-imagine how architectural spaces can evolve.

As more architects turn to computers as design tools, it is important that we understand the fundamentals behind the design to make us stronger candidates. A rigorous body of work that shows not only end result but design investigations and processes will be recognized and set apart from those that are purely form.

THE ABCs OF CV RÉSUMÉ 3

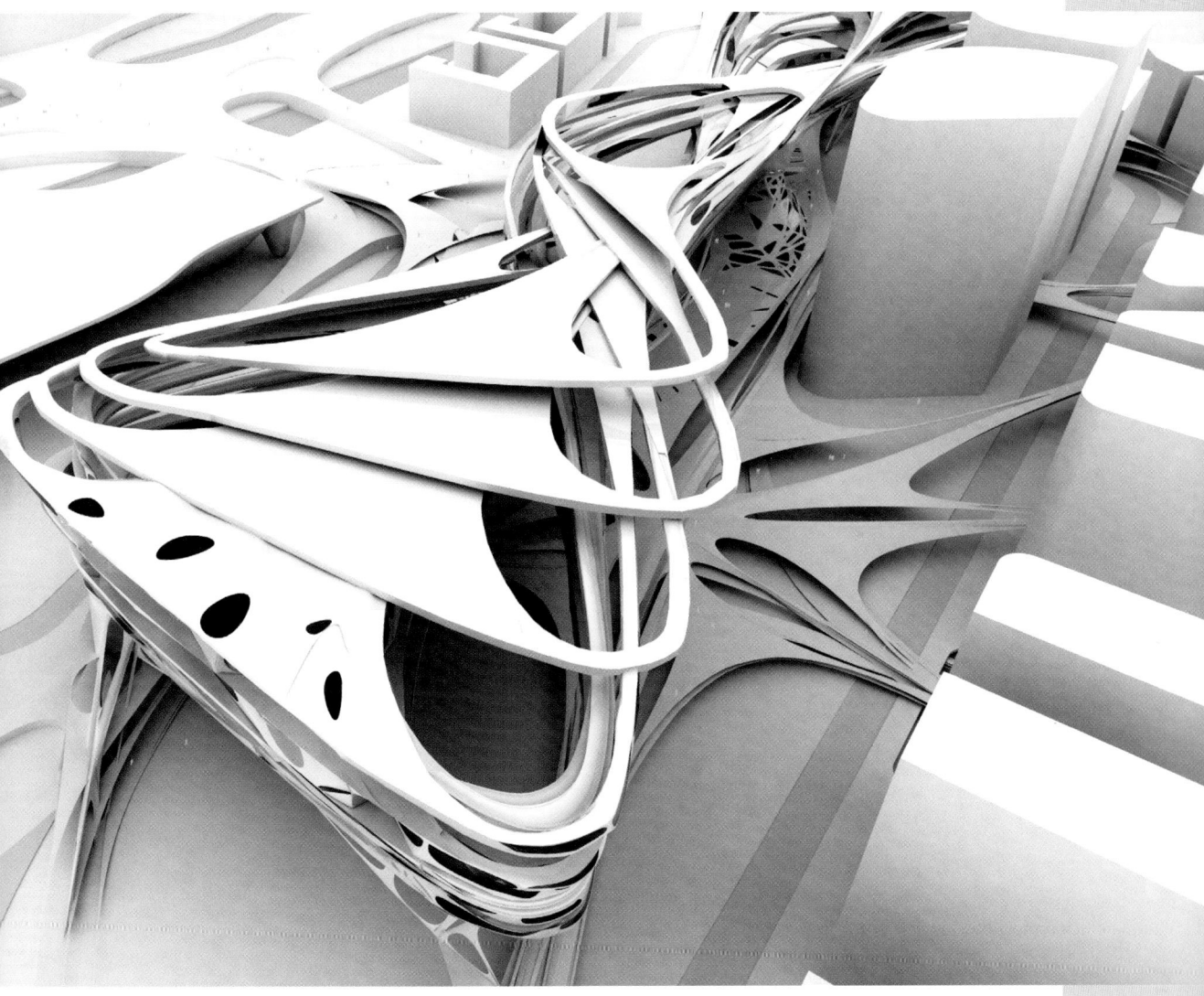

FROM BOOK TO WEB

At the end of our graduate program, Flotsam compiled a book to document work over the 18-month period. Following the book, we decided to publish a website to display our work. While material is presented linearly in books, on the web there is opportunity for information to branch out in a dynamic and interactive way. Thus we reorganized the data and developed an outline that would be clear and concise to navigate. In this case, branching is not too extensive because the website is designed for one specific project. If the website were expanded to display multiple projects, branching could grow to become more complex.

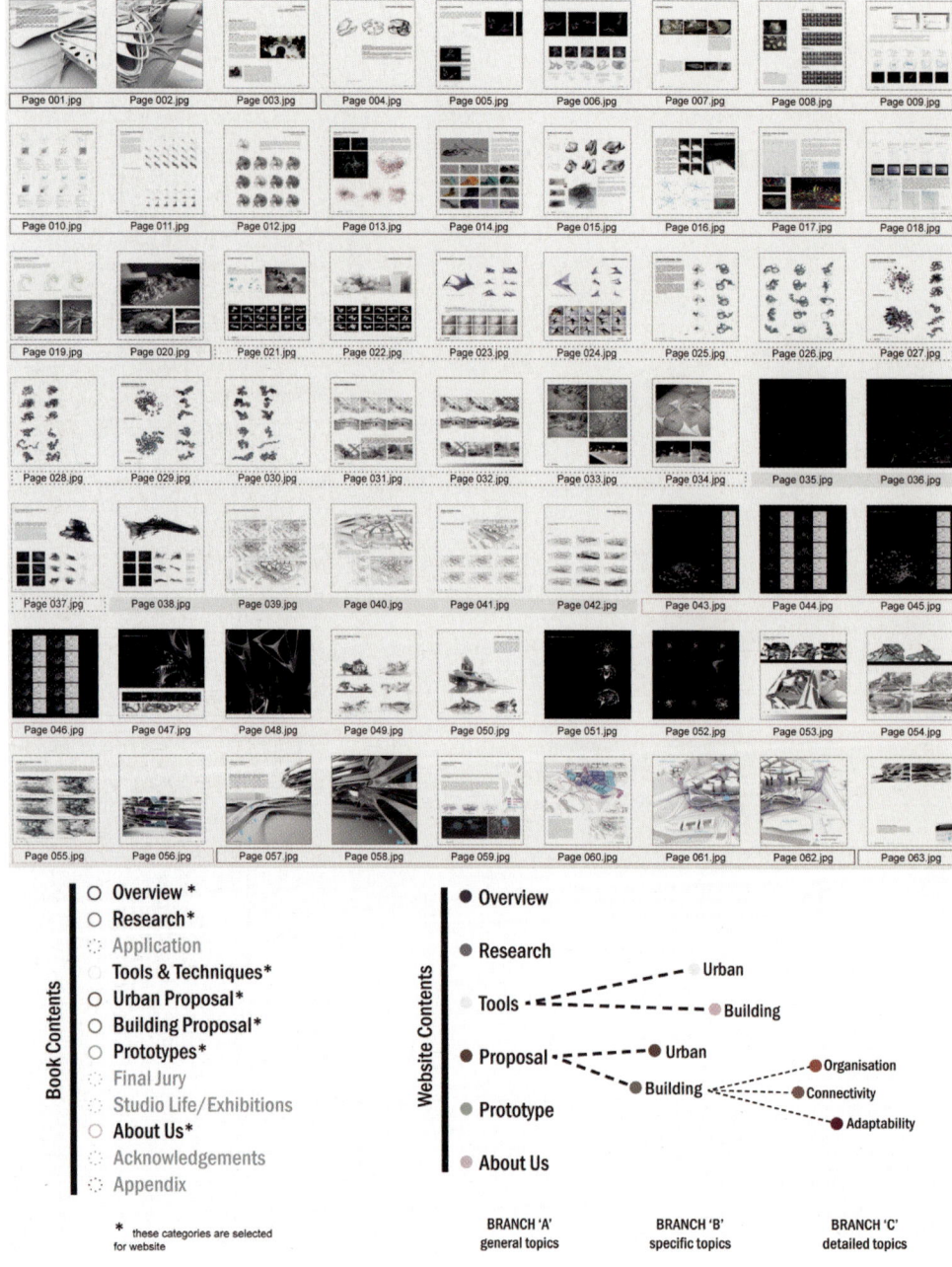

INTERFACE

With the content organized, we designed the interface in which to display the work. By keeping the organization clear and simple, we allow the work to speak for itself as the point of interest.

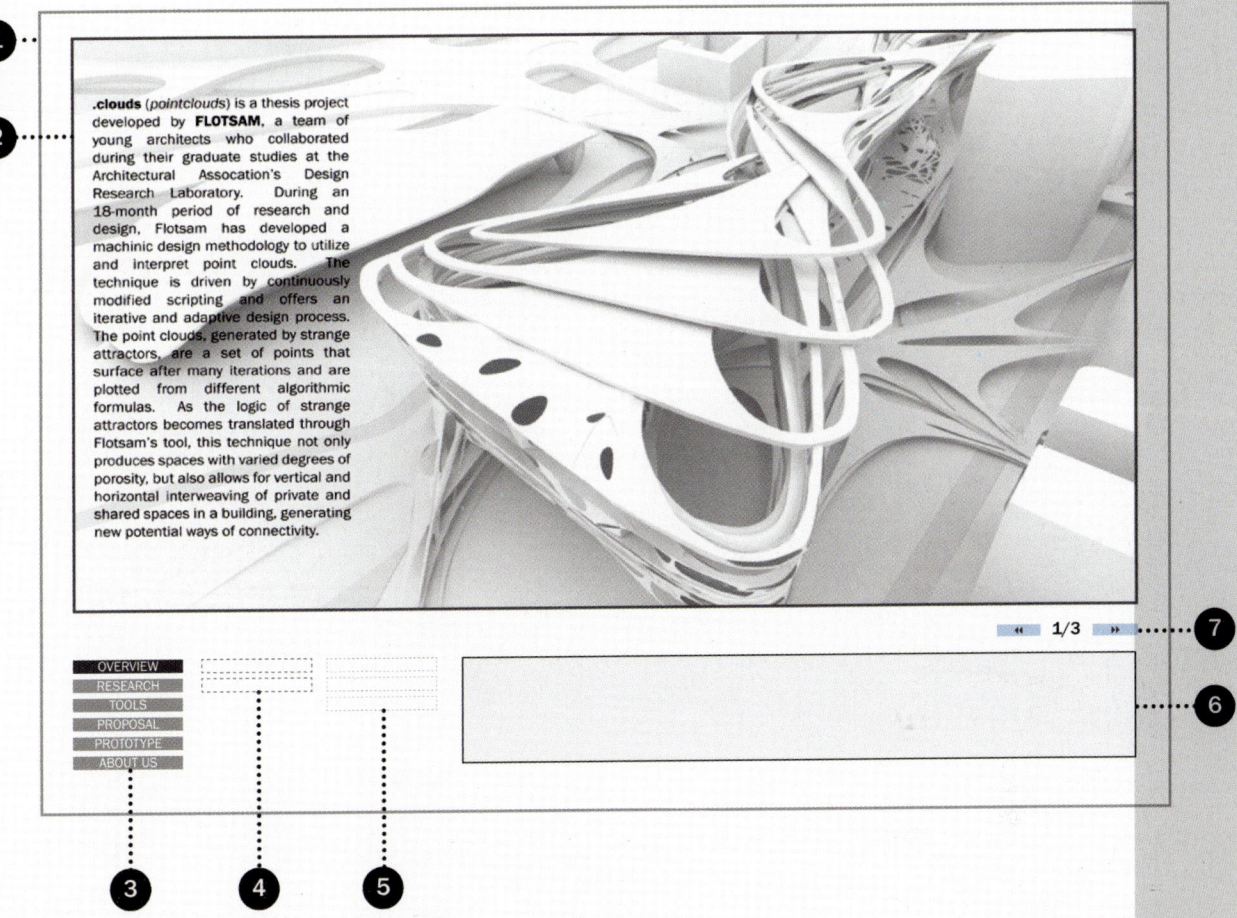

1 WINDOW FRAME

2 IMAGE BOX [DISPLAYS SLIDES AND VIDEOS]

3 BRANCH 'A' BUTTONS [ORGANISE SLIDES ACCORDING TO CATEGORIES & SUBCATEGORIES]

4 BRANCH 'B' BUTTONS [RELEVANT BUTTONS APPEAR UPON PRESS OF BRANCH 'A' BUTTON]

5 BRANCH 'C' BUTTONS [RELEVANT BUTTONS APPEAR UPON PRESS OF BRANCH 'B' BUTTON]

6 CAPTION BOX [HEADING & DESCRIPTION]

7 FORWARD/BACKWARD BUTTONS & SLIDESHOW COUNTER

ORGANIZATION

Consider the choreography of how text/images appear. Unlike text in a book, as a designer you can control the sequence in which information is displayed. Bear in mind that there are multiple paths the user can take, not just one. The purpose of branching out into subcategories is so that the viewer is not forced to scroll through a slideshow of consecutive images. Instead they are broken down into categories and the viewer can browse by topic – allowing more flexibility and control to the reader.

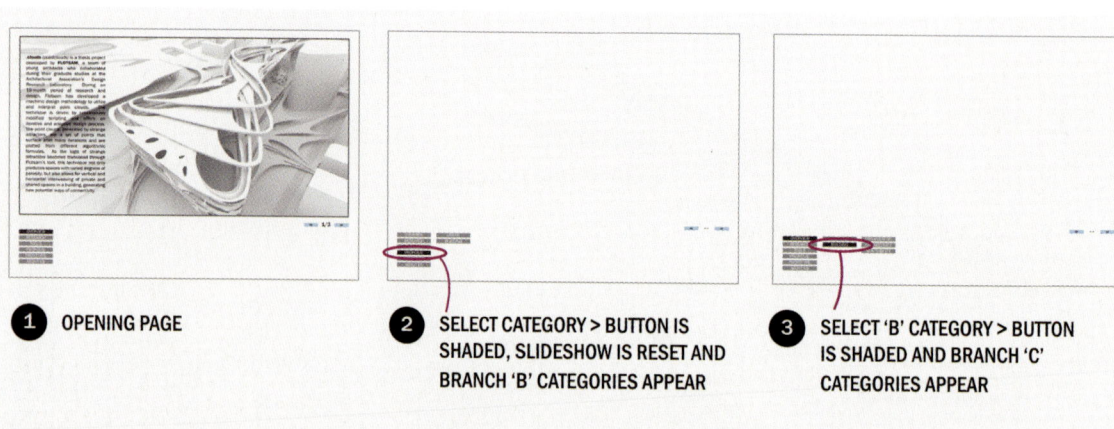

① OPENING PAGE

② SELECT CATEGORY > BUTTON IS SHADED, SLIDESHOW IS RESET AND BRANCH 'B' CATEGORIES APPEAR

③ SELECT 'B' CATEGORY > BUTTON IS SHADED AND BRANCH 'C' CATEGORIES APPEAR

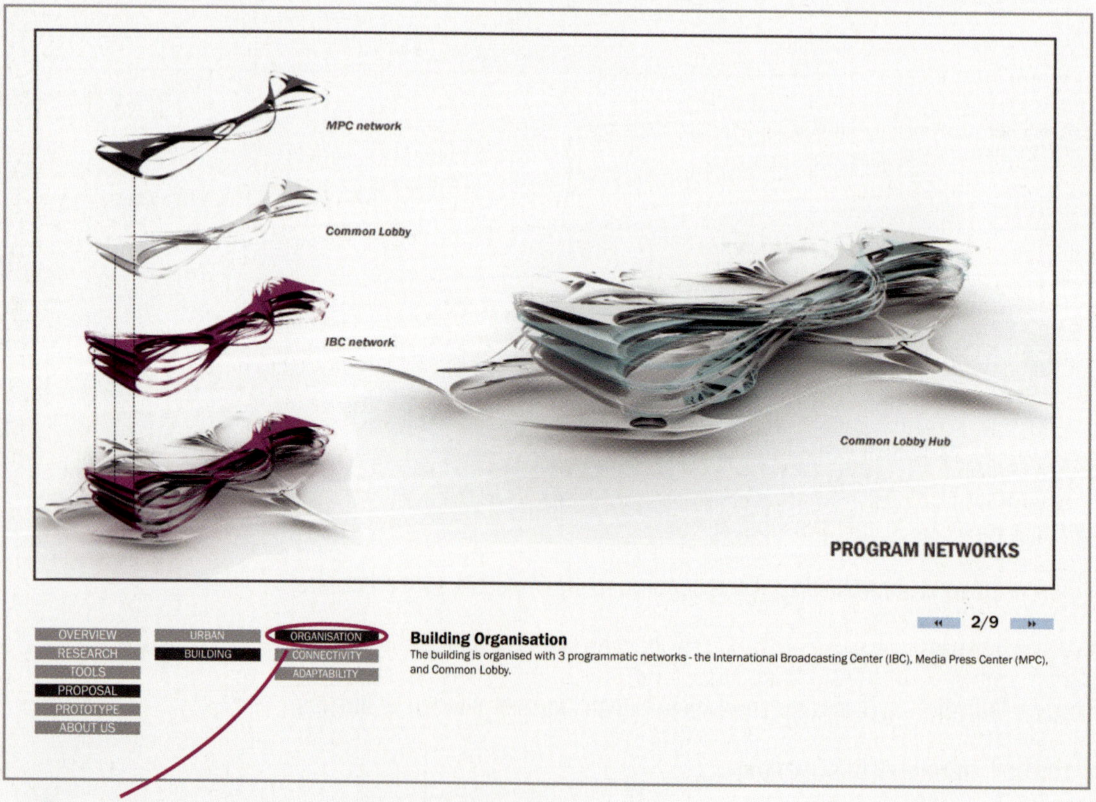

④ SELECT FINAL CATEGORY > SLIDESHOW IS LOADED AND CAPTIONS APPEAR
> COUNTER DISPLAY UPDATES ACCORDING TO CURRENT SLIDE

THE ABCs OF CV RÉSUMÉ

CONTENT

As design processes evolve with digital techniques, it is of interest to highlight steps along your process. Consider that you are not selling the design alone, but your skill too. Think about how you can capture and convey your skill to the reader. In our case, we highlight two aspects of the design process – research and design tool.

The research aspect is quite straightforward – showing different experiments made with a series of formulas and varying results obtained when changing parameters of the formula. This can be broken down as input and output.

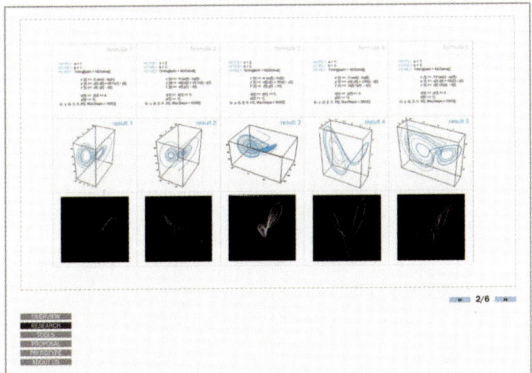
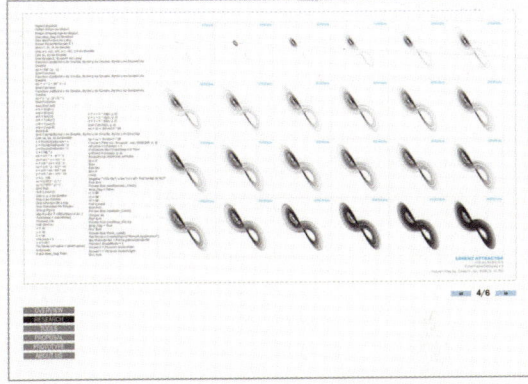

The top row contains the input, middle row displays the output, and bottom row renders output from a different angle.

On the left, we display the "input" parameters - considering growth, time and iterations.
On the right we display the output which are stillshots showing different stages along the growth, while changing parameters.

The images below show how we have applied our research towards a design tool which is ultimately used to generate the design proposal.

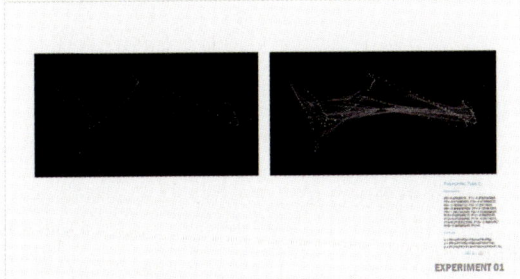
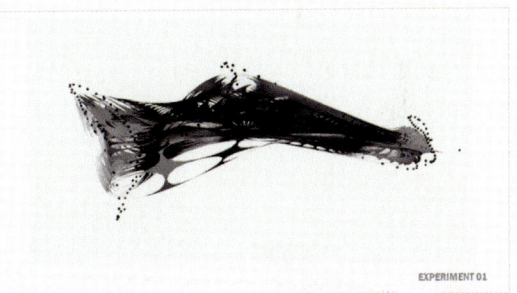

Step by Step process of applied tool

Result of applied tool

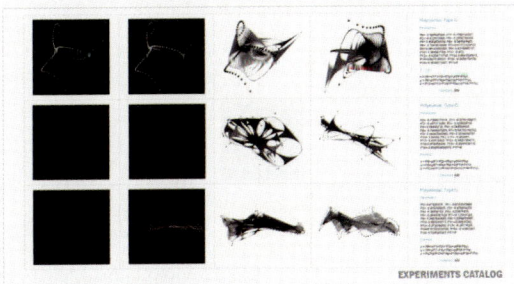
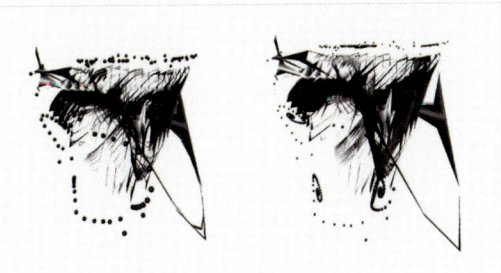

Catalogue of other examples

Animation showing application of tool

ANIMATIONS

Videos and animations are a useful tool to explain your work. Capture the attention of your audience from the onset with an eye-catching video. Placing it at the introduction of your site, use it to summarize the essence of your work. If the viewer is interested to know more, they can freely navigate through your site.

Animations are a lot more telling than still frames. Take advantage of your medium and make use of videos and animations.

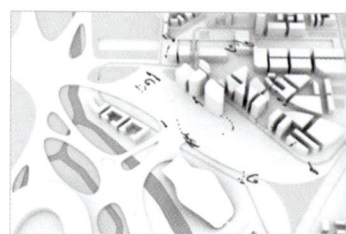

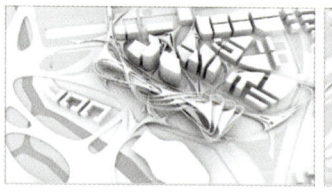

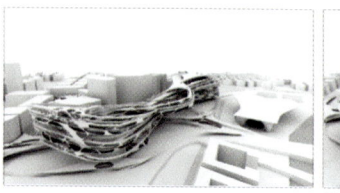

THE ABCs OF CV RÉSUMÉ 3

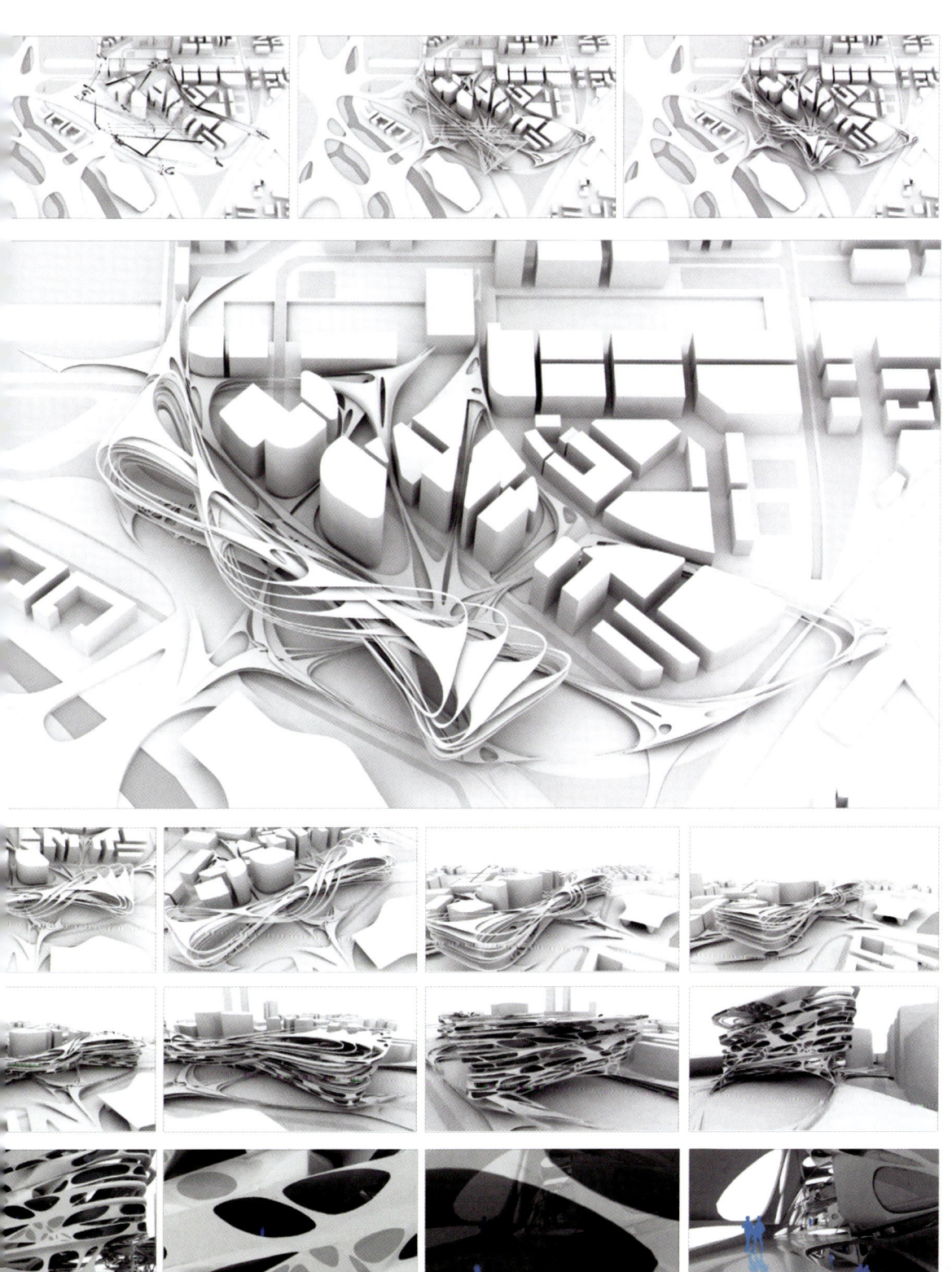

4

**MAPPING
A MARKETING
STRATEGY**

SELF-MARKETING MEANS COMMITMENT TO YOUR CRAFT When we talk about "self-marketing" we are referring to those varied activities undertaken in order to make yourself known and sought after in the marketplace, usually (though not exclusively) for the purpose of obtaining gainful employment. Self-marketing has been practiced for decades by public figures of every ilk – from actors, to sports heroes, pop stars, and politicians. Today the potential power, methods, and practice of self-marketing are being embraced by an increasing number of leaders in the corporate world. We also find self-marketing principles currently being used in an academic context – specifically in the support provided by career specialists employed by educational institutions to help graduates seek employment or develop a career plan.

☐ THE KEYS TO BRANDING: SELF-ACTUALIZATION, EFFECTIVE DEVELOPMENT, AND RECOGNIZABILITY

The concept and theories of self-marketing were taken one step further in Tom Peters' 1997 article for *Fast Company* magazine titled "The Brand Called You". In this article Peters explicated the concept of developing an individual brand and single-handedly incited the branding craze. With the advent and continued flourishing of the free-market economy and free-agency or project-based entrepreneurialism, personal branding is essential for career success. In his follow up book *The Brand You 50: Or: Fifty Ways To Transform Yourself from an 'Employee' into a Brand that Shouts Distinction, Commitment, and Passion!* (1999) he explains the free agent paradigm that applies particularly well to online environments, where companies must remain dynamic, and grow and change quickly to succeed. In a free-agent world, workers aren't necessarily loyal to a company; instead, they are always looking ahead to the next project. In fact, the rampant job-hopping in the Internet economy has been one of the original drivers of the free-agent workforce. Establishing a recognizable reputation, networking and continually positioning your brand to be as visible as possible continue to be critical skills in our dynamic, free-agent economy.

The concept of personal branding is essentially an attention-getting tactic that is frequently depicted as the key to helping the aspiring professional achieve a competitive advantage in an increasingly competitive marketplace. According to Davenport and Beck (2001) the emerging online environments of the Internet and social media represent an increasingly competitive "attention economy" which poses a significant challenge for those who wish to be known and have their voice heard in the business world.

An integral component of branding involves high-energy, immediately recognizable, attention-grabbing techniques used by prospective candidates to market themselves and their services. According to most proponents of self-marketing and personal branding, the process mirrors the product or corporate branding process, and should follow three broad stages, which Arruda (2012) summarizes as "extract, express and exude." First, you are encouraged to look inside yourself to discover your key identifying attributes, or "your unique promise of value." Then you can construct a compelling "personal brand statement" inspired by and concentrated on this attribute set. Finally, you must develop a strategy for making the brand visible to the marketplace. Roffer (2002) summarizes this process as follows: "Branding is about finding your 'big idea', the core you, and putting it out in the universe to fulfill itself" (p. 2).

MAPPING A MARKETING STRATEGY 4

Through the use of dynamic and distinctive promotional techniques, small and medium sized companies can also develop their own unique brand. For example, in case study three André Tavares – editor at Dafne, a small architectural publisher based in Portugal – writes about establishing his niche publishing house and subsequently developing a greater presence within the Portuguese architectural arena. Dafne's objective was to provide a communication venue for a new generation of architects and critics in a format free from many conventional restraints. After five years of publishing the works of Portuguese and Brazilian contributors, Tavares contends that Dafne has achieved its primary objectives of remaining relatively small, while still providing a canvas for provocative architectural arguments, and continually increasing the firm's visibility within Portugal. The team at Dafne has achieved these objectives by creating a dynamic office philosophy, a viable corporate identity, unique product development, an original, easily accessible, and recognizable company website, a distinctive corporate brochure, and an exceptional sense of team spirit.

☐ BRANDING: A HOW AND WHAT TO DO

The topic of branding is also taken up by Kansas City-based Senior Architect and Project Manager at Burns & McDonnell Amy Slattery in her essay, "A Strategic Case Study: A Virtual Brand". In this piece the 2011 recipient of the AIA Young Architects Award provides a straightforward, step-by-step approach to developing a branded persona. By breaking down the process into five, easy-to-understand actions – establish, define, identify, diversify, and maintain – Slattery guides her readers through the creation of a unique individual brand through the effective use of strategies such as microblogging and digital portfolios. She posits that self-marketing in the digital world via connected systems of unique content is the future of professional networking and job procurement. Slattery also reminds readers that public consumption of our online identities is a 24/7 activity: even when we unplug, our online selves remain engaged in defining and representing us and how we fit into the global schemata of connection and opportunity.

In both self-marketing and personal branding, intuitive and informal approaches often dominate professional literatures and the marketplace. The starting point in most perspectives on personal branding tends to be the same key idea: personal branding is the "natural" and "obvious" result of extending the idea of branding from the commercial realm (which involves marketing products and services) to the personal realm – which involves individual people. For better or for worse, the possibility of obtaining a single, career-defining, long-term position with one company is very small. For this reason you need to evaluate what your skills and interests are and market them. It is also crucial that you network and promote yourself as the brand behind the recognizable, noteworthy, and impressive projects you've worked on. By turning everyday work into interesting and inspiring projects, Peters believes workers will become more self-motivated, completed projects will become more innovative, and companies will become more dynamic.

An example of one such company is Mecanoo Architects of Delft, in the Netherlands. This architectural firm has taken Peter's advice and applied it to their collective work. In his essay in this chapter Henk Döll discusses founding a new Rotterdam office for Mecanoo in 2003. Döll describes how he met the challenge of fostering a team spirit with a diverse talent pool of young architects. Döll also describes how defining a specific office philosophy and maintaining a central focus on the notion of "Reflective Practice" has incited dynamic productivity and cohesion. By recognizing and promoting the unique skills of his team, Döll created a distinctive corporate identity that could be branded and marketed to clients.

Know yourself. Be proactive. Define yourself. Sell yourself. Network. Take responsibility for your future career direction and your success. Contrary to most popular beliefs, your "brand" isn't your logo or tagline. Your brand is all of the emotions that other people feel when they think about you. Tom Peters and others indicate that those emotions are often triggered by your individual ethos and other people's experience with you as a "product". Therefore, it will prove beneficial for you, first and foremost, to concentrate on defining who you are and what you have to offer while building a strong and relevant network of relationships.

☐ RELATIONSHIPS, RELATIONSHIPS, RELATIONSHIPS

Relationships develop over time as you build mutual credibility and trust. Relationships, in turn, build networks. If you enter a relationship giving more than you ask, the networks you foster will become your most valuable marketing tool. In addition, always be on the lookout for ways you can further expand and strengthen your network.

The basics of professional networking based on relationship-building include: building a simple, effective, and compelling website; maintaining a blog; and being active on social networking sites. However, be realistic and keep in mind that it would probably take a super-human effort to maintain a strong presence on all social networking sites. Maintain your sanity as well as your professional ethos by focusing your talents on maintaining a quality presence on a handful of established and respected social networking sites.

Keep in mind that different web outlets offer different opportunities to connect. Using different social media outlets (such as Twitter, Facebook, Linkedin) gives an impression of you in a variety of different contexts. Using social media also gives others a chance to interact with you outside of the hiring process. Therefore, make sure you carefully craft an engaged and intelligent online persona. If you're consistently insightful and thoughtful in your comments while remaining passionate about your field, you'll build credibility and professional esteem. At a minimum, by being active on relevant social media sites you'll connect with people you can turn to for professional advice – not to mention prospective employers or clients.

Always maintain your professionalism, but don't forget to have fun with your self-marketing campaign. For example, Brussels-based architect Pascal Monniez of M Architecture distinguishes himself by taking a humorous approach to the pedestrian concerns of business marketing. While viewing self-marketing and personal branding as a practicality rather than a product, Monniez agrees that representation of one's individual architectural practice, personality, and abilities is necessary for the professional communicative purposes. Using simple line drawings and internationally recognizable turns of phrase, Monniez creates whimsical comic strips illustrating the necessary evils of architecture commodification.

Taking the initiative to make yourself known to a prospective employer – through social networking or through more traditional interactions – can certainly work to your benefit. If a manager knows you from direct, positive experience, they're likely to prefer you to a similarly qualified candidate who is completely unknown to them. However, bear in mind that no employer is going to hire you on the basis of your social media presence alone. You also need to be a strong candidate offline too. Therefore, make sure that you don't neglect the more traditional aspects of your job search: write the best, most professional, most compelling résumé and cover letter; and present yourself as the most qualified, competent, engaging, and driven candidate in your interview.

HOW SOCIAL MEDIA CAN HELP YOUR CAUSE ... AND HOW IT CAN HURT

Like all technologies, social media is a tool that is only as good as its user. These are some of the mistakes that social media users frequently make when looking for a job:

- **creating a Twitter account and waiting for prospective employers to contact you,**
- **indiscriminately sending your résumé to hiring managers through Linkedin;**
- **creating an online video résumé.**

But here's how the intelligent and strategic use of social media could help:

- Learn to use blogs effectively. Being a smart, thoughtful commenter on blogs relevant to your field will illustrate that you are well educated, intellectually curious, engaged, a competent writer, and passionate about your discipline. Being able to show your prospective employer a history of insightful, carefully crafted blog posts can truly work to your benefit.
- You can even create a blog of your own – and then get the word out. Just as you have done with your own unique skill-set and experiences, make sure you market your blog. Designing and writing for your own blog takes a significant amount of effort, persistence, and preparation, but it can go a long way in impressing an employer.
- Use Twitter and Facebook professionally. Follow, connect with others, and establish relationships with others in your field while maintaining your professional integrity. Engage with others in thoughtful, insightful, and meaningful ways.

☐ TWO ADDITIONAL TOOLS FOR SUCCESSFUL SELF-MARKETING CAMPAIGNS: THE PRESS KIT AND THE ELEVATOR SPEECH

THE PRESS KIT

The press kit is a set of editorial and promotional material provided to members of the press at a news conference or before the release of a new product, service, or candidate. While the press kit (also known as a "media kit") is a specialized tool originally developed and used by public relations teams, the idea of having a tool in print and/or digital format to quickly and comprehensively communicate key facts about a subject to an audience is worth learning from and appropriating.

Traditional press kits often contain bios, pictures, a mission statement, press clippings, and endorsements. Creating your own press kit is definitely a worthwhile endeavor for a number of reasons. For example, it forces you to be brief and to compact your professional self. It forces you to focus on only those most important and beneficial aspects of your professional self that you want to present to a prospective employer. The key to a press kit is its compactness: a press kit is essentially a compression of information to the most salient, essential things you want others to know about you.

Keep in mind that the full press kit should be available for anyone searching the Internet. Potential clients should be able to access it quickly and easily. Therefore your press kit should be linked to your social networking sites such as LinkedIn, Facebook, Twitter, or to your personal website.

THE ELEVATOR SPEECH

Another strategic key to mastering self-marketing is to perfect an eloquent and descriptive introduction of yourself and your position. This indispensable tool, commonly known as the "Elevator Speech," can be your best approach to entering professional networking situations. It can also prove incredibly valuable during those extraordinary moments when opportunities arise to create productive new professional contacts. Katharine Hansen, speechwriter and author of *A Foot in the Door: Networking Your Way into the Hidden Job Market* (2004), describes this tool as "A clear, concise bit of communication that can be delivered in the time it takes folks to ride from the top to the bottom of a building in an elevator. Whatever the exact origin, the Elevator Speech is an exceptionally useful and versatile tool in numerous situations" (pp. 69–70).

We have all had the experience of being introduced to someone who seems less than enthusiastic about their profession. There is little that deflates a room or an individual faster. This perception of dejection is often a result of a poorly delivered and ineffective elevator speech. If you sound apprehensive, doubtful, or self-effacing, it's difficult to become engaged in who you are and what you do. As you have probably guessed, this is not the sort of brand you want to project. Instead, learn to value and highlight your achievements while projecting self-confidence and enthusiasm.

The basic format of a good elevator speech generally includes your name, title, and your area of expertise. You can enhance your speech and make it more memorable by adding a statement about the benefits derived from your services or the unique qualities that set you apart from your peers. You can also include a brief statement outlining why your job is important, what specific capacities you offer, or what problems you can help your prospective employer solve. This information will maintain interest and incite further inquiry.

References

Arruda, W. (2012) 360°Reach – Personal Brand Assessment, Retrieved July 25, 2012, from http://www.reachcc.com/reachdotcom.nsf/bdf8f1dec3dadac0c1256aa700820c2c/d8c1129d558414edc1256af5000ca667!OpenDocument

Davenport, T. H. and Beck, J. C. (2001) *The Attention Economy: Understanding the New Currency of Business*. Boston: Harvard Business School Press.

Hansen, K. (2004) *A Foot in the Door: Networking Your Way into the Hidden Job Market*. New York: Ten Speed Press.

Peters, T. J. (1997) "The Brand Called You" *Fast Company*, 10, 83. Retrieved July 25, 2012, from http://www.fastcompany.com/magazine/10/brandyou.html

Peters, T. (1999) *The Brand You 50: Or: Fifty Ways To Transform Yourself from an 'Employee' into a Brand that Shouts Distinction, Commitment, and Passion!* New York: Knopf.

Roffer, R. F. (2002) *Make a Name for Yourself: Eight Steps Every Woman Needs To Create A Personal Brand Strategy For Success*. New York: Broadway.

CASE STUDY 1

TITLE: A STRATEGIC CASE STUDY: A VIRTUAL BRAND
AUTHOR: AMY J. SLATTERY

A VIRTUAL BRAND

Self-presentation is no longer simply about credentials. Professional self-presentation is now about advocacy, leadership, and expressing a point of view. And, with the advent of social media, it is about how and where you present yourself – and the influence and reach that you have. Whether you are presenting yourself to potential employers or potential clients, experience only goes so far. Impact is increasingly what sets you apart from your peers.

The following is my personal example of how to establish a recognized brand – both virtual and personal – through the strategic presentation of credentials and an active point of view in social media, online publications, websites, and blogs.

The process is relatively simple and can be broken down into the following steps:

- Establish goal/message and target audience.
- Define credentials: collect and document content.
- Identify desired impact, point of view.
- Diversify outlets.
- Maintain a voice and presence.

MAPPING A MARKETING STRATEGY 4

THE TARGET AUDIENCE AND STRATEGY (FIRST ESTABLISH WHY)

The market was terrible in 2009. At the time, I was with the award-winning firm, BNIM. Our projects were stopping and there wasn't much on the horizon. We all began to focus our collective energies on the pursuit of work. My advocacy work for women in architecture and visibility on a high-profile project gave me the potential to establish a more recognized leadership brand. My personal strategy was to become known as a leader in two areas: complex project execution and diversity advocacy in the architectural profession. My goal was, through the development of an online personal brand, to expand my own virtual network (and therefore that of the firm) and contribute to and enrich the firm's proactive business development and communication efforts. The target audience was potential clients and collaborators, with the ultimate goal to produce more work.

Now four years into this process, I find it can be harder than you think it will be and you have to keep the ultimate goal in sight. The initial impetus was for firm value, but it is an individual endeavor. As I recently made the transition to a new firm, I discovered it is even more important that you enjoy the process, relish making new connections, and continually ask how this could be leveraged into opportunities and ultimately work. Because ultimately within the context of a firm, it's about your contributing value to the bottom line. Otherwise, you can continue to blog/tweet/chat with no real results.

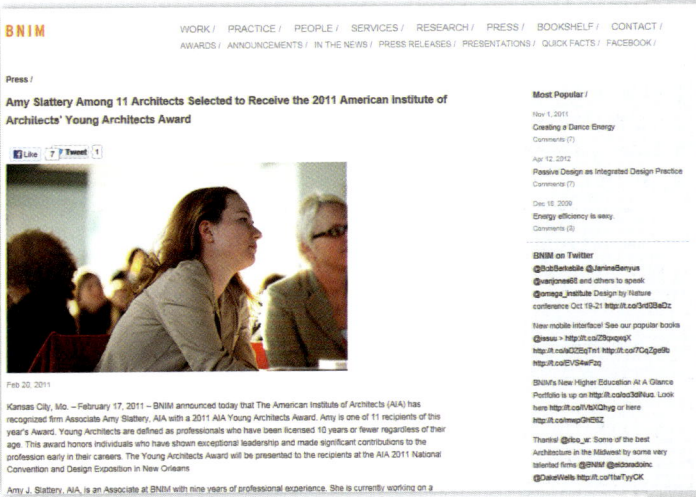

This is a process of leveraging each step along the way. My personal process is still in the connections realm. Opportunities are coming, but continuing to leverage these into work is tough.

Potential → recognition → connections → opportunities → work

You must have a starting point. Understand what sets you apart, where your talents are, what your impact is to take it from merely potential to results.

Find a good starting point. For me it was applying for the AIA YA Award. After 9 years in the industry, I had amassed enough work, leadership, and volunteerism to consider this opportunity. This was the start of leveraging my potential to recognition. Following this recognition, connections were easier to make, and this became the basis for the launch of my online brand.

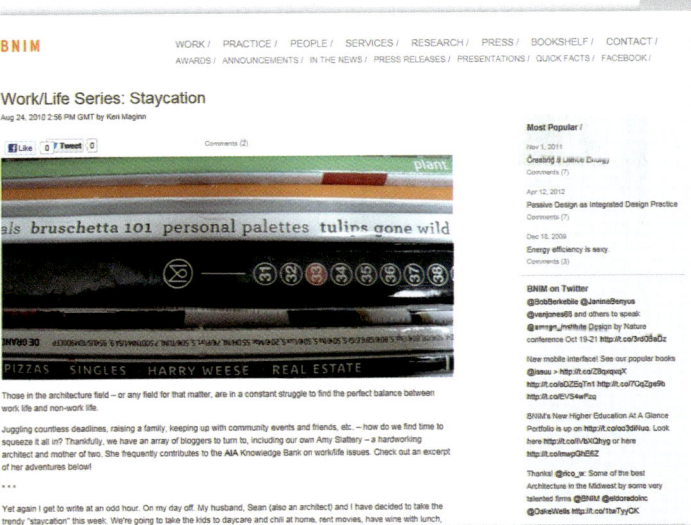

THE CONTENT: CREDENTIALS (DOCUMENT YOURSELF)

Since developing the Young Architect Award application, I have maintained a folder of information that serves as the source for all online content. The core document in this source folder is an active CV file in word format that I update following each lecture, event, publication, and project. The source folder also includes the best images that have defined (and are defining) my career, including projects, event photos, the media and publications that have noted the projects. I update my biography and keep it in two forms: a long (1 page) and short (1 paragraph format). I also save a print-ready and web-ready headshot. As opportunities for presentations, writing, and other outlets become available, I fine-tune these biographies and edit the CV to a shorter résumé format to suit the audience. For instance, a biography used for the American Institute of Architects (AIA) will definitely include detail of leadership positions I've held within the institute, while a Commercial Real Estate bio will be more focused on my practice and advocacy for women in the profession. However, this information is the consistent base file for all virtual outlets and will continue to be the source of information that I will continue to update for the rest of my career.

Keep an updated base file:
- Print-ready headshot (300 dpi, 8 x 10)
- Web-ready headshot (72 dpi, 4 x 5)
- Brief biography (1 paragraph)
- Long biography (1 page)

Maintain a current digital source folder:
- Comprehensive CV (3–5 pages)
- Notable professional accomplishments
- Professional registrations
- Firm leadership
- Community leadership
- Representative projects and descriptions of the projects
- Education
- Awards
- Academia
- Speaking engagements
- Publications and other writing
- Network
- References
- Quotes from clients and colleagues
- Résumé (2 pages maximum including some project imagery)
- Defining imagery
- Projects
- Events
- Media
- Publications

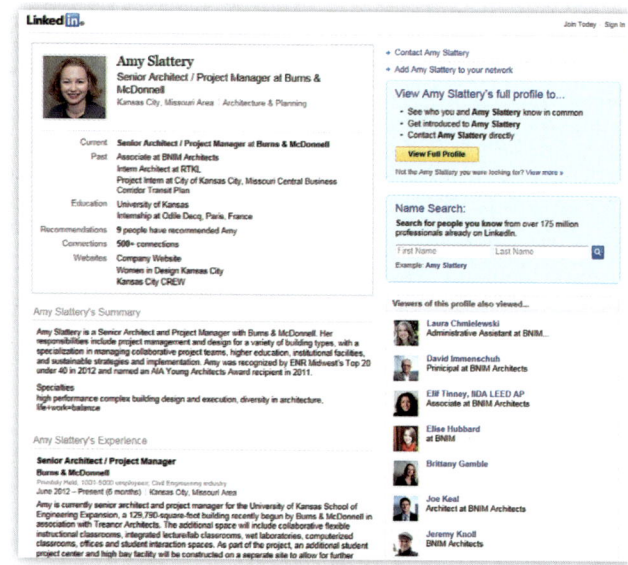

MAPPING A MARKETING STRATEGY 4

THE CONTENT: POINT OF VIEW (IDENTIFY YOUR IMPACT, ASSESS YOUR POTENTIAL)

The application process for the AIA Young Architect Award was not only a great starting point for the collection and documentation of my work experience, but also an opportunity to collect and measure the impact of that work. This was an opportunity to reflect, refine, and focus the next steps in alignment with the key points of my emerging platform or brand. The content of my work thus far was clear in two areas: complex project execution and advocacy for diversity in the profession. The potential was to leverage this project and leadership experience into connections.

TIP

Take a look at your portfolio and develop a key focus so that you can focus your impact on targeted areas. Ask a friend, colleague or mentor to give you another opinion if you have a difficult time discerning your focus. Sometimes, outside perception is different than your own.

FACETS OF A COMPLETE PERSONAL BRAND

Most if not all virtual outlets have the opportunity to share your credentials and write about your expertise and point of view. However, some have more potential than others, some are more time consuming, and inevitably a different audience frequents each. Therefore, understanding your time availability and commitment and establishing diversity that is accomplishable is the best strategy. To maintain the focus on your core purpose and strategy in this endeavor, all outlets should feed back to your company website or the place that gives you context and relevance related to your career. Your core message can be presented there.

- Content = credentials + point of view.
- Feeds all outlets and website.
- All outlets direct to website.

Virtual Brand

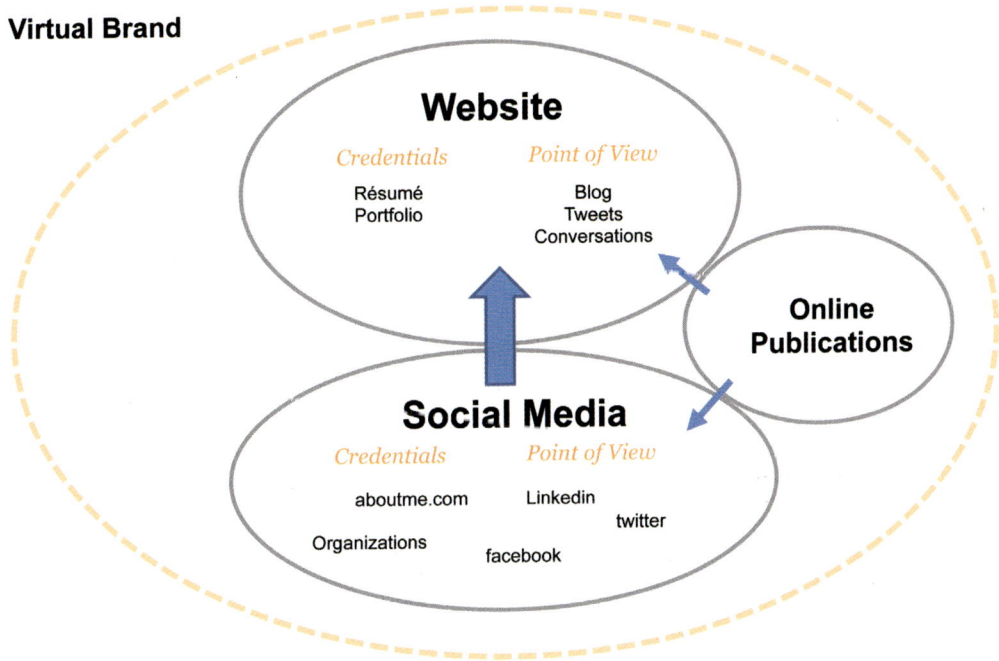

ONLINE PRESENCE

BNIM's company **website**, BNIM.com, is home base. It is home to their blog, press page, and project info – and all virtual networks direct traffic back to the website. Social Media is where we connected and found more and more collaborators, as well as leveraging opportunities to promote leaders within the firm. The key is that online communications is a complete and diverse package – with a website, Twitter account, Facebook, vimeo, LinkedIn, and other content sharing accounts being critical to delivering a variety of content to your core audience.

This is one package that is linked and tied together within BNIM's website. Press posts for key events, awards or milestones are developed to increase search engine optimization on various subjects and keywords, and drive visitors to the site in promotional efforts.

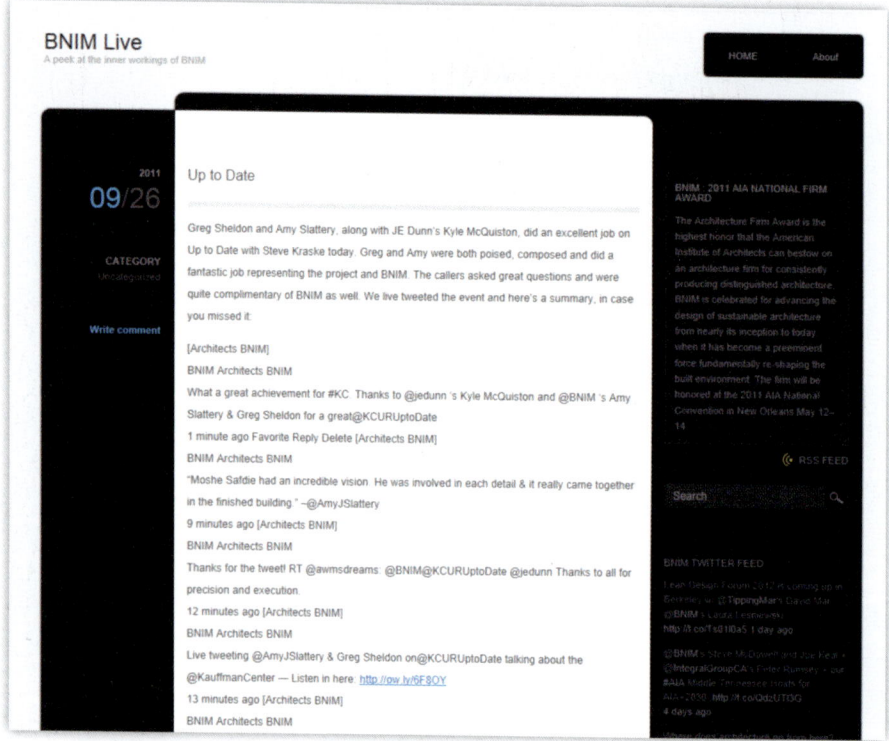

Blogging is an opportunity to write and share what you are currently working on. This is another outlet for your expertise and a way to create an expert leadership platform. It does take time to craft a thoughtful, informational post. Be sure your blogs are consistent with your point of view and that you stay on point.

CONTENT SHARING OUTLETS

LinkedIn.com is where jobs are found and created. It's also a place to note everything related to your career, even when you are not in an active job search. I have had more contact with potential employees via LinkedIn and introductions through connections in this online space than in any other network. I use my short bio and translate my CV to their format. Opportunities for dialogue are growing on LinkedIn; there are many groups available, so seek out groups related to your target areas. The Women in Architecture LinkedIn group has been particularly interesting related to my advocacy work. The weekly updates from groups are useful, and recommendations can be great connecting tools.

About.me is a simple graphic splash page that can be tailored to the amount of information you wish to share beyond a Twitter profile. I post my short biography and links to the Burns & McDonnell website, my Twitter and LinkedIn. I found this resource after following Cameron Sinclair (co-founder of Architecture for Humanity) on Twitter. It's also a great quick summary to send to anyone you meet.

Twitter is my current fix. The opportunities are hard to categorize, but the potential is outstanding. This is the place to be contributing to and leading dialogue. I try to tweet daily, or weekly at a minimum, and to split my tweets along the following guidelines developed at my firm: half about the architecture and engineering design work we do at Burns & McDonnell, 25 percent retweets of others, and 25 percent relevant to advocacy for diversity and work/life balance. Again the ultimate goal is to drive activity to the website, but it is also helpful for making connections and introducing new people to our work.

I have a few personal rules for Twitter that may be a guide to consider. Craft your Twitter biography carefully. This is brief, but is what others see when they look for you. Change your name to how you want others to know you ... right now I'm Amy@BurnsMcD. If you don't have anything to say, don't say it. Don't talk about what you ate for dinner. Have something to say. And say it consistently. Some say you must tweet daily, others say up to 20 times a day (which I personally think is too much). But, do it at least weekly. Create dialogue and contribute to the virtual community by retweeting those you find interesting. Mention others. Be generous. The followers you will receive will surprise you. Don't do it if it doesn't come naturally. Fitting a square peg into a round hole isn't easily done, so if this medium doesn't come naturally to you, find another. Or, just give it time. It might grow on you.

BNIM is now using live tweets to drive website hits during special events. During the AIA Convention in 2011, they ran a live blog that featured the BNIM attendee tweets. Architect Magazine Online picked up our thread and we had so many hits it shut our website down for a day. Below is a live tweet that was done during a live radio interview I participated in during the opening of the Kauffman Center.

Facebook is where professional and social lines can be easily blurred. BNIM has an active Facebook account, again to drive connections to their website. I personally use it primarily for communication to my family and friends. What I say to my family is different than what I say to my potential clients and collaborators, but others use this medium solely for professional relations. The choice is yours.

ORGANIZATION NETWORKS

Almost any member organization now has an internal virtual network where you can set up a profile, connect with others, and post conversations. AIA has Knowledge Net that is open to both members and non-members and we are now using this system to connect women in architecture groups across the country. CREW (Commercial Real Estate Women) uses a members-only system and now collects all member information on this internal network called CREWBiz. These networks provide job and deal opportunities in addition to information sharing. I post my long biography and update the relevant information from my CV:

LEVERAGING ONE OUTLET TO THE NEXT

In addition to using these social networks to increase visitors to your website, other content sharing applications can increase the opportunities for personal presentation.

- ISSUU
- VIMEO
- YOUTUBE
- FLICKR
- PINTEREST
- TUMBLR

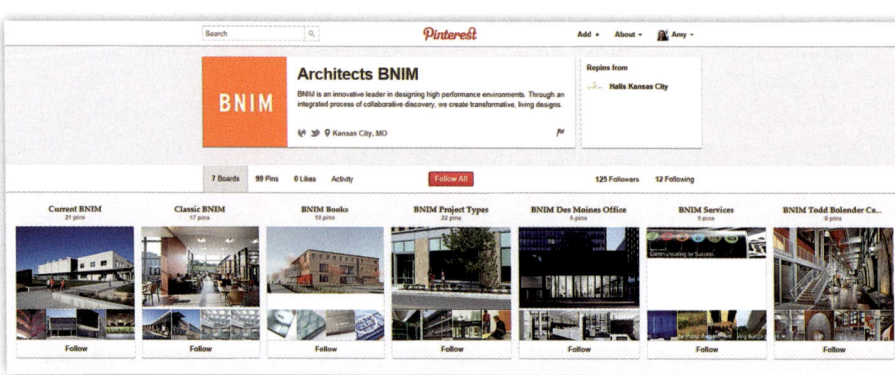

MAPPING A MARKETING STRATEGY 4

RESULTS

Once you have established a platform, it's surprising what comes up. When Architect Barbie was announced in 2011, Architizer did a brief promotion article on their website where they interviewed all recent women who received the Young Architect Award. At the 2011 convention, I participated in a podcast that was then posted on the AIA website. All commentary and online articles are opportunities to push your expertise and thought leadership.

WHAT'S NEXT

It's my opinion that online reach and influence is the future of self-presentation. Soon, we won't simply be communicating virtually, we will be working online. BNIM is just beginning to see this in their work. Through crowdsourcing sites such as MindMixer the BNIM teams are engaging our communities in a more active and meaningful way and in real-time. The work we do will act as the door to more connections and future work, not just our description/ presentation of it. In the future look for more in the realms of Augmented Reality and Open Source Design.

ADVICE DEFINING OPPORTUNITIES AND CONSEQUENCES

Because of the potential time commitment and rigor required for success in these endeavors, you must establish a definite hierarchy and always self-check the focus on connections back to the firm, the work, and the leveraging of these connections to opportunities to create work.

Almost everything we do as designers involves some form of self-presentation. What we wear, what time we arrive at work, the conversations we have, and ultimately the presentation of our work to our clients, our collaborators, and our community. All of these areas are what define your professional personal and others' perception of you.

This reality has now been extended to the virtual realm for public consumption 24/7, even when you are not intentionally networking. Be self-aware. Defining opportunities – and, as a result consequences – are out there. The world is small, and it can be surprising where the right (or wrong) impressions and connections are made. So, control what people see when they google you. Get out there and make your mark in the virtual world, but also use a dose of caution to control your message. Google yourself.

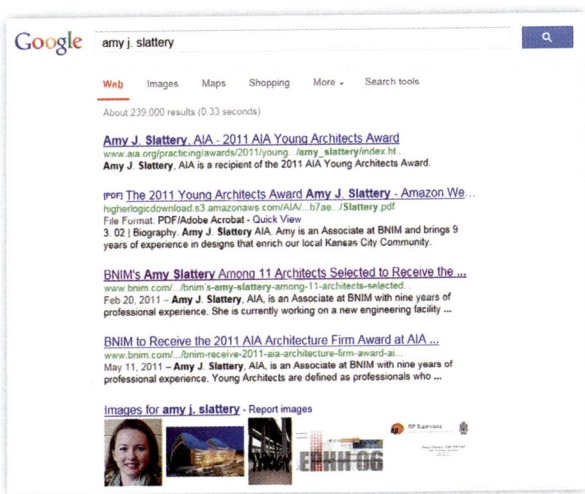

Here's what comes up when I google myself. And yes, I did adjust my Facebook privacy settings shortly after this screenshot.

115

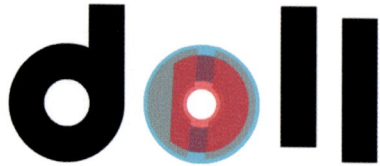

CASE STUDY 2

TITLE: HOW TO CREATE IDENTITY FOR A NEW ARCHITECT'S OFFICE?
AUTHOR: HENK DÖLL

SETTING UP A NEW FIRM

After being a founding partner in Mecanoo Architects (Delft, the Netherlands) for over twenty years I founded a new office in Rotterdam in 2003 with a group of twenty architects and staff. Finding a suitable and representative office space, setting up a new computer network structure (with the first Apple office network at that time in the Netherlands) and creating a team spirit within an international group of young professionals were obvious challenges. Defining the office philosophy and creating a new corporate identity were means of an effective self-presentation that were more fundamental and had to be tackled simultaneously.

CREATING IDENTITY

Central focus was (and still is) our understanding of the notion of 'Reflective Practice',[1] and one aspect in particular: the dialogue with our clients and future users. This is reflected in our office philosophy and in the way we communicate. From the beginning the main focus was on the presentation of the new office to (potential) clients and the architect's community in the Netherlands and abroad. In several inspiring sessions we further defined our office philosophy, the mission and vision and our management operating principles.

This was worked out in statements on (among others):
- the dialogue with our clients and future users;
- cross-over networks with other professionals in the field of art, architecture and planning;
- our architectural design philosophy;
- the office as an incubator for new talent.

Based on this philosophy we defined our core activities: architecture, urban planning and interior design. In the past ten years we realized a great variety of projects in these fields, from small-scale interior renovations to large-scale urban master plans. The next step was to define our ambition to broaden the architect's field of work into the fields of research and product development. This resulted among others in the book *Ground-Up City – Play as a Design Tool* [2] and the development of the Sustainable Dance Club™. The energy generating dance-floor is the most promising feature of this sustainable concept and is currently further developed into a broad applicable flooring system: 'Energy Floors'.

Parallel to defining our office philosophy we developed concepts for the graphic design and graphic presentation of our corporate identity through the house style and website. The quality of the graphic design was remarked: together with the graphic designers of Dietwee we won the Dutch Design Prize 2005.

MAPPING A MARKETING STRATEGY 4

henk   erica   alijd

annelies   albert   blanca

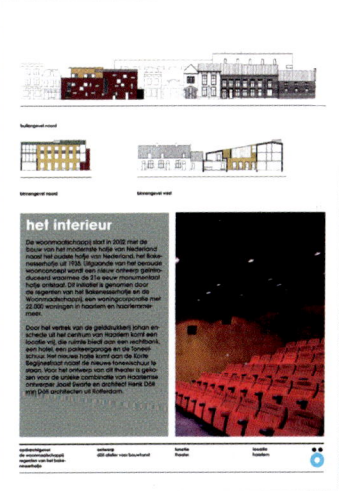

LEVELS OF COMMUNICATION

The first expressions of communication were a series of mailings in 2003 with (intriguing) announcements on the new office, followed by a brochure with the office philosophy and the office statements. This small square brochure with its blue wrapper served as an easy handout and was used for many years. At the same time we managed to attract interest from the (architectural) *press* in the Netherlands and caught free publicity. The principle of mailings has been repeated on several occasions since, as well as press releases on specific topics, such as prize-winning competitions and openings of our buildings.

From the beginning our website (www.dollab.nl) has played an important role in our communication and currently it is our main level of communication. At present the structure may be slightly outdated, but the site is still regularly updated and shows the basic office information, the latest news and projects.

Our portfolio with project documentation is designed within the concept of the overall graphic style. It consists of four (or eight) pages per project (in hard-copy: double printed A3 format). On the front cover one can find the project's name (title), the project's slogan (subtitle) and a short description, along with a characteristic picture. On the inside spread(s) one finds a further explanation of the project, both in text, plans, sections and pictures or images. On the back cover an overview picture (preferably air view) and the project's credit information can be found. Each project can be downloaded from the website in a PDF-format. The short project description and a selection of the projects can be found on the website as well. For each specific question, for instance from a (potential) client, we put together a tailor-made loose-leaf set of projects in a special Döll A4- or A3-wrapper, which is again a product that matches our graphic house style.

For a quick overview on our main projects we have developed a series of A4 pages. On these pages the projects are categorized in: urban planning, supervision, housing, buildings, interior design and research. These overviews are used as handouts and work quite well in conversation with (potential) clients and other interested parties and people.

PLATFORMS

As architects our personal relations with our clients are crucial. Therefore, most of our communication and presentation is face-to-face, in (personal) meetings, presentations, real estate fairs etc. The hard copy overviews and project documentation are used to illustrate our concepts and work, as well as PowerPoint presentations or animations. Free publicity through (international) publications in architectural magazines and books help to reach a wider audience and become known to a larger crowd of clients in the field.

EFFECTIVE SELF-PRESENTATION

To us effective self-presentation is expressed in the corporate identity and the way of working in a reflective practice. It is the ultimate result of the office (design) philosophy.

Notes
1 Schön, Donald A. (1983) *The Reflective Practitioner: How Professionals think in Action*, Basic Books; Döll, H. (1999) 'The Reflective Architect', in Annette W. LeCuyer (ed.) *Mecanoo*, Michigan Architecture Papers 6, Ann Arbor: Michigan.
2 Lefaivre, L. and Döll, H. (2007) *Ground-Up City: Play as a Design Tool*. Rotterdam: Nai Publishers.

DÖLL ARCHITECTS – COMPANY INTRODUCTION (CURRENT VERSION, UPDATED 2011)

Company name Döll Groep / Döll Architects, Rotterdam, the Netherlands
Established 2003
Contact Henk Döll, CEO / Chief Designer

OFFICE PROFILE

The notion of 'reflective practice' lies at the basis of our office philosophy. It stands for an attitude whereby we deploy creativity and innovation in order to tackle projects in an undogmatic way. The focus is on the interaction between the brief and the design in an open communication between clients, future users and architects. Our core activities are architecture, urban planning and interior design. The expertise comprises urban design (master planning, supervision), buildings (schools & universities, offices, retail, town halls, theatres etc.), housing (apartments and houses) as well as interior design (offices, retail, housing). We are specialized in the transition between these scales: between urban context and architecture and between building and interior layout. Our qualities are especially in the designs for specific groups, innovative accommodation and work concepts and reconstruction of urban areas and buildings.

PARTNERSHIPS AND JOINT VENTURES

We work from our base in Rotterdam. The majority of our work has been realized in the Netherlands, but we are also involved in various projects in other countries, such as Germany, Switzerland, Spain and China. The increasing amount of work in Germany resulted in a partnership in Hamburg in 2006: Coido architects (Cordsen Ipach + Döll GmbH, www.coido.de). Since 2010 Döll has had a joint venture with the Joint Business Center of International Design Union in Shenzhen (www.jbdidu.com).

NETWORK

Working with different design disciplines is important to us. We cooperate with professionals in other disciplines, trying to deepen the profession by looking for cross-overs and by addressing social issues from an architectural point of view. It enables us to provide the right expertise for each specific task. We regularly work together with external specialists and maintain a wide, international network of (landscape) architects, engineers, designers, artists and researchers.

DESIGN PHILOSOPHY

In an overview of the main Dutch architectural firms in the Dutch Architecture Yearbook 2009/10 our work was placed between modern and avant-garde. The style can indeed be characterized as modern with a modest use of architectural resources and mixed with (local) tradition. To us designing means giving form to identity. Whether large- or small-scale, every project requires a unique solution. That is why we analyze the particular characteristics of the project, its location, its nature and its users. Creativity and innovation are essential in our design work. We develop solutions for topical and social issues, such as new use concepts and trajectories of change within organizations. To achieve this we create new models or apply tried and tested typologies in an unconventional way. To us, this is the challenge of design.

ARCHITECTURE

Spatial experience is often undervalued in architecture practice. Our plans are characterized by a clear structure in which the experience of mass, light and space acquires form. By putting attention to designing within the sections of a building, unique and powerful spatial compositions are created. The way our buildings look reveals a certain modesty, with surprising elements and subtleties in the details. Classical architectonic concepts like composition and principles of proportion are just as important as the use of material and color. Details are designed with great concern and knowledge. We think we can justly talk about the art of building, about architecture.

DIALOGUE

Communication does not go in one direction. The contemporary process of designing and building is characterized by the involvement of a large number of people, many of whom have different, sometimes contradictory views and interests. Excellent projects are not achieved by working in an isolated way. A carefully designed project is the result of an inspiring collaboration with the clients, users, advisors and the people carrying out the work. We have experience in bringing together different demands and wishes into an integrated plan. Instead of looking for quick, hasty solutions, we discuss different aspects of a design assignment. Dialogue is thus essential for the design process. The primary factor is a critical attitude on the part of both client and architect.

CULTIVATION

We strive to excel in our profession and we see our studio as a place to cultivate talent. The openness that we aim for in the contact with external parties also characterizes the atmosphere within the office. Space is made for the creative involvement of staff in projects, workshops and interactive presentations. Since the office consists of people with different nationalities and backgrounds, projects are constantly looked at from varying perspectives. Everyone is stimulated to continue developing him or herself personally and to extend their boundaries. Members of staff are expected to contribute to design discussions and to keep abreast of developments in the field.

MAPPING A MARKETING STRATEGY 4

HENK DÖLL

Architect Henk Döll (Haarlem, the Netherlands, 1956) graduated in 1984 at the Faculty of Architecture at Delft University of Technology. As a result of winning and realizing the Kruisplein housing competition in Rotterdam (1980–1985), he was already working during his studies as an independent architect, together with Francine Houben and Roelf Steenhuis. This cooperative firm was transformed in 1983 into Mecanoo Architects, in which he was partner for over twenty years. In 2003 Henk Döll made a new step forward by founding the Döll Group/Döll Architects in Rotterdam. The increasing amount of work in Germany resulted in 2006 in a partnership in Hamburg: Coido architects (Cordsen Ipach + Döll GmbH). Since 2010 Döll has a joint venture with the Joint Business Center of International Design Union in Shenzhen.

Henk Döll has received various prizes and distinctions, such as the Rotterdam-Maaskant Prize for Young Architects in 1987, 'for the innovative contribution to housing architecture'. His work has been shown at numerous exhibitions in the Netherlands and abroad and is often published in Dutch and international magazines and books. He publishes articles, gives guest lectures and presentations and teaches at various architectural schools, both in the Netherlands and in other countries worldwide. His appointments have included a guest professorship at the Institut für Städtebau, Raumplanung und Raumordnung of the Technische Universität Wien (1995) and the Eliel Saarinen Chair at the College of Architecture + Urban Planning of the University of Michigan (2000, 2001). Henk Döll has served on numerous competition juries and boards. Currently he is a board member of the 'Atelier HSL Foundation' (Art and Design for the new High Speed Lines in the Netherlands) and of the Dutch Architects Register. This is the authority established by the Governmental Architects Title Act to maintain the Register and is designated as the Competent Authority in the Netherlands for the application of the EC Directive on the recognition of professional qualifications. ∎

CASE STUDY 3

TITLE: *OPÚSCULOS:* TALKING ABOUT ARCHITECTURE
AUTHOR: ANDRÉ TAVARES

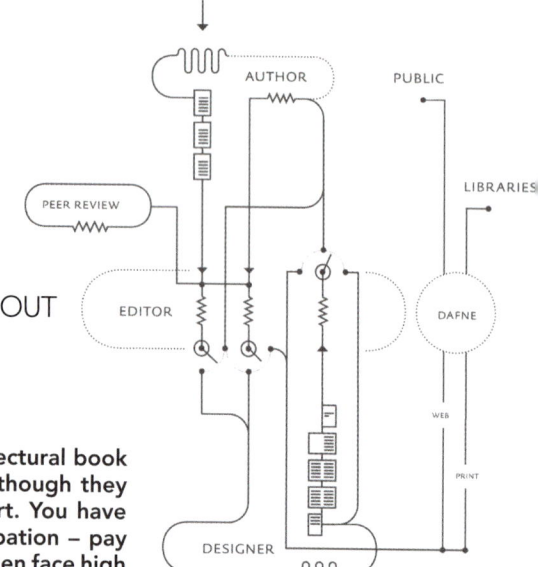

OPÚSCULOS

We were a small architectural publisher in an even smaller architectural book market. Books did not sell what they should (they still don't, although they are great and wonderful books). Making a book is a lot of effort. You have to prepare large amounts of material – a time consuming occupation – pay royalties and clear image copyrights, carefully design pages and then face high printing costs. A small publisher doesn't want to publish lots of books per year otherwise it would no longer be small. But at the beginning, we needed to have a more intense presence within the Portuguese architectural arena.

Opúsculos, the so-called 'small literary constructions on architecture', did respond to that objective. They also allowed to a younger generation of architects, mostly architectural critics, to present themselves in a not so constrained format.

We were not seeking to establish a theoretical agenda, neither to promote a certain trend or architectural idea, but mostly to push forward the ways you can talk about architecture. How can you talk about it? It does not necessarily need to be the awkward marketing advertisement, nor the eventually cryptic theoretical discourse, nor the naive or presumptuous architect description of its own design. So how could it be?

With three initial texts produced in different contexts (n.4, n.1 and n.2) we established the layout of the series – sufficiently tight to keep a regular layout but able to adapt itself to contents we were expecting but we did not know how they would be.

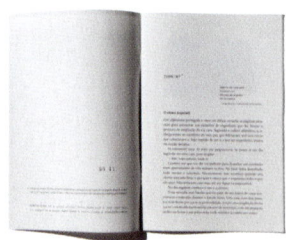

When we launched the series we asked for 'unpublished' texts that would fit with the aims but very few came. But as just one adventurous and talented young writer came to us, we had to challenge a lot of potential contributors to move on towards number 5 and 6. Then, a few months after when the option to download PDFs for free attracted a large public to our website, we began to have lots of people interested in publishing their own Opúsculo. We then were faced with the hard practice of selection, trying to manage the way we wanted to move on with the series, because most of the contributions we received by then were really not the kind of thing we wanted to publish. That was the hardest moment; we had to find more and more contributors, challenge some people we knew would be able to do wonderful things (as some did) to keep publishing what we wanted to when everybody wanted to publish what we did not want to. Quite a paradox, but it revealed the most fruitful moment for the series.

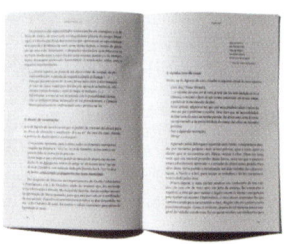

MAPPING A MARKETING STRATEGY 4

In the beginning we thought of doing 24 numbers, one per month on an irregular basis. Obviously too ambitious for a small publisher with no resources, we then decided to do it for 4 years, instead of 2. We spent 5 years doing that, and when we decided to finish we noticed we would have to go until number 26. All contributors were Portuguese except for 2 issues that were done by Brazilian colleagues (we asked for contributions from some other European colleagues, but with no success).

Although there was a certain regional concentration of the content production, at a first glance no coherence came out of the contents, one might say there is no coherence in Portuguese architectural arguments. But the major objective was achieved, we managed to publish very different and thought provocative architectural arguments, and increase Dafne's prescence in the Portuguese cultural arena.

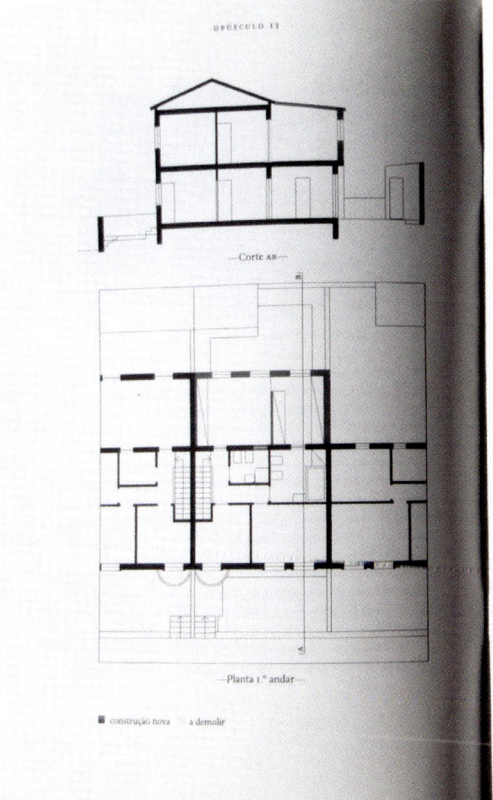

contre le marketing

CASE STUDY 4

TITLE: CONTRE LE MARKETING (I'M NOT)
AUTHOR: PASCAL, MONNIEZ

TRANSLATION: EPILOGUE

Ideologically, we are against architecture marketing, and the Order of Belgian Architects strongly regulates any form of advertising. For us, architecture is not a product to be marketed, as it is not designed to meet the needs of all consumers. Rather, architecture is a practical response to a specific need and not a commodity to be reproduced ad infinitum.

Despite this, business realities inevitably lead us to an awareness of consumer interest in and communication about our production. It is therefore by devious means and purely mercenary intentions that we are working "against the marketing."

The drawing, the humor, the derision, and lightness are our chosen media here. It is through these means that we express ourselves and attempt to give a lighthearted introduction to the world of architecture. ■

I'm not

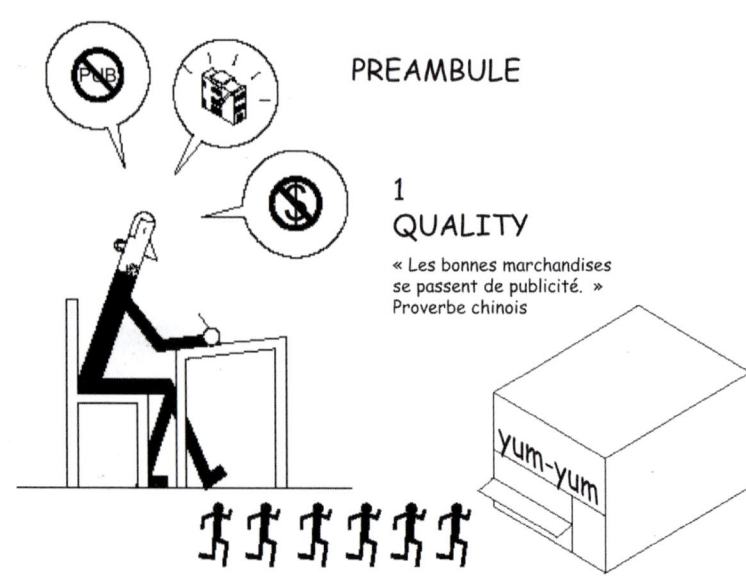

PREAMBULE

1
QUALITY

« Les bonnes marchandises se passent de publicité. »
Proverbe chinois

MAPPING A MARKETING STRATEGY 4

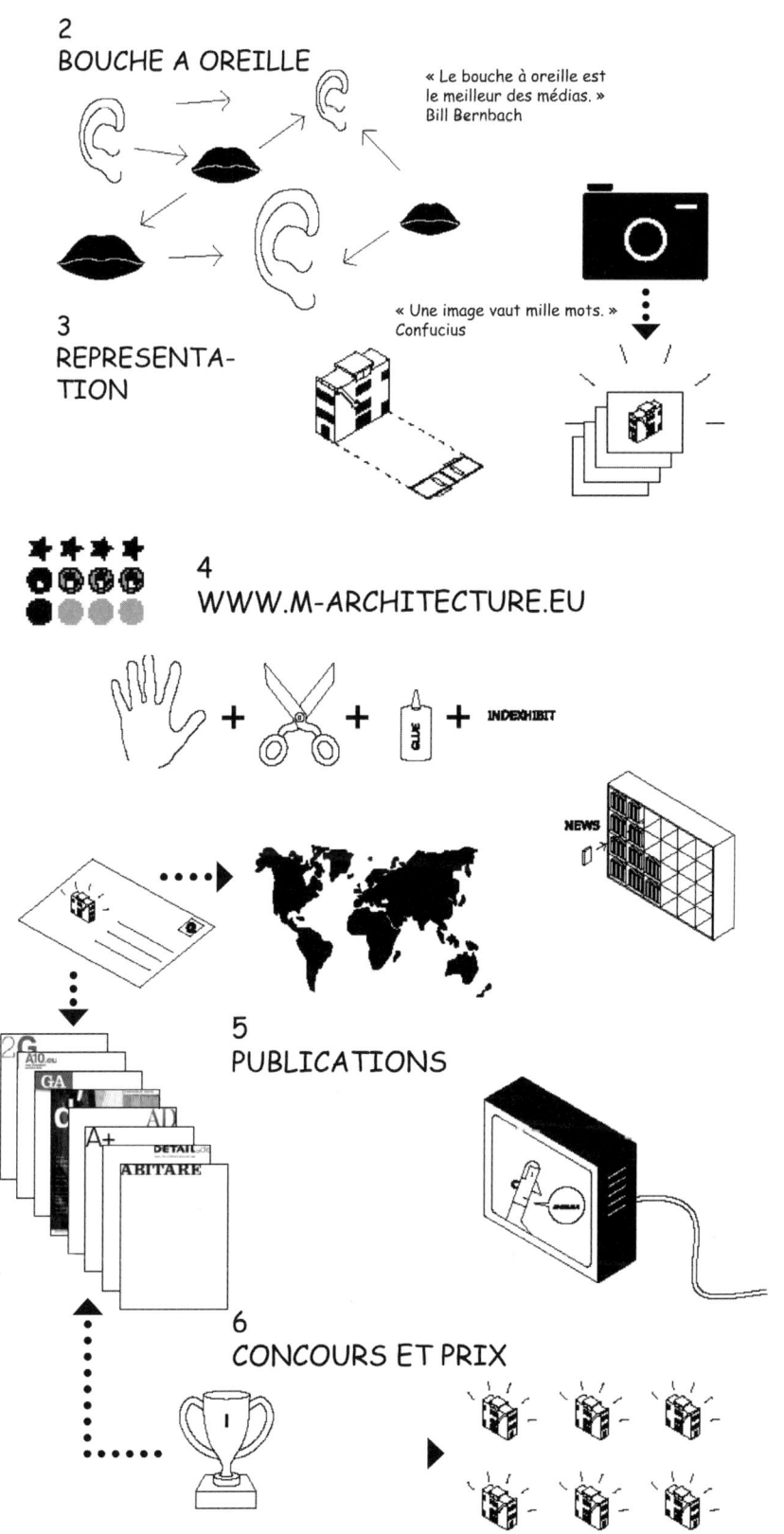

5

MAINTAINING
AN EDGE

DON'T STAND STILL ... BE ACTIVE In order to establish yourself in the market, you need more than talent alone – you will also need tenacity and endurance. You must always strive to remain relevant by ceaselessly developing your contacts and ideas.

Whether you are aware of it or not, you're presenting yourself every day in various ways in social media forums. Your friends, future employer or clients are also tweeting, blogging, emailing, texting, posting, uploading, sending emails, and exchanging information online. All of this activity will undoubtedly shape your self-presentation campaign. Conscientious control of your virtual persona is one way of successfully marketing yourself while maintaining an edge in the growing field of entrepreneurial designers.

Like your peers and competitors, as a burgeoning talent bursting onto the creative scene, you need to move forward on multiple fronts. Vertical or ladder approaches to career mapping are no longer viable realities in today's marketplace. Linearity is out. Instead of straight shots to a predetermined destination, today career maps are labyrinths that force you to maneuver sideways, forward, slide on the diagonal, and even move backwards. Director of Intern Development at Gensler, Andrew Caruso, advises us to, "Get comfortable with the unknown" (Caruso, 2009). In order to remain active, competitive, and relevant in today's competitive professional world you will need to teach yourself new skills, gain new expertise, learn new ways of communicating that expertise, develop new capabilities, and constantly reinvent your brand.

An innovative example of reinventing a professional identity and career path is Gensler's "Make Your Mark" campaign (2010). "Make Your Mark" is a talent acquisition campaign that focuses on career versatility and is designed to seek out a broader platform of talent. Many participants also have the advantage of interacting with prospective employers in non-traditional ways. Gensler's initiative has created numerous professional opportunities for individuals to build connections and network. Gensler's talent brand campaign re-makes the firm's brand by operating on three levels: 1) it reinforces his firm's brand identity; 2) it resonates with the core design disciplines of the organization's professional practice community; 3) and it subtly repositions the firm in opposition to common misconceptions about it being overly "big" or "corporate".

MAINTAINING AN EDGE 5

☐ STAY FOCUSED EVEN THROUGH A RECESSION

I believe there are at least three key areas you need to focus on while striving to maintain an edge in today's "Creative Economy World" – and during a recession. My inspiration for this three-prong approach came directly from Andreas Kluth's book *Hannibal and Me* (2011). In *Hannibal* some of Kluth's advice for maintaining a competitive edge while leading a purpose-filled life includes: (1) never confuse means with ends, (2) always have "young" ideas, and (3) maintain self-discipline.

☐ NEVER CONFUSE MEANS WITH ENDS

Keeping one's priorities straight is almost always easier said than done. "Never confusing means with ends" means maintaining your perspective and keeping your ultimate objective in focus. This initiative refers to any action, behavior, or object you consider in terms of its results rather than in terms of its value, in and of itself. In other words, nearly every single action has an end other than itself, and it is important to keep this ultimate end in mind. For example, many people often see money as an end in and of itself, rather than a means to some other ultimate, more meaningful purpose.

Current editor in chief of www.edgargonzalez.com, a tangential weblog on architecture and design, Edgar Gonzalez has contributed a great deal to the importance of distinguishing ends from means in mass digital media. Gonzalez contends that by "liking" something on Facebook we are often confusing means with ends. He argues that in this age of over-information it is easy to end your reading or inquiry by clicking on the thumbs up icon, which gives a sense of jurisdiction over the media and the information we are being inundated with. With the advent of the "like" button, or pinning something, or the ability to re-tweet, comes a sense of agency and egalitarianism: everyone has a voice and everyone's voice is equal. However, Gonzalez argues, it may also create a great deal of chaotic, distracting noise. If we are to create discussions of consequence and meaning in global dialogues, perhaps not everyone's contributions are in actuality or should be considered of the same value. "Like" should be a means to some greater end, rather than a means in and of itself.

☐ ALWAYS HAVE "YOUNG" IDEAS

Having "young ideas" means avoiding having your creativity and innovative, imaginative potential stifled by social norms and mores. In addition, always be aware of and tapped into the technical and cultural activities of industry by connecting with up and coming designers, creators, builders, and writers. Another way of cultivating fresh and innovative ideas is to be aware of trends, new product development, and marketing campaigns. Feed and stimulate your brain with fresh ideas every day to stay ahead of the game.

Brain storming and mind mapping are excellent, tried and tested ways of accessing your creative potential. Like other traditional ways of harnessing the innovative, these exercises are primarily comprised of two distinct stages that you can take and apply to your own thought process: a free-thinking stage and an organizing stage. Below are details on how to apply these mind-exercises to your own thinking.

STEP 1

BRAINSTORMING = FREE THINKING → PRODUCING IDEAS

- Write your topic (names of architect, designer, terms, etc.) in the center of a blank page.
- Use colors, pictures, words and symbols to record any other ideas, topics, authors, theories or anything else associated with the topic. You can put these anywhere on the page. Associate freely and do not block out any ideas. Throughout the brainstorming process anything and everything could prove productive by inciting a breakthrough idea.

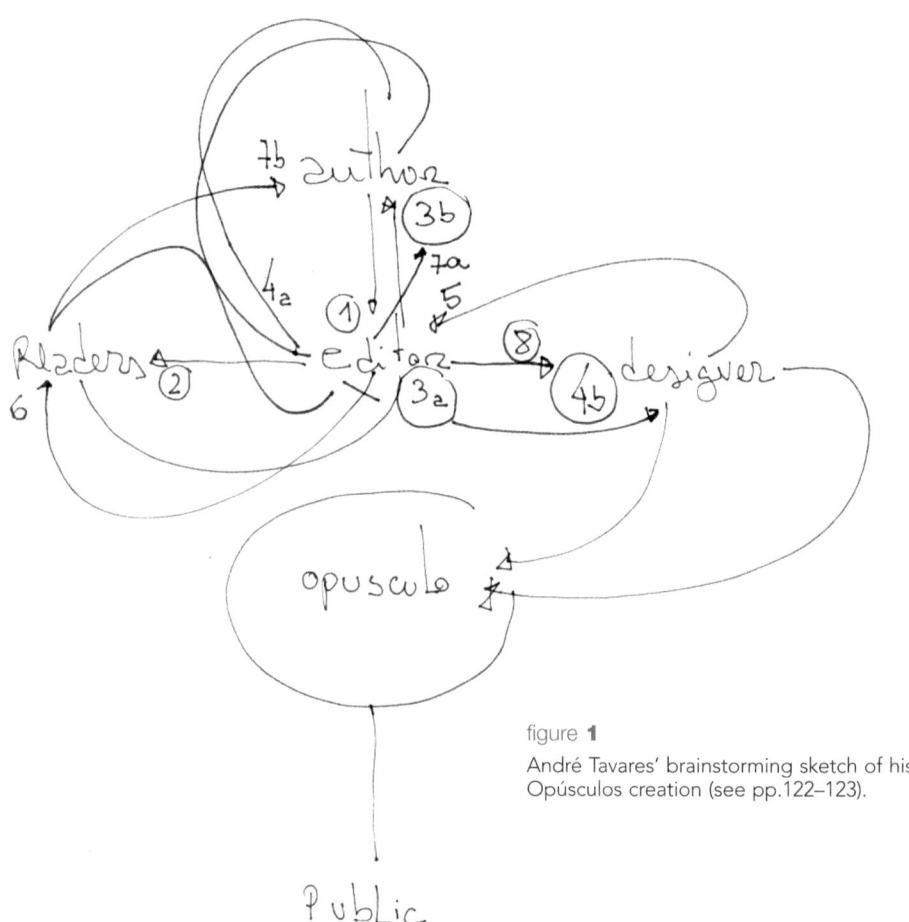

figure **1**
André Tavares' brainstorming sketch of his Opúsculos creation (see pp.122–123).

STEP 2 MIND MAPPING = IDENTIFYING RELATIONSHIPS → ORGANIZING IDEAS

- Map the relationships between the ideas or key points using lines, arrows, colors and words to link them.
- Identify the type of relationships between points: contrast/similarity/cause/effect. Spend some time thinking, in depth, about these connections. Then, articulate these connections and inter-relationships along the connecting lines. Finally, use this map to organize your thinking. Arrange items in a logical order to create the structure of your innovative thinking.

In addition, there are now websites like DAYTUM (http://daytum.com/) that help you connect with fresh ideas by collecting, categorizing, and communicating your everyday data in figurative and graphic format. Tools such as these may lead you to extraordinary opportunities or to discover a new, exciting passion.

A great example of turning "young" ideas into realities can be found in the Chicago-based Spirit of Space collective, which documents and communicates ideas about architecture via digital media. In their essay presented in this chapter "Film is More: Architecture + Storytelling + Film", Goss argues that the audience for traditional architectural discourse is limited to those within the discipline's ranks. By cinematically capturing architecture in the act, Spirit of Space interfaces with the larger public by using the common languages of imagery and sound, effectively making architecture accessible by imbuing it with an egalitarian ethos.

Detailing his three-stage production process as storyboarding/research, filming, and editing, Goss describes the new opportunities discovered during the final phase of video manipulation. Goss advises would-be filmmakers to embrace new media as a vital component in the evolution of architecture, to develop a design point of view that will inform their efforts with concrete objectives and a personal vision, and to dive in without reservations. Goss writes, "Once the camera is rolling, time and space are being sequentially captured, and there is no looking back". Goss contends that the acts of filming and editing his film afforded him fresh new perspectives and opportunities for innovation.

SOUND OFF!

In the space below, creatively introduce yourself. Show us what inspires you, sketch your next big idea or describe your personal design point of view.

Be original. Be inspiring. Be memorable. A picture is worth a thousand words. When you're done, e-mail a PDF to us at recruitment@gensler.com.

NAME

SCHOOL

EMAIL

figure **2**

Gensler's request for the creation of a mind map style submission for intern applicants as part of their recruitment initiative.

Gensler

© Gensler 2011

MAINTAINING AN EDGE 5

☐ MAINTAIN SELF-DISCIPLINE

Even though many of us are under constant threat from layoffs due to outsourcing, off-shoring, right-sizing, downsizing, and bankruptcies, you must continue to express yourself, what you can do, and what you stand for to everyone in your professional network. Do this constantly and consistently with various audiences – your neighbors, your friends and friends of friends, your family, your colleagues, or even the man on the street – it will lead to new opportunities.

Maintaining a sense of discipline by staying on top of your self-presentation is another way to generate excitement and fresh thinking. Think out loud by starting a blog, a twitter account, or your own website where you can post projects and exhibitions. In his essay The Architect Who Blogs: Notes from on the Road, James Benedict Brown presents an introductory overview of how user-generated web content, including professional profiles and portfolios, creates a state of constant flux. The ubiquity of the Internet has allowed us to move from static to dynamic content. The sand underneath our feet is constantly being carried out with the tide; therefore, to avoid sinking and to remain relevant we need to catch a wave and ride the tide.

Brown credits the popularity of blogging with ushering in the era of active users driving the content of online spaces while also pointing to public networks, such as Facebook and LinkedIn, as critical to student and professional self-presentation and self-promotion. However, he advises users to conduct audience analyses before engaging with any social media. Finally, Brown encourages us to maintain conscious distinctions between professional and personal interaction. The digital world and waging an effective self-presentation campaign within this world demands a significant amount of self-discipline.

References
Caruso, A. (2009) "The $100,000 Question." Retrieved July 26, 2012, from http://www.gensler.com/uploads/documents/The_$100,000_Question_11_20_2009.pdf

Gensler (2010) "Make Your Mark Campaign." Retrieved July 26, 2012, from http://www.gensler.com/xtr/pdf/Gensler_StudentGraduateGuide.pdf

Kluth, A. (2011) *Hannibal and Me: What History's Greatest Military Strategist Can Teach Us About Success and Failure.* New York: Riverhead Books.

CASE STUDY 1

TITLE: ARCHITECTURE + STORYTELLING + FILM
AUTHOR: ADAM GOSS

WE ARE CONTRIBUTING TO ARCHITECTURE

Spirit of Space uses digital media to communicate ideas about architecture. We seek to establish a heightened awareness of designed environments, making architecture accessible to everyone. For us, video is the most effective tool to communicate the value of design. Each member of the Spirit of Space team studied architecture. Making architectural films, we have realized that it is possible to meaningfully contribute to the profession in alternative ways. We love architecture. We love motion pictures. And Spirit of Space merges the two. Offering expert services to those involved in the profession and education of architecture, Spirit of Space bridges professional architectural ideas with public understanding through the production of short films featuring the design process and finished works of architecture.

EVERYONE KNOWS HOW TO WATCH A FILM

Film transcends time, space, language, and culture, generating a connection with viewers through sight, sound, and emotion. But at the same time, cinema is a contrivance. It is not reality. Because of privileged perspectives, editing, and manipulation of time, film is full of connections that do not exist. Consequently, film is not in competition with reality. And a film about architecture can never replace true, physical existence.

   Nevertheless, cinema can influence reality, and an architectural film can reveal an infinite number of truths about a space. Cinema penetrates one's thoughts and imagination, which in turn can affect one's lived experiences. Empathetically viewing a film stimulates cognition, activating the process of learning and the generation of new memories. When a space, an experience, or a detail is depicted in a film, one internalizes this information, and newly acquired knowledge can be directly translated into affecting how one might experience a space. Thus, viewers can empathize with what is being projected onto a screen. Architectural films initiate curiosity and discovery while encouraging more meaningful lived experiences.

   Traditional forms of architectural communication are quite effective for disseminating the particulars of a project within the profession. However, the general public understands and relates to architecture through direct, human experience. When explaining a design process with traditional forms of architectural representation, it is difficult to discern whether or not an audience is attentive or if they even understand what is being presented. Film is an exceptionally powerful medium, because it induces architectural understanding while captivating the attention of an entire room. By fixing the experience of time and restricting the field of vision, a film presents a common experience, allowing a space or an idea to be visually and aurally perceived in a similar manner by the eyes and ears of an entire audience.

MAINTAINING AN EDGE 5

FILM IS MORE

SPIRIT OF SPACE

WE SEEK TO CAPTURE ARCHITECTURE IN THE ACT

In the creation of every film, one wears three primary hats: planner, observer, and editor. Often starting with a storyboard, the planner must figure out how to capture and represent a three-dimensional space in a two-dimensional format. Wearing the observer's hat requires strategically determining how to capture that information with the lens of the camera. And finally, the editor is immersed in a process in which he compares the storyboard to the actual footage, making critical decisions to piece together the best narrative.

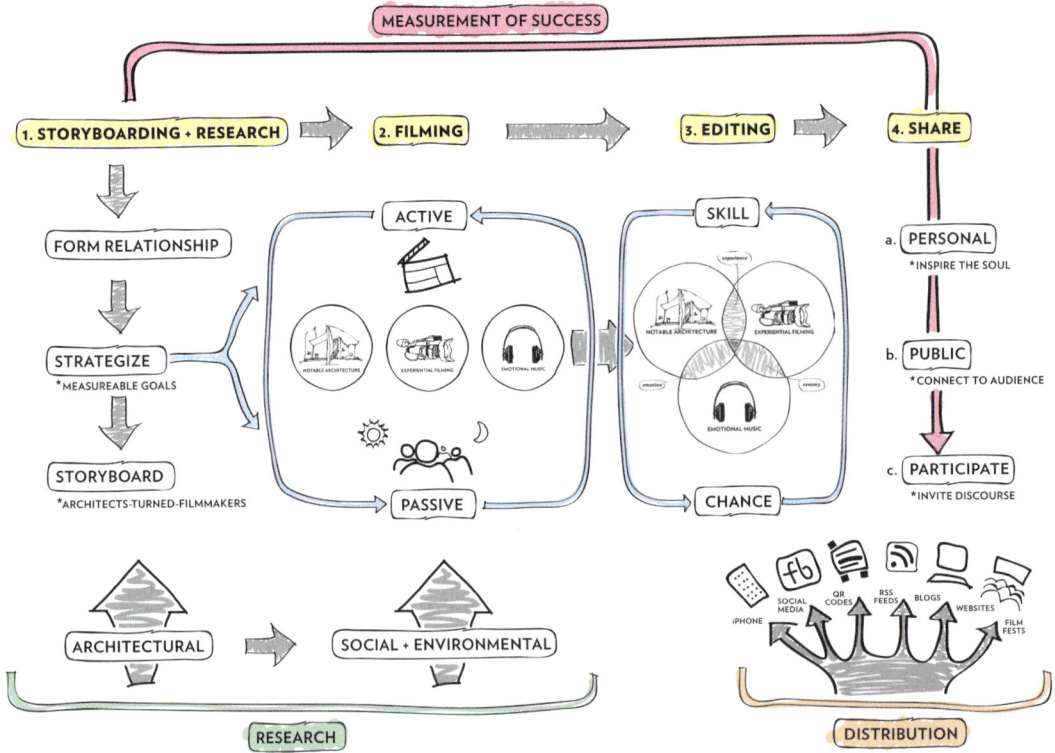

+ STORYBOARDING AND RESEARCH

We want to share our architectural experiences with everyone. But being cognizant of people's time, we understand that we must be efficient and insightful with our message. Therefore, it is very intentional that our films are quite short. Although every space can tell a million different stories, crafting short films reveals necessary constraints. Research generally guides the way, as it is essential for us to only focus on what is best for a specific project and for an individual client. In addition, while drawing up our storyboards, it is imperative that we work closely with the architect early on in the pre-production process. Establishing a working relationship, it is much easier for us to determine a strategic vision that tells the story from the architect's perspective. But at the same time, it is our task to ensure that the architect's story is told in such a way that everyone will understand.

+ FILMING

Working as architects, we must empathetically recognize that most people do not possess the same sensitivity to detail or even a heightened awareness of design. So, to begin to understand the varied perspectives of the general population, we often conduct several on-site interviews, spending ample time observing and "living" in the space.

MAINTAINING AN EDGE 5

We take great pride in the compositional quality of each frame, but some of our most beautiful scenes are never planned. They couldn't be. Filming is unpredictable, and patience is always rewarded. Spirit of Space attempts to reveal an exchange of actions and emotions within a space. It is an investigation into what a space provides and means to its users. While experiencing and documenting various layers of an architectural space, idiosyncrasies unfold, presenting themselves to the camera lens. And the time devoted to capturing this interaction results, serendipitously, in a unique film.

Our methodology is a process of discovery where skill and chance seamlessly work together. It is up to the architectural cinematographer to be confident enough in his skills to allow chance to indicate where the next shot should be, being adept enough to intuitively follow an unexpected path. The space reveals itself.

+ EDITING

In the editing room, we often like to say, "this is where the magic happens," but we must also clarify that the amount of time dedicated to research, storyboarding, and filming allows for this "magic" to happen. Once again, both skill and chance are crucial in guiding the editor through this part of the production process. Creating a thoughtful narrative about a space, the editor stitches together privileged perspectives and temporal manipulations. During the editing process, we often discover new opportunities and angles that we may not have been aware of while filming on set, because these fortuitous surprises can only be realized afterwards.

In addition, sound is vitally important to any motion picture, and Spirit of Space generates its own melodic beats inspired by the filmed architecture. Musical tracks help communicate architectural space aurally. Each soundtrack establishes a mood and sets a tone for every Spirit of Space film.

Finally, we want to ensure that our videos are accessible to as many individuals as possible. Effective architectural communication is essential, and we are simply using the latest digital technology to set a new standard for how architecture is perceived and understood.

+ ADVICE

While still students, we began the initial efforts that eventually led to the inception of Spirit of Space. At that point in our education, we had the academic freedom to push ourselves in an experimental direction, and consequently, we saw how effective film could be. Architecture has become more specialized than ever, and digital media is a vital part of this evolution.

Over and over again, we have observed that students who are making architectural films have an immense yet simple fear of pushing that little red button. But at the same time, advancements in photographic technology have established a newfound ease in the point-and-shoot phenomenon for still images. With a seemingly limitless amount of digital memory, less and less subjectivity is required, because multiple shots can be taken, ensuring that at least a few of the shots will be compositionally pleasing and in focus. On the other hand, while cinematic technology has evolved, the actual process of filming is pretty much the same as it was for the Lumiere brothers. Once the camera is rolling, time and space are being sequentially captured, and there is no turning back. Further, subjectivity has always been a part of the process, since the filmmaker is essentially telling a story. Thus, it is up to the individual who is actually holding the video camera to make all of the critical decisions while crafting an imaginative perspective.

In response to these observations, our advice is threefold. One. Subjectivity ought to be embraced by simply trusting one's instincts. In the profession of architecture, it is expected and encouraged for a designer to have a point of view. Two. Prepare for the film shoot. Storyboarding and research will ease much of the anxiety by establishing clear intentions and a creative vision for the final film. Three. Hit the little red button. ■

CASE STUDY 2

TITLE: THE ARCHITECT WHO BLOGS: NOTES FROM ON THE ROAD
AUTHOR: JAMES BENEDICT BROWN

The evolution of computing technology is perhaps most visible in the experiences of the successive generations who use it. Many of the authors in this book grew up with the desktop computer: what first appeared as a solitary terminal with a command line interface in the corner of my primary school classroom had by the time of my graduation from university become a daily feature of my online life. In turn, those born less than decade later have grown up not with the internet limited to their homes or schools, but with them in their pockets. The internet is everywhere, and the very existence of the traditional desktop computer seems to be threatened by the shift to the cloud. Today, the most popular activities on the internet are social – those platforms which allow individual users to connect to one another, sharing their media, making recommendations and forging connections with "friends," "contacts," and "followers." In the architectural "blogosphere," BldgBlog[1] typically receives between 5,000 and 8,000 unique hits a day,[2] while ArchDaily[3] has more than half a million fans on Facebook.

But where did this social side of the internet begin? How did the obscure art of HTML programming evolve into a market of platforms that allows anyone to express themselves online? Some date the birth of the social internet to 17 December 1997, when an Ohioan writer called Jorn Barger added a "weblog" of links to his personal website.[4] Acting as the human editor behind his constantly updated list of recommended links, Barger created a new online medium, one that was chronological[5] and that presented an edited, thematic, and personalised face to the internet. Within less than a decade, integrated platforms such as Blogger, LiveJournal, TypePad, and Wordpress had brought blogging to the masses, making it as easy to publish a blog as it is to write longhand in a diary. While the names of proprietary social media platforms such as Facebook and Twitter have entered common parlance, the diversity of platforms and accessibility of the internet have ensured that blogs remain popular. This case study focuses on blogging, presenting personal reflections on this medium and considering the steps the architect can take to use blogging in developing both their personal and professional profile.

MAINTAINING AN EDGE 5

TO BLOG OR NOT TO BLOG

I started blogging in 2005, when I registered a site on Blogger called On the Road.[6]

It started as a hybrid diary and round-robin email, written to keep British friends and family at home updated during a year abroad in Canada. I started by writing posts just like emails, even signing with my initials. I published photographs from my travels as uncaptioned "snapshots." Oddities of everyday life in a foreign country could be described, illustrated and shared. Informal restaurant reviews were interspersed with rants about the Canadian tax system or the strange quirks of keeping pets; poignant moments alone at a bus stop or on a street corner became prompts for reflections on architecture, food and romance. The blog became an extension (perhaps an exaggeration) of the personality I wanted to present to the world. Without a particular reader in mind posts became open-ended, written for an audience of anyone and no one in particular. On the Road remains a personal blog, often with first name references to friends or lightly anonymised references to work situations. Uncertain of the voice to adopt when discussing matters of politics, religion or (heaven forbid) architecture, the On the Road archive is a varied and occasionally revealing account of how, just when I thought I was all grown up, I started to grow up again.

figure **1**
On the Road screengrab.

WHO ARE YOU SPEAKING TO?

Shuffling between the different aspects of my life for such a diverse audience made On the Road a rather incongruous reading experience.

So when, in 2006, I took time out from work to take a month-long rail trip through the USA and Canada, it seemed only appropriate that my blog should spawn a distinctive sister. With long hours to pass on cross-country trains to kill, I had all the time in the world to write about what I could see out of the window or who I had met on my journey. On The Rails[7] was born: a dedicated travelogue of photographs and entries describing the trip as I went along. This new blog quickly built an audience that was different from On the Road. Having made contact with travel experts and even some trainspotters during the planning stages of my trip, it made more sense to invite them to read and comment on a blog that was focused on our shared interests. After all, if an architect designs a new house, he or she will describe it in different ways to different people. When talking with a builder, the architect might describe the structure or technical specifications. When talking with the client, the architect would more likely describe the functions of the different spaces or the finishes of the different surfaces. We change the way in which we speak to different people dozens of times a day, often without noticing. In order to really capitalise on the potential of social media, a similar adaptation of one's voice is necessary. Being a medium that was basically free (aside from the cost of accessing the internet), I was able to write two blogs that served two different audiences, and which therefore took on two different personas.

figure **2**
On the Rails screengrab.

MAINTAINING AN EDGE 5

BLOGGING IN THE ACADEMY

When I returned to the UK in 2006, blogging remained a peripheral activity to much of my professional life. Out of an awareness of the confidentiality of my work, let alone the potential boredom of my readers, I had never let blogging stray too far into the realm of my work. But back at university, my experiences of the medium began to suggest opportunities that could support other collaborative projects. One such blog became a collaborative archive of a research driven live project that investigated other live projects[8] at the University of Sheffield.[9] Another (No Words No Action)[10] was a personal journal focusing on the research informing my Masters dissertation. It used the chronology of the blog as a means to maintain personal discipline and accountability by publishing snippets of my research and work in progress. This included instalments from research interviews with comic artists in the Netherlands and the USA, reporting not only the findings of my research but also the broader experience of traveling abroad to conduct such research. These blogs all had the facility for readers to lodge comments or questions on individual posts. With only a small audience, however, these blogs remained exercises in thinking "out loud," although as audiences grow so can the potential for feedback.

Steve Parnell, an architectural historian and critic, recalls how he found that blogging "was effective for quite quickly knocking out an idea in a short essay format of up to around 800 words." Without the pressure to produce a formal piece of published writing, we had both discovered the inherent appeal of writing on a blog and receiving feedback from those who shared our interests. Parnell explains how "I used to enjoy getting feedback (through the comments) and I admit to initially becoming quite obsessed with visitor statistics. I also used to like being part of a small circle of architectural bloggers who would respond to each others' posts and build upon each others' ideas … In retrospect, I can see that I was informally beginning a research project that ultimately resulted in my PhD." Even without the benefit of immediate feedback from our audiences, blogging had provided both of us with an online sketchbook for new work.

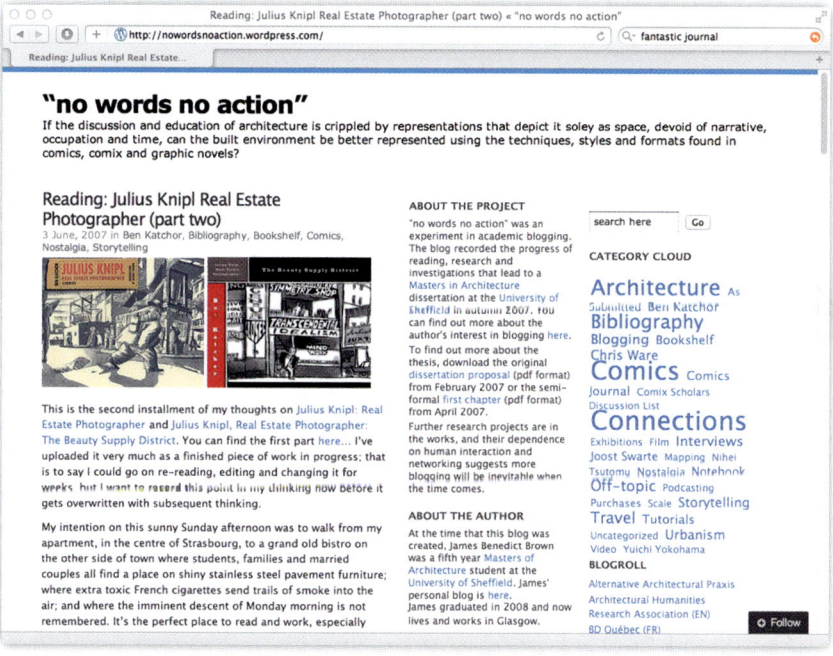

figure **3**
No Words No Action screengrab.

BUT WHY SHOULD ANYONE LISTEN TO YOU?

Just as Steve Parnell found that blogging began to tease out ideas for future research, my Masters level blogging lead in 2009 to the blog that supported my doctoral research. Learning Architecture[11] has been an invaluable space for more public thinking, writing and reflection on my doctoral research. As an early-career academic, having the facility to share tentative ideas with like-minded people around the world has immense potential to increase both one's confidence and productivity. But like any form of communication, successful blogging depends upon a meaningful connection between author (or editor) and reader. As a student of architecture, using the Live Project Live Project blog to support the community-based activities of a student live project was particularly insightful, as our first instinct as students was to use it as a space to reflect critically upon architectural processes. These blog posts were, however, of little interest to the communities with whom we were working. Just as an architectural portfolio can be unintelligible to someone without an architectural background, blogging can find its greatest value when the author shares a vocabulary and field of interest with his or her audience. Time and again, I've found that the success of blogging depends upon recognising and speaking to one's audience. .

This is also true for other forms of social media. Few people, for instance, will have exactly the same selection of "friends" on Facebook as "connections" on LinkedIn. By distinguishing the various audiences of your online social presence, you can tailor your voice as appropriate. In more practical terms, that means photographs of you in the bar at two o'clock in the morning don't get presented to potential employers. But while social networks such as Facebook and LinkedIn present closed networks that allow users some degree of control over who sees their activity, a blog demands careful consideration of what one writes.

Steve Parnell and I both use the chronological journal format of a blog to support our academic and critical writing: publishing progress updates, highlight others'

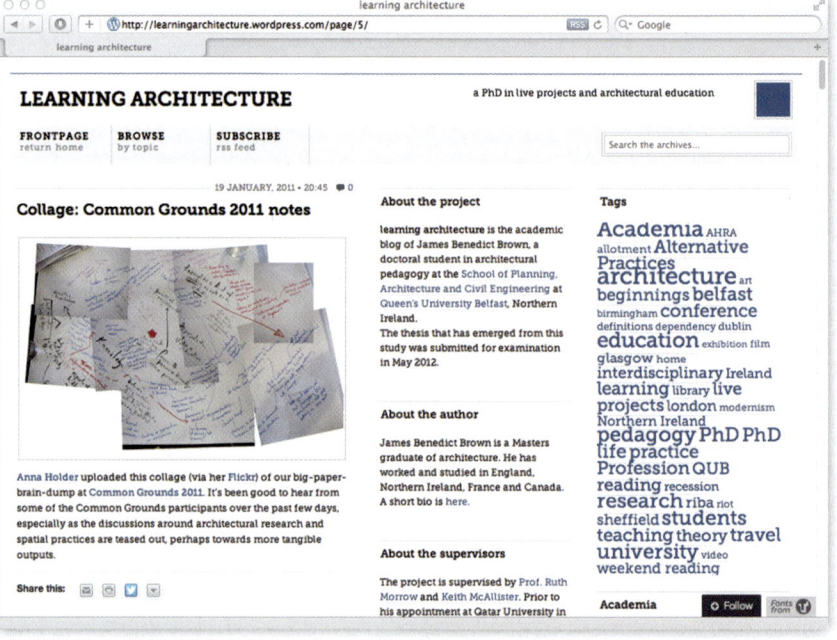

figure **4**
Learning Architecture screengrab.

research and even to just practice the art of writing itself. But it is not only academics who can benefit from blogging their theoretical explorations. Given that a significant proportion of design is research, architects can also take advantage of blogging to collate inspiration, develop ideas and test out research. Charles Holland, architect and director of London-based practice FAT (Fashion Architecture Taste),[12] explains how writing his blog Fantastic Journal,[13] "is more about developing a set of general interests around the subject." He describes how "a decade or so after graduating, during which time we had developed the practice and built some buildings, it was refreshing to re-engage with theoretical questions again."

MAINTAINING AN EDGE 5

KNOWING WHEN TO MOVE ON

But what happens when an academic or architect begins to lose interest in a blog? Although he now acknowledges that the short-form of "Twitter has stolen my blogging mojo," Steve Parnell's early explorations in blogging lead to an "accidental career" as an architectural critic in the traditional (i.e. printed) architectural press, including the *Architects' Journal* and *Mark* magazine. He notes how "it's great that people like me, who would never have previously considered breaking into the architectural press, have been able to do so. Blogs are more meritocratic like that." However, the result has been that he now writes less online and more in the traditional media of architectural magazines and academic journals.

Now that my own PhD thesis has been submitted for examination, Learning Architecture is beginning to outlive its original purpose – just as On the Rails described a single trip and Live Project Live Project supported a defined six-week student project. Charles Holland broaches the possibility that blogs have limited lifespans by noting that because "a blog is a place to put speculative thought which then leads to more formulated writing, it also suggests a time span for a blog too." Parnell also notes that "now I've done the PhD, and now that I'm regularly writing for the press, I don't feel I can be as informal about my writing, so I end up not blogging at all."

So does this mean that blogging is ultimately too limited for architectural practice? A blog provides a stepping stone for both ideas and careers, but in so doing it can also reveal itself to be expendable. Parnell explains that "writing for the paper media still has more gravitas and authority. Not because of audience, but because it's edited and less ephemeral. Somebody else is expending paper and ink on your thoughts (often at the expense of other people's) and others are paying to read it, so it's more valuable." While "mainstream" blogs such as BldgBlog and ArchDaily may be accused of attempting to overthrow architectural print media, independent bloggers can use the form to develop their research and their practice before moving on to "more valuable" media. So while blogs can sometimes burn out or fade away, in so doing they support the development of an individual's creative practice. Like a bookshelf filled with old sketchbooks, archived blog entries (even across multiple blogs) can provide a remarkable legacy of an architect's creative practice. ■

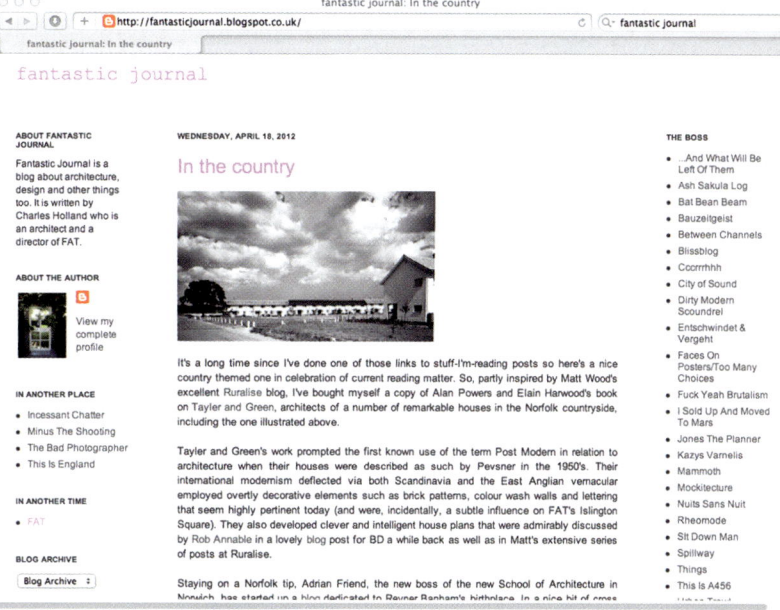

figure **5**
Fantastic Journal screengrab.

Notes
1 http://bldgblog.blogspot.com/
2 Peters, T., 2012. Idea Hunting. *Mark*, 38, pp. 192–197.
3 http://www.archdaily.com/
4 http://www.robotwisdom.com/
5 Or rather anti-chronological, because the page would always present you with the most recent post first.
6 http://jamesbrownontheroad.wordpress.com/
7 http://jamesbrownontherails.blogspot.com/
8 A design studio project that engages students with a "real" client and a "real" project as part of their academic studies.
9 http://liveproject.wordpress.com/
10 http://nowordsnoaction.wordpress.com/
11 http://learningarchitecture.wordpress.com/
12 http://fashionarchitecturetaste.com/
13 http://fantasticjournal.blogspot.co.uk/

INDEX

A
About.me, 133
academic research, 26
accessibility, viii, 6, 10, 53, 138
action, 5, 16, 17, 20, 21, 22, 24, 28, 34, 35, 38, 47, 75, 103, 129, 137, 141
activism, 50
advertising, 51, 52, 124
Aesop, 3
agora, 23
application, 13, 24, 25, 26, 27, 28, 29, 44, 67, 68, 71, 74, 77, 110, 111, 114, 121
aptitudes, 2, 6, 10, 29, 39
Alexander, Christopher, 47
alternative lifestyles, 51
ambition, 19, 43, 44, 116,
American Institute of Architects, 84, 86, 110
animation, 98, 118,
ArchDaily, 138, 143
Archigram, 50
Archinect, 13
Architects Journal, 51, 143
Architectural Association (AA), London, vii, 50, 52, 54, 55, 92
Architectural Design (AD), vii, 51
archispeak, 53
Architizer, 115
architectural
 communication, 54, 134, 137
 -critics, 122,
 -discourse, 131
 -film, 134, 137
 -publishing, vii, 27, 47, 50, 51, 53, 103, 122, 141, 142
 -values, viii, 3, 34, 35, 42, 43, 44, 48
Architecture for Humanity, 48, 113
art history, vii, 60, 62
Art Institute of Chicago, vii, 60, 61, 62
Amsterdam, vii, 60
Axel, Nick, vi, 16-23

B
base file, 110
basic skills, 40
Becker, Alton L., 29, 30, 31
Bentham, Jeremy, 23
beyond, 46, 47, 52, 58, 71, 113
blogger, 138, 139, 141, 143
blogging, 21, 103, 112, 128, 133, 138, 139, 141, 142, 143
Blueprint, vii, 51, 52
blunders, 30
bouche a orielle, 124
BNIM, 109, 112, 113, 115
Bolles, Richard N., 36, 41
brain storming, 129
Brazil, 103, 123
British Architecture Students Association, 50
British Pavilion, 58
Broadgate, 52
Brown, James Benedict, vi, 133, 138-143
Burrough, Tom, 50

C
career change, 66
career plan, ix, 34, 35, 36, 37, 38, 102
Cesal, Eric J., vi, 34, 35, 36, 42-49
cinema, 54, 131, 134, 137
cinematic architecture, 55
Clifford, Brandon, vi, 24-27, 31
Clip-Kit, Ltd., 50, 51, 53
Clerkenwell Architecture Biennale, 52
cloud, 71, 82, 92, 138

competencies
 -profile, 38, 40
communications, vii, 52, 53, 54, 60, 61, 77, 112
computer-aided design, 66, 82, 92
computational design, 92,
connectivity, 92
construction, vi, vii, 8, 43, 48, 61, 62
construction management, 44, 45
core values, viii, 34, 43
curiosity, 31, 35, 66, 134
courage, viii, 10, 35, 48, 102, 133, 137
cover letter, 16, 18, 19, 68, 70, 71, 105
CREWBiz, 114
CV, ix, 10, 13, 16, 18, 19, 54, 66-71, 110, 112, 114

D
Dada, 62
Dafne Editora, vii, 103, 123
DAYTUM, 131
DIY, 35
defining imagery, 110
delivery method, 77
design, 113, 115, 116, 118, 119, 120, 121, 122, 124, 128, 129, 130, 131, 132, 136, 137, 140, 142
design process, 62, 92, 97, 120, 134
Design Museum, London, 51
De Stijl, 62
developing a professional profile, 30, 31, 33, 138
dialogue, 28, 29, 31, 34, 73, 112, 113, 116, 120, 129
digital source folder, 110
diversity advocacy, 109
discovery, 24, 28, 29, 31, 45, 134, 137
Disney, 34
digital media, 129, 131, 134, 137
documentation, 24, 25, 26, 27, 111, 118
Döll, Henk, vi, 104, 116-121
Down Detour Road, vi, 45, 46, 49, 77
dRMM, 55

E
Eames, Charles and Ray, 8
editing, 25, 26, 27, 50, 62, 131, 134, 136, 137
email, 12, 17, 27, 54, 61, 66, 72, 74, 77, 78, 82, 128, 132, 139
energy conservation, 51
environmental issues, 51
embedded marketing, 24
empathy, ix, 2, 4, 24, 28, 29
Esterson, Simon, 51, 52
events of circumstance, 19
evolution of architecture, 131
exhibitions, vii, ix, 52, 53, 55, 62, 84, 88, 121, 133
exit strategy, 37
expertise
 -collaboration, 40
 -negotiating, 40
 -planning, 40
 -presentation, 40
 -organization, 40
 -special, 40

F
fabrication, 25
Facebook, 61, 104, 105, 106, 112, 113, 115, 129, 133, 138, 142
film, 55, 131, 134, 136, 137
flat space, 22
Flickr, 114
Flotsam, 71, 92, 94

Florensky, Olga and Alexander, 56
formal introduction, 19
free thinking, 129, 130
functionalities of architecture, 43
Futurism, 62

G
Gehry, Frank, 51
Gensler, 52, 128, 132, 133
Georgian buildings, 55
goals, 11, 29, 34, 36, 37, 38, 48, 136
Gonzalez, Edgar, 129
Google+, 15
Goss, Adam, vi, 131, 134-137
graduate school, 25, 26, 43, 44, 45
Graphic Thought Facility, 60
Greeks, 29
Grimm brothers, 3

H
Haiti, 42, 47, 48
Haitian earthquake, 47
Harvard University, 21
Herzog, Werner, 54
hierarchy, 76, 82, 89, 115
Hogrefe, Alex, vi, 10-14, 30, 31
Holl, Steven, 60, 61, 62, 63
House of Cards, 8
Hudson Yards, 52
human
 -interaction, 22, 73, 105, 119, 133, 137
humanitarian architecture, 47
hypothesis, 29

I
icon, 52, 129
ideas, ix, 2, 3, 5, 16, 23, 29, 30, 34, 45, 47, 50, 52, 53, 55, 58, 73, 92, 128, 129, 130, 131, 134, 141, 142, 143
identity formation, 12, 17, 18, 19, 21, 22, 23, 34, 45, 46, 103, 104, 116, 118, 119, 128
IE School of Architecture, Madrid, 53
illumination, 4, 29
improvisation, ix, 5, 8
incubation, 29
infographic, 82
International Commerce Center, 52, 119, 121
invention, 28, 29, 30, 31
isolation, 46
Issuu, 114

J
Japanese bathhouse, 55, 56
job postings, 13

K
key focus, 111
King, Stephen, 3
Kluth, Andreas, 129

L
leadership, 39, 40, 108, 109, 110, 111, 112, 115
LeFevre, Karen Burke, 29, 31
Lifschutz Davidson, 55
LinkedIn, 10, 13, 104, 105, 106, 112, 113, 133, 142
Lipton, Stuart, 52
list of projects, 54
Liu, Lillie, vii, 71, 92-99
Lloyd, Jordan J., vii, 67, 76-83
London Festival of Architecture, 38, 52
Longs, Richard, 54

M

M.Arch, 45
Mackey, Bill, vii, 67, 84-91
Mari, Enzo, 56
Matisse, Henri, 7
manifesto, 34, 46
manifestation, 22, 23, 29, 34
Masdar City, 52
Matter Design, 25
M.B.A., 44, 45
Marketing, viii, ix, 5, 6, 10, 13, 24, 26, 28, 38, 52, 53, 84, 102, 103, 104, 105, 106, 107, 122, 124, 128, 129
McKeogh, Nick, 52
McGee, Wes, 25
meaning, ix, 2, 4, 5, 6, 10, 24, 28, 29, 30, 43, 44, 46, 47, 71, 77, 105, 115, 129, 134, 142
Megascope, 50, 51
middle class, 42, 43
milestones, 35, 38, 112
mind mapping, 129, 131
Monniez, Pascal, vii, 105, 124-125
Murray, Peter, vii, 38, 50-53, 54
Muse, 29, 30, 31

N

narrative(s)
  -of space, 136, 137
network presence, 18
networking, 10, 11, 20, 24, 25, 26, 27, 72, 102, 103, 104, 105, 106, 107, 115
New London Architecture, 52
New London Quarterly, 53
new opportunities, 18, 131, 137
New York University, 60
Norwood, Vanessa, vii, 35, 54-59
Nova, 51

O

online communication networks, 18, 22
online presence, 12, 22, 112
online social networks, 16, 18, 20
Opúsculos, 122
open source, 115
organization networks, 114
original(ity), ix, 28, 30, 31, 34, 60, 63, 67, 70, 73, 77, 82, 102, 103, 106, 132, 143

P

painting, 62, 63
paper cut-out model, 7
paths of becoming, 18
passion, ix, 4, 29, 31, 34, 35, 54, 55, 76, 91, 102, 104, 105, 131
Passion to Build, A, 53
Pegram-Pieper, Alexis, vii, 28-31
personal website, 10, 12, 23, 106, 138
personality profile, 41
Pidgeon, Monica, 51
Pink, Daniel H., 2, 4, 24, 28, 29, 31
Pike, Kenneth L., 29, 30, 31
Pinterest, 114
photography, 56, 58, 61
Platonic, 29
play, ix, 2, 5, 8, 10, 55, 61, 63, 73, 116, 118
portfolio, 3, 5, 6, 13, 16, 18, 26, 30, 31, 48, 68, 77, 103, 111, 118, 133, 142
Portugal, 103
point clouds, 92
position, 4, 18, 21, 23, 35, 36, 39, 41, 42, 43, 45, 46, 47, 61, 62, 63, 66, 68, 69, 70, 71, 73, 74, 75, 80, 88, 90, 91, 102, 103, 107, 110, 120, 128, 137

postmodern identity, 19
PowerPoint, 3, 5, 118
preparation, 3, 25, 29, 47, 73, 105
Price, Cedric, 50, 82
print to web, 110
privileged perspectives, 134, 137
press manager, 60, 61, 62
profile
  -competence, 40
professional, 34, 36, 37, 39, 43, 46, 51, 52, 66, 67, 68, 69, 70, 71, 72, 73, 74, 75, 77, 92, 102, 103, 104, 105, 106, 107, 108, 110, 113, 115, 116, 119, 121, 128, 133, 134, 138
professional life, 35, 141
programmatic approach to life, 42
project preparation, 3, 25, 29, 47, 73, 105
propeller Z, vii, 6-9
publications, 26, 53, 88, 89, 108, 110, 118, 125

Q

quality, 6, 53, 63, 68, 72, 104, 116, 124, 137
Quintana de Uña, Javier, 53

R

Reading Landscape, 56, 58
relationships, ix, 4, 16, 24, 28, 39, 72, 104, 105, 131
release, 25, 27, 61, 106, 117
representation, 18, 23, 24, 55, 62, 69, 105, 124, 134
research, 7, 25, 26, 29, 52, 62, 71, 73, 81, 82, 88, 92, 97, 116, 118, 119, 131, 136, 137, 141, 142, 143
résumé, ix, 11, 12, 13, 17, 30, 31, 53, 66, 67, 68, 69, 70, 76, 77, 78, 79, 80, 81, 84, 88, 89, 92, 105, 110
rhetoric, 5, 28, 29, 31
Romans, 29
Royal Academy, 51
Royal Institute of British Architects Journal, 51
Royal West of England Academy School of Architecture, 50
Russians, 56

S

self-actualization, viii, 3, 16, 29, 30, 31, 34, 48, 102
  -actualizing, 34
self-determination, 34
self-discipline, 129, 133
self-presentation, viii, ix, 2, 3, 4, 5, 6, 10, 11, 16, 17, 20, 21, 22, 23, 28, 29, 31, 54, 108, 115, 116, 118, 120, 133
Shanghai Tower, 52
Shard, The, 52
shared symbolic space, 21, 23
shared spaces, 92
Shumon, Basar, 54
skills
  -methodological, 39, 40
  -personal, 39, 40
  -social, 39, 40
  -technical, 39, 41
Slattery, Amy J., vii, 103, 108-115
social
  -equity, 48
  -media, viii, 10, 13, 26, 27, 61, 102, 104, 105, 108, 112, 128, 133, 136, 138, 140, 142
  -networking, 10, 11, 72, 104, 105
Socrates, viii, 34

Stirling, James, 51, 52
story
  -boarding, 131, 136, 137
  -telling, 3, 131, 134
student, ix, 21, 24, 25, 26, 27, 28, 45, 46, 48, 50, 53, 72, 85, 86, 133, 137, 142, 143
studio culture, 46
subconscious, 29, 30
Sudjic, Deyan, 51
subjectivity, 137
symphony, ix, 2, 4, 16, 29

T

Taipei 101, 52
target, 38, 69, 79, 108, 109, 111, 112
Tarkovskys, Andrei, 54
Tavares, André, vii, 103, 122-123
technology, 2, 40, 50, 53, 76, 121, 137, 138
theme(s), ix, 3, 8, 28, 30, 34, 68, 82
threads, 16, 30, 56
time management, 39, 40
Tschofen, Philipp, vii
Tumblr, 114
Twitter, 13, 15, 18, 22, 23, 61, 104, 105, 106, 112, 113, 133, 138, 143

U

UK, 58, 66, 69, 82, 141
unexpected path, 137
understanding, viii, 3, 4, 19, 29, 30, 35, 41, 44, 51, 56, 76, 111, 116, 134
United States, 21, 66, 70
University of Chicago, 60
University of Sheffield, vii, 141
unpaid internships, 19
urban design, 60, 62, 119

V

Van den Hout, Julia, vii, 36, 60-63
Venice Biennale, 52
Venice Takeaway, 58
Venturi, Robert, 47
verification, 29
video, viii, 13, 62, 98, 105, 131, 134, 137
Vimeo, 112, 114
virtual brand, 103, 108
virtual job fair, 10, 13
Vitruvious, 54
visual rash, 77, 80
visual and performing arts, 54

Y

Young Architects Award, 103
Young, Richard E., 29, 31
YouTube, 114

W

Wallpaper, 52
web design, 12, 23, 53, 61, 71, 77, 94, 103, 104, 106, 108, 110, 111, 112, 113, 114, 115, 116, 118, 122, 133, 136, 138
Wilson, Robert, 54
women in Architecture, 109, 110, 112
WordPress, 138, 143
World Trade Center, 52
word of mouth, 47
web hosting service, 12, 13

Z

Zumthor, Peter, 63